I0815215

Joy and Fear
An Illustrated Report on Modernity

Theo Deutinger

Joy and Fear

An Illustrated Report on Modernity

Lars Müller Publishers

Author's Note

I encountered the book *De Moderne Mensch Ontstaat*, the Dutch version of *Modern Man in the Making*,[1] in Rotterdam about 20 years ago. I saw it in my favorite antique bookstore directly opposite my house. The book was expensive, and its contents were mesmerizing. At home I googled the author, Otto Neurath, and discovered the impressive story of a fellow Austrian who, like myself, spent several years in the Netherlands. Immediately I felt a strong connection. I don't remember how many times I crossed the street just to go through the book. When I finally bought it some months later, I already knew its contents by heart.

What fascinated me about the book was its attempt to describe the emergence of modernity – a time long gone, as I thought. Being educated in the '90s and '00s, I'd been led to believe that we are living in post-modern times. Somehow, I'd always taken the prefix "post-" very literally – as a time after modernity. It had always felt a bit like post-mortem (after death) to me, thus a little sad. Working on the book, I've come to understand that "post" actually means "let's stop and question"[2] (post = critique) modernity. Hence modernity had not ended; it had simply entered a phase of self-criticism.

I would argue that post-modernity started with the events in Hiroshima and Nagasaki in 1945, six years after Neurath published his book. Our world has not been the same since the pilot of the *Enola Gay* released Little Boy, the first atomic bomb used to kill people (primarily civilians), on August 6, 1945.[3] I have the feeling we are still feeling the shockwaves of that first nuclear explosion. Powers were released that are far beyond the human sense of time and space. Some of us awoke and asked ourselves: What have we done?

We have developed supernatural powers we should not use. Paradoxically, the struggle with supernatural powers is an eternal, almost religious, dilemma that eclipses the logic of modern thinking. Almost every religion revolves around a god or demigod who is worshipped because of powers that are at the same time a curse. Jesus was nailed to a cross for resurrecting the dead and walking on water. Thor had a dubious relationship with his hammer. Zeus could not always restrain his anger. There is a fine line between the use and the abuse of power.

Humans' paradoxical relationship to the powers released by nuclear energy clearly reveals the dilemma facing the modern human. While "being modern" was desirable in Neurath's time, it has turned into an imperative today. There is no alternative: in the same way that "we must be nuclear," "we must be modern" and thus knowingly put our existence at risk. If we stop modernizing and slow down the acceleration, we will lose out to others and fall behind. We know that we can't gain much anymore, but if we don't try, we might lose everything.

The initial idea for this book was simply to take Otto Neurath's book *Modern Man in the Making* and extend its illustrations from the 1930s to today. But once I entered the world of Isotype, I was carried away by cars, horses, and ships, almost crushed by gearwheels, and haunted by figurines. I got too entangled in Otto Neurath's thinking – an intellectual from the Industrial Age. To continue his story, I had to detach myself from the man and cling more to the method of Isotype. After several attempts, I managed to escape – not without help from my collaborators and my publisher. "Don't dive; surf" was the advice to follow, and so it turned out that this book you hold in your hands became much more of a dialogue between us, contemporary humans, and Neurath, the man from the past.

Dear reader, I hope you enjoy reading this book as much as I and my colleagues have enjoyed writing it. It has indeed turned out to be a story of joy and fear.[4]
I truly hope that it contributes to a better understanding of the times we are living in.
I hope it inspires a future that confronts fear and inspires joy.

About This Book

Joy and Fear enters into dialogue with Otto Neurath's book *Modern Man in the Making*, a book that chronicles the developments of humanity from the 1800s to the late 1930s.[5] Some of the subjects of modernity (such as steel production, urbanization, and healthcare) which Neurath introduced have continued their developments till the present day. Others, however (such as employment, political regimes, and sites of production), have changed course since the 1930s. Furthermore, a large proportion of the subjects of modernity gathered here in this book are entirely new, having begun only in the time since the publication of *Modern Man in the Making*. Topics such as nuclear energy, the Internet, and the rise of China did not yet exist in Neurath's time, and so they call for new narratives, alongside new illustrations and new Isotype.

The recurring pictograms in the Isotype from Otto Neurath's, Marie Neurath's, and Gerd Arntz's work have been modified in *Joy and Fear* as little as possible, and any newly created pictograms maintain a style consistent with the originals. This creates dilemmas, however, as the depiction of people is often tangled up with questions of identity politics. In Neurath's work, all figures representing humanity are men – unless they very specifically aim to present a woman, in which case they are wearing a dress. Further, Native Americans are printed in red, and Asians wear conical rice hats. In negotiating this dilemma, certain changes needed to be made: for starters, the pictogram for the human, a figure which ideally represents all humans, not only males, has been made more androgynous so that all sexes might feel represented by it and feel comfortable using it. It must also be acknowledged that while giving an earnest attempt to remove sexist, racist, and other exclusory biases in the illustrations in *Joy and Fear*, we cannot pretend to have done so perfectly, as the Isotype is by nature a generalizing form of representation.

Global South and the West

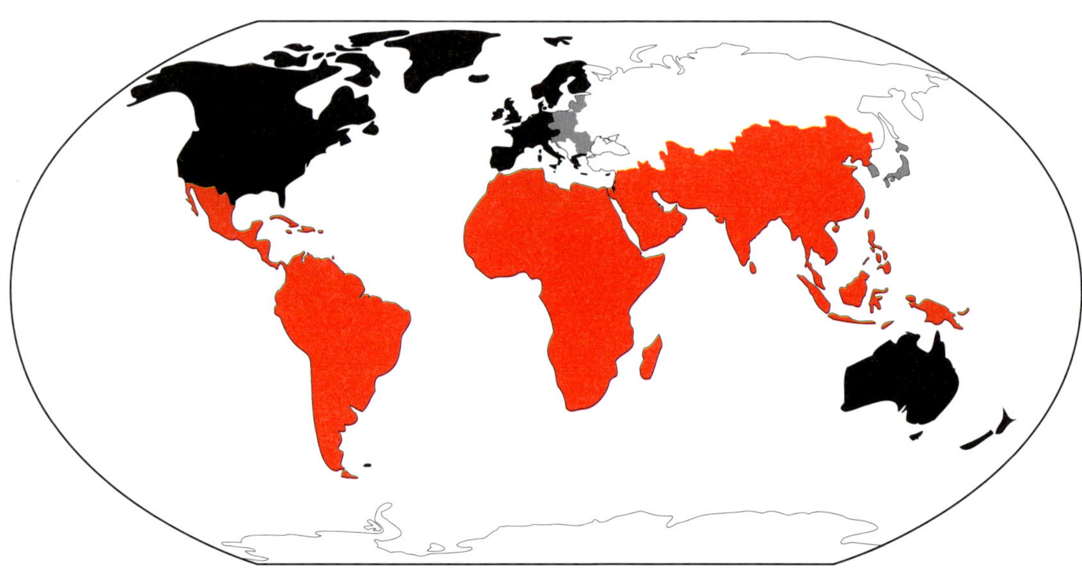

black: the West
gray: countries more recently joining the West
red: Global South

The text frequently uses the terms "Global South" and "the West." This map specifies these generalizations. If data is mentioned in combination with these two specific terms, the data concerns the areas highlighted on this map.

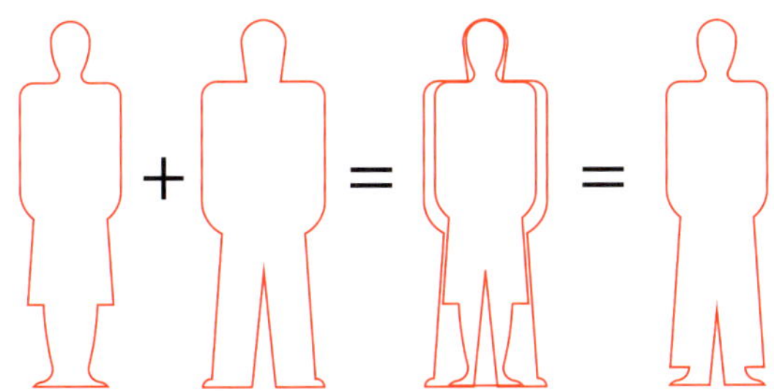

To develop a general pictogram for a human, the female and male pictogram have been merged. Throughout the book, this pictogram is used to represent a human. In a few cases where a specific distinction between men and women is made (e.g., age pyramid, Olympic athletes), the specific pictograms have been used.

Isotype is the name of the method developed by Otto Neurath, Marie Neurath, and Gerd Arntz.
Isotype charts are the individual diagrams and maps.
Pictograms are the individual elements of which an Isotype chart consists.

Regional Division

United States and Canada	Europe	CIS
Latin America	Southern Territories	Far East

In his book Modern Man in the Making, Otto Neurath divided the world roughly into six regions. For most of the illustrations, these have been left like that for the simple reason of being able to compare the Isotype charts from the 1930s to those of today.

Europe = the geographical continent of Europe
CIS (Commonwealth of Independent States) = Armenia, Azerbaijan, Belarus, Kazakhstan, Kyrgyzstan, Moldova, Russia, Tajikistan, and Uzbekistan
Latin America = all countries of the American continent except the United States and Canada
Far East = China, Taiwan, and Japan
Southern Territories = all countries not included in the other five regions

An Isotype pictogram in the lower right-hand corner indicates that the illustration is a reproduction or a direct continuation of a diagram from Otto Neurath's Modern Man in the Making

Annual Chicken Consumption

each symbol represents 1 kg (~1 chicken) consumed per person per year

The selection of the countries Brazil, Chad, China, Germany, India, Iran, and USA for certain comparisons is based on Neurath's selection plus the addition of countries that were nonexistent in his time that are representative of a region or continent. Sometimes, if the original selection had to be extended in order to make a point, the countries chosen (e.g., England and Wales) have been kept for the sake of continuity.

This book analyzes the past 80 years and describes the transition from an industrial to a digital society, providing a glimpse into the form of modernity in which we live today. Since 1939, humanity has created a society that, at its core, is conjoined by electronic media and at the same time estranged by it. Modern media – e.g., the radio program (television was not yet known to Neurath, but follows the same principle as radio) – is replaced by live streaming, and modern production sites – e.g., factories – are employing fewer and fewer people, who are being replaced by robots and computers.

Today, pictograms are important for a different reason than Otto Neurath intended. Pictograms don't provide people with information in an easy and universal way, but are mainly a reference, and very often a nostalgic reference. The symbol for "e-mail" is a letter, the one for "save" is a floppy disc, and that for "phone" is an old dial phone from the 1930s (just take a quick look at your smartphone). The gearwheels of modern technology are hidden and too small, and their shapes are so unintelligible that pictograms of devices that are now in museums must explain their usage.

The fact that technology kept on accelerating while iconography stagnated made updating this book a bit easier. The vocabulary Otto Neurath, Marie Neurath, and Gert Arntz left behind was good for about 90% of the Isotype charts. The remaining 10% are drawn in a similar style and are rather indistinguishable. The result is a fascinating hybrid, and in the book one often has the feeling that people from the past are trying to explain to us the times in which we live.

Modernity Kills

The Manhattan Project

Published in 1939 and titled *Modern Man in the Making,*[1] Otto Neurath's book chronicled the development of modernity in the preceding century. Neurath's work focused on the years between the 1800s and the 1930s. It was the time of radical transition from a peasant to an industrial society; it saw the radical growth of European cities and the colonization of large parts of the world by European powers which was enabled by huge advances in technology. At the time of publication, the technology and science-hungry modern man as described in Neurath's book was developing the atomic bomb using nuclear fission under the Manhattan Project. In 1945 the United States of America, backed by the United Kingdom and Canada,

Fat Man Bomb Victims

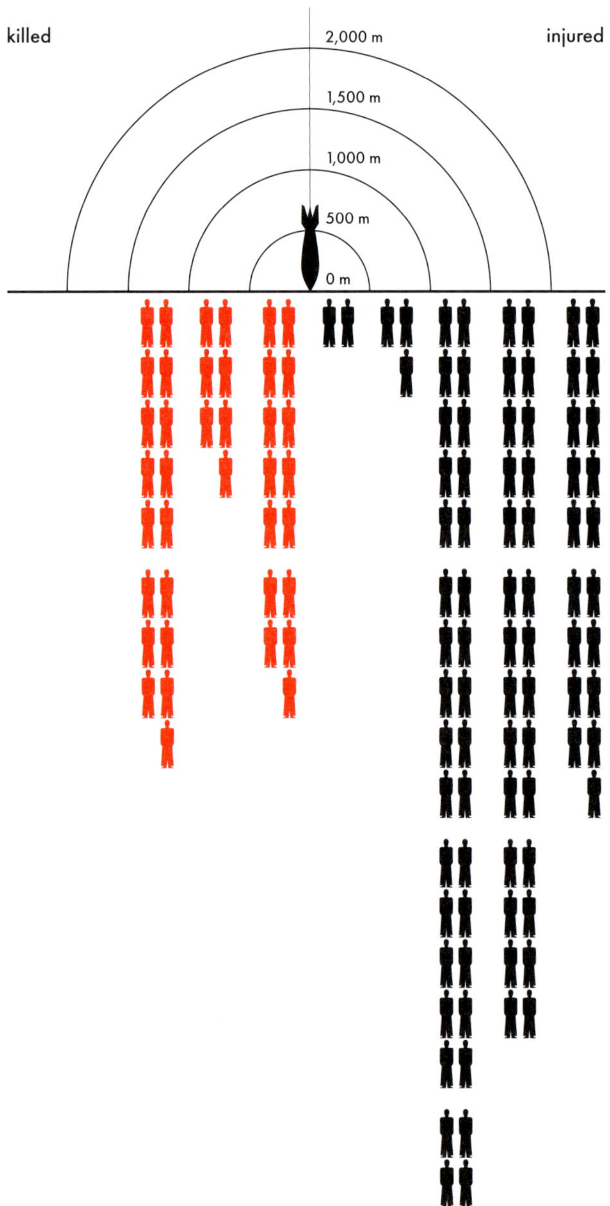

one symbol represents 500 direct casualties from the air-burst explosion
red: killed
black: injured

had reached the point at which the Manhattan Project could perform its first nuclear test, named "Trinity" by Robert Oppenheimer.[2] Allegedly, he drew inspiration from John Donne's poem "Hymn to God, My God, in My Sickness." The poem tells the tale of a man on the brink of death, though not afraid – knowing that heaven awaits him.[3]

It was a mere three months later that the USA dropped the atomic bomb "Little Boy" on the town of Hiroshima in Japan, using a B-29 bomber named after the pilot's mother, Enola Gay, bringing about the death of approximately 64,500 people and the injury of a further 72,000. Only three members of the *Enola Gay*'s crew knew what the real nature of the mission was; the others were given black goggles to avoid being blinded by the big flash that was about to occur. Three days later, the USA dropped a second atomic bomb called *Fat Man* on Nagasaki, killing a further 39,000 people.[4] Additional atomic warheads were being readied to be dropped in the weeks ahead if Japan did not surrender.

In 1947 the Manhattan Project was dissolved and succeeded by the US Atomic Energy Agency. Former scientists of the Manhattan Project then created the *Bulletin of the Atomic Scientists*, showing the "doomsday clock"[5] on every cover of their annual magazine. Paradoxically, the same people who were part of the team that developed the first nuclear bomb to be used also invented the doomsday clock, a metaphorical clock that depicts how close humanity is to a man-made global catastrophe. While at its start, the estimation of minutes to midnight was based on nuclear threats, it now also includes risks arising from climate change, bioterrorism, and artificial intelligence. In 1947, the year it was introduced, the clock was set at 7 minutes to midnight. Today (2023) the clock is set at 90 seconds to midnight, the closest we have ever been to total annihilation since its inception.[6] While Neurath chronicled the making of the modern man, the introduction of the atomic bomb would in turn promise to be the fastest method for the modern human to unmake itself.

***Fat Man* Bomb Mortality**

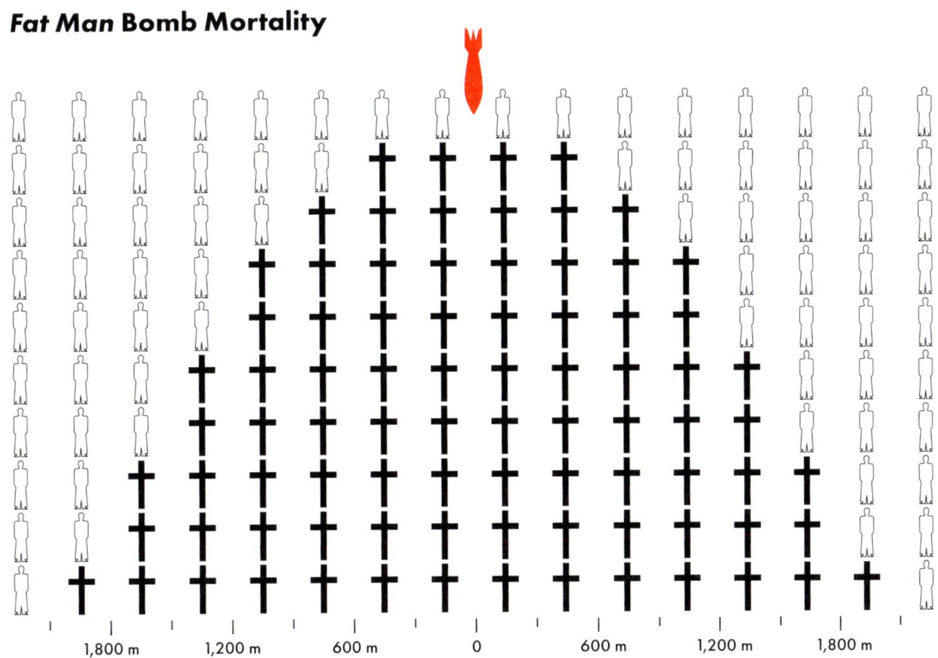

one cross symbol represents 10 per 100 people killed per distance by the *Fat Man* bomb in Nagasaki

Doomsday Clock: Minutes to Midnight

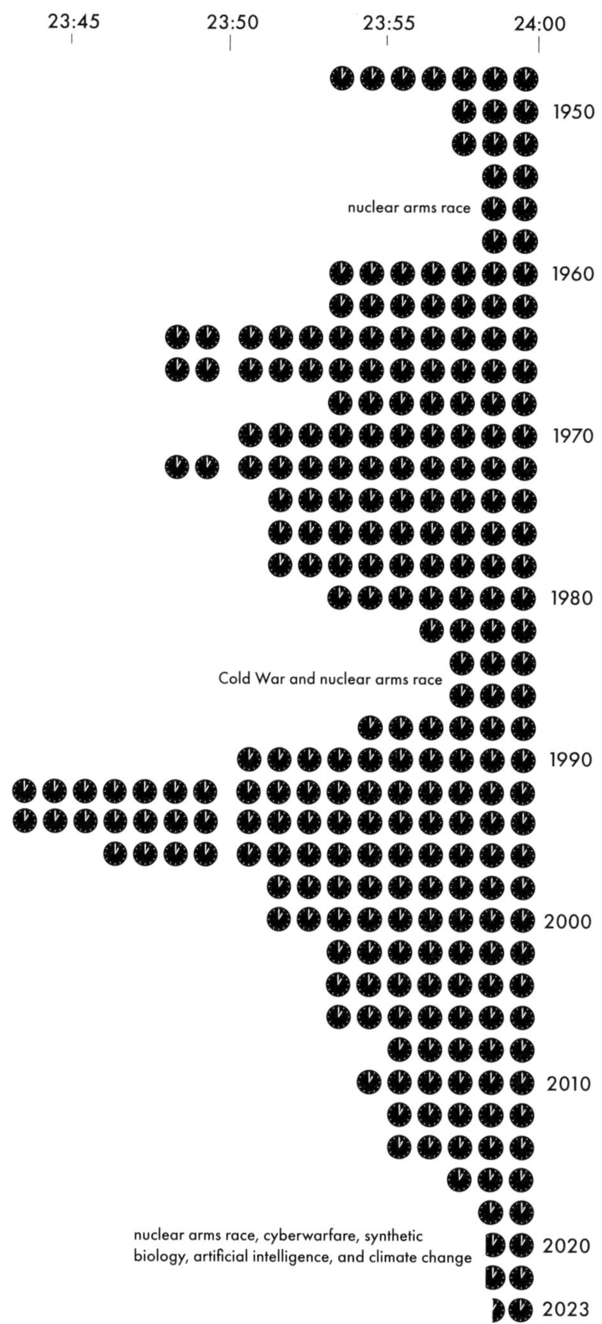

each clock represents 1 minute (60 seconds) to midnight

The Big Extinction

Apocalypses are nothing new to planet Earth. Long before *Homo sapiens* left their first traces, Earth was prone to many ups and downs. One of the five big extinction events, the Permian-Triassic extinction, occurred some 250 million years ago, wiping out an estimated 96% of all life at that time.[7] It took 10 million years for life to recover. As we speak, humankind is working on the planet's sixth big extinction, the first extinction in history to be caused intentionally by "intelligent" creatures, rather than by external forces of the universe.

Mass Extinctions During the Past 500 Million Years

each bar represents 10% of marine extinction intensity

The bars show the apparent percentage (not the absolute number) of marine animal genera becoming extinct.

It is widely believed that we are living in the Anthropocene, in a time when human actions have such an impact that they influence the present and future of planet Earth as a whole. While the Anthropocene Working Group has not yet formally defined the Anthropocene as an epoch in the geologic time scale, the organization has marked it as beginning in the mid-20th century, coinciding with the time the doomsday clock was introduced. Nuclear activity, the burning of fossil fuels, the dumping of plastic waste in the oceans, and the genetic modification of plants and animals are some of the factors that define the start of the period in which the Earth bears witness to a drastic increase across nearly all measures of human activity – a time known as the Great Acceleration.[8] One of the most pertinent results of this acceleration (in today's discourse) is climate change caused by the burning of fossil fuels. Greenhouse gases that have been captured underground in the form of oil and gas are emitted into the atmosphere, changing its composition. One of the earliest scientific and best-known warnings was the report *The Limits to Growth*,[9] released in 1972 by the Club of Rome, a group of selected politicians, diplomats, scientists, economists, and business leaders from around the globe. Although the report drew much attention and led to the rise of "green" political parties all over the globe, nothing was done. On the contrary, ever since then, plastic waste and fossil fuel burning has increased with each and every year.

Humans tend to forget the fragility of their species. Pandemics, earthquakes, volcanic eruptions, and meteors are very real threats that can impact the Earth at any time. In 1815, Indonesia's Mount Tambora volcano erupted, sending the Earth into a two-year-long winter.[10] The loss of harvests caused the starvation of millions of people around the world. Nature, however, recovered swiftly. Past extinctions show that any future extinction caused by the Anthropocene poses little danger to life on Earth as a whole, yet will likely be fatal to humans. Earth's other species, however, might not see humanity's extinction as a reason to mourn. Through modernity, a surplus has been created, but humanity is also risking its very existence.

Nuclear Times

Ever more people with ever more electronic devices need ever more energy. In the 1930s, households had radios and electric lighting, but no dishwasher, washing machine, vacuum cleaner, or electric toothbrush. Coal, the main energy source at that time, was already known to be an unhealthy energy source. The ever-increasing accumulation of appliances led to a steady increase in coal consumption, which eventually turned lethal. During the six days of the Great Smog of London in 1952,[11] thousands of people died.

Therefore, the harnessing of nuclear energy was welcomed as a huge step for humankind toward an endless source of clean and cheap energy. Architects designed houses that could walk, and novels and comics commonly depicted humans conquering outer space. Yet the promise of clean, unlimited nuclear energy was in fact merely the silver lining of a very dark cloud; nuclear energy is only cheap and clean as long as it is safely contained. People knew it could go wrong, and it inevitably did.

On April 26, 1986, nuclear fission in reactor 4 of the Chernobyl nuclear power plant in what is now Ukraine spiked out of control, resulting in a core meltdown.[12] The result was devastating. The wind carried a radioactive cloud over central and western Europe, threatening the health of millions of people. In the years leading up to the disaster, the KGB had been tasked with taking measures to prevent "panic and provocative rumors" regarding a leak in 1982 and other emergencies in 1984.[13]

Nuclear Fallout as a Result of the Chernobyl Disaster

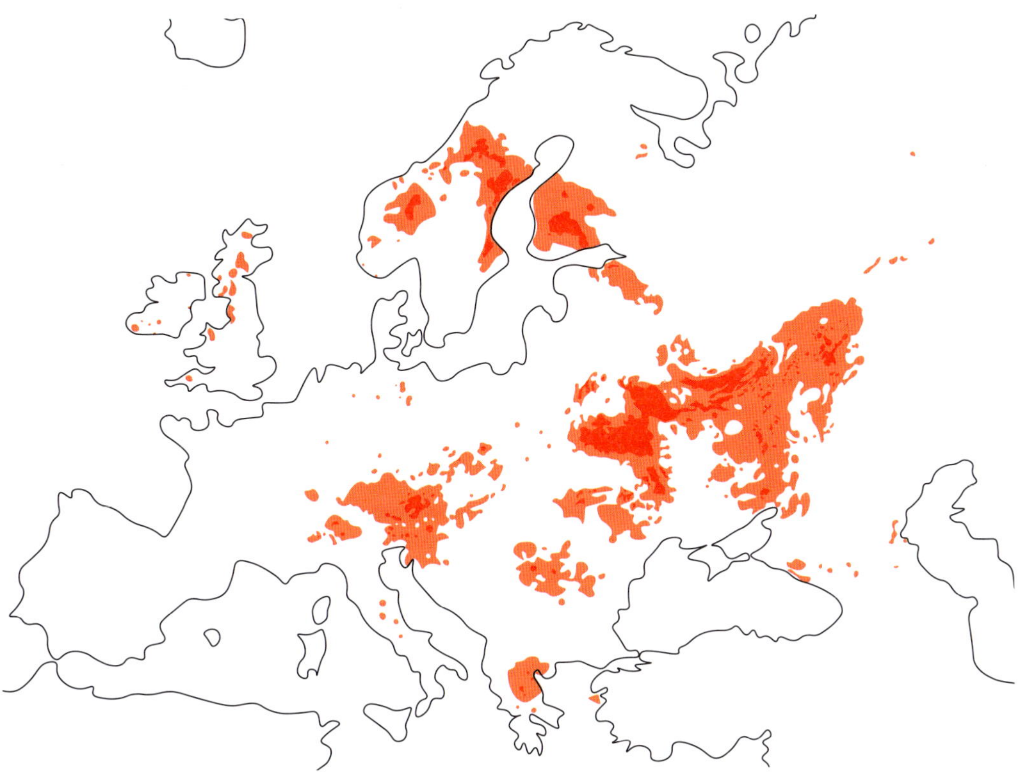

As the Chernobyl nuclear power plant melted down, the USSR cut all intercity telephone networks to the nearby town of Pripyat, preventing word from getting out, and workers at the plant were told not to speak of the disaster to family and friends.[14] While the spread of the word could be controlled to an extent, the spread of radiation could not: when radiation reached Sweden, some 1,000 km away, the rest of the world got wind of the disaster not from the Soviets, but from alarmed nuclear scientists in Sweden.

This occurrence inspired other countries such as the Netherlands to suspend their nuclear programs or to terminate nuclear energy altogether, as in Sweden and Austria. Although Chernobyl is today the worst nuclear disaster the world has seen, it was not the first time that things had gone wrong – in fact, that medal belongs to the British. While the Chernobyl disaster is well-known, the UK had already borne witness to one of the worst nuclear accidents to date in 1957. The Windscale Fire happened at Unit 1 at Windscale, Cumberland. The catastrophe created a fire in the nuclear plant which burned for three days and released radioactive fallout that spread across the UK and mainland Europe, contaminating these areas with toxic polonium-210. Then-Prime Minister Harold Macmillan ordered the disaster to be strictly censored. The UK government played down the incident and continued to build nuclear power plants. The area around the plant was not evacuated; however, in 500 square kilometers of the surrounding countryside, milk contaminated with dangerous levels of iodine-131 was dumped into the Irish Sea for about a month.

One byproduct of the nuclear fission process used by the Windscale nuclear plant is a radioactive element called tritium. This is a core ingredient in the making of

Nuclear Power Plants

before 1970

1970–1979

1980–1989

1990–1999

2000–2009

2010–2020

every symbol represents 5 nuclear power plants

blue filled: USA & Canada
blue outlined: southern hemisphere (Argentina, Brazil, Mexico and South Africa)
black filled: Western and Central Europe
black outlined: Eastern Europe (Belarus, Ukraine, Russia)
red filled: China
red outlined: Asia (without China)
green filled: Japan

thermonuclear warheads. Winston Churchill had committed the UK to continuing its testing of thermonuclear bombs before international test bans came into effect. Under a very tight deadline, pressure was placed on the Windscale power plant to produce tritium for the UK's hydrogen bomb tests. In order to meet this deadline, the power plant was misused and heated beyond its limits to produce the tritium at a higher rate than would otherwise be possible. This misuse of the plant resulted in its eventual failure and is suspected to have led to an estimated 240 cancer-related deaths.[15]

Since the 1990s, the years following the Chernobyl catastrophe, the USA and Europe have kept their stock of nuclear power plants constant. Some countries like Germany decided to become nuclear-free after the second-largest nuclear power plant disaster in Fukushima, Japan, in 2011. While many thousands died from the tsunami and the earthquake that caused the disaster, no immediate deaths from acute radiation syndrome were reported. However, more than 100,000 people were evacuated from their homes, and official figures report 2,313 disaster-related deaths (in addition to the 19,500 caused by the natural disaster).[16]

While this seemed like the definitive end of nuclear development, the moment the West stopped building new nuclear plants, China started. Since 1991, China has been ramping up its arsenal of nuclear plants and announced in 2021 that it would construct 150 new reactors in the next 15 years – more than the whole world has built in the past 35 years. At the moment, more than 50 nuclear power plants are under construction.[17] Although the first nuclear power plant went on grid in 1954, no country in the world has a permanent storage site for its nuclear waste. All high-level radioactive waste from the past 70 years is in temporary storage facilities, while the half-life of plutonium is 24,000 years. For the 12,000 tons added every year, the time needed to decay completely would be more than 200,000 years.[18]

Nuclear Waste Dumped in the Ocean between 1946 and 1993

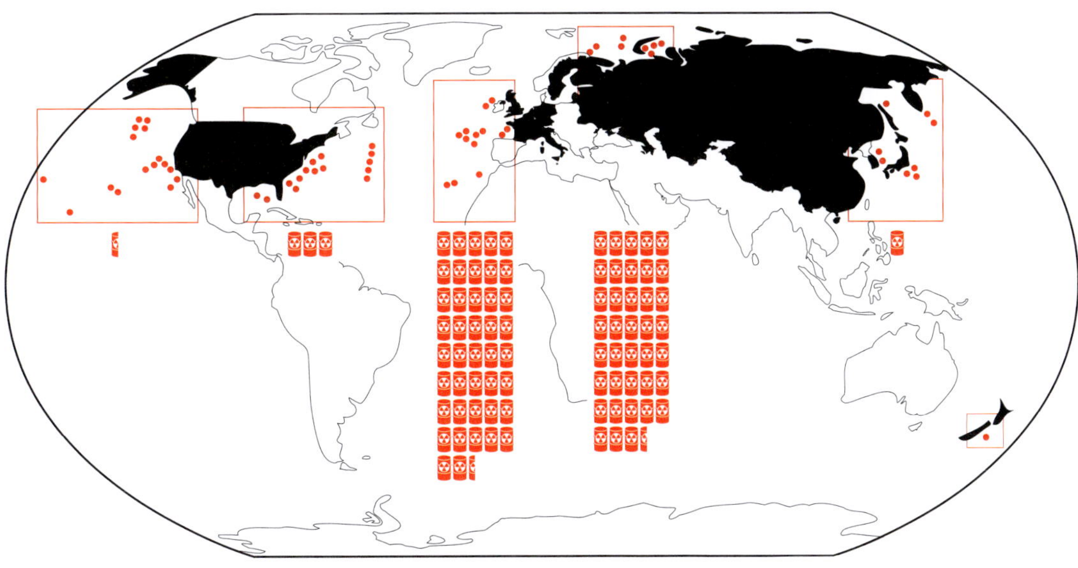

red barrels: one symbol represents 1,000 terabecquerel of nuclear waste dumped per region
red dots: nuclear waste dumping locations
black: countries that dumped nuclear waste

Until 1994, radioactive waste could legally be dumped into the oceans. Only then did the International Maritime Organization (IMO) ban this practice for solid radioactive waste. Prior to the ban, a reported amount of 85,000 tons of radioactive waste had been dumped, with the USSR, UK, Switzerland, USA, and Belgium being the top five contributors.[19]

Other strategies for long-term waste disposal include underground depots, future reuse, and disposal in outer space. Some nuclear waste is still being dumped in international waters when no one is looking. Off the coast of Somalia, while civil war has raged since the 1990s, European companies broker deals with local warlords for the disposal of nuclear waste. Children in coastal towns are born without limbs, and widespread cancer and other diseases appear that are symptomatic of radiation sickness, while Europe gets to indulge in its high-tech nuclear energy.[20] The prosperous and powerful countries invest and profit from relatively cheap nuclear power, while the risks are shared with the entire world, thus also with the poor and burdened.

Nuclear Weapons

black filled: USA
black outlined: France & UK
red filled: Russia
red outlined: China
blue filled: Israel
green filled: Pakistan
green outlined: India

one symbol represents 100 nuclear warheads

Fat Man Versus *Tsar Bomba*

Fat Man – dropped on Nagasaki on August 9, 1945

Tsar Bomba – tested on October 30, 1961

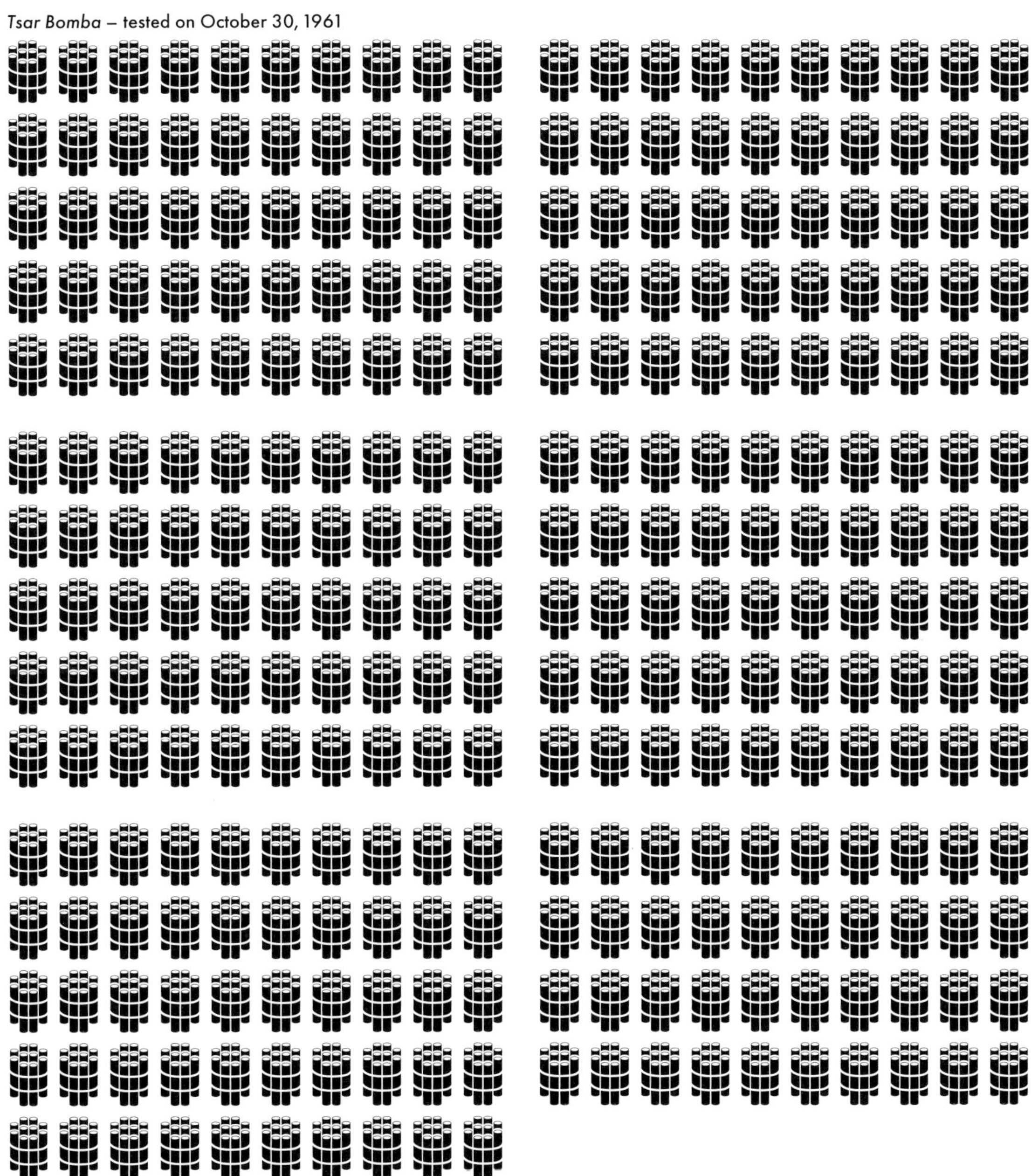

each single stick symbol represents 20 kilotons of TNT equivalent
each bundle symbol represents 200 kilotons of TNT equivalent

Multiple Threat Scenario

The bombs dropped on Hiroshima and Nagasaki by the USA in 1945 were not only the biggest war crime by a democratic country in modern times; they also prompted a discussion about humanity's capability of self-destruction. Instead of placing a global moratorium on nuclear weapons, the most powerful countries, with the USA and the USSR at the forefront, started a nuclear arms race, adding 64,450 nuclear arms to stockpiles during a 41-year crescendo; that boils down to 30 new weapons of mass destruction per week.[21] Negotiations to curtail arms production began in the 1980s with the START I bilateral treaty between the USA and the then Soviet Union to reduce and limit the use of *strategic* offensive arms such as nuclear warheads and ballistic missiles. START I was implemented in 1991 and expired in 2009. Subsequent START treaties didn't come to fruition until 2010, when Russia and the USA signed the New START, which eventually was extended in 2021 till 2026, limiting the number of nuclear warheads on deployed intercontinental ballistic missiles, submarine-launched ballistic missiles, and heavy bombers to 1,550.[22] On February 21, 2023, the president of Russia, Vladimir Putin, announced that Russia would be suspending its participation in New START.

Depleted Uranium Weapons

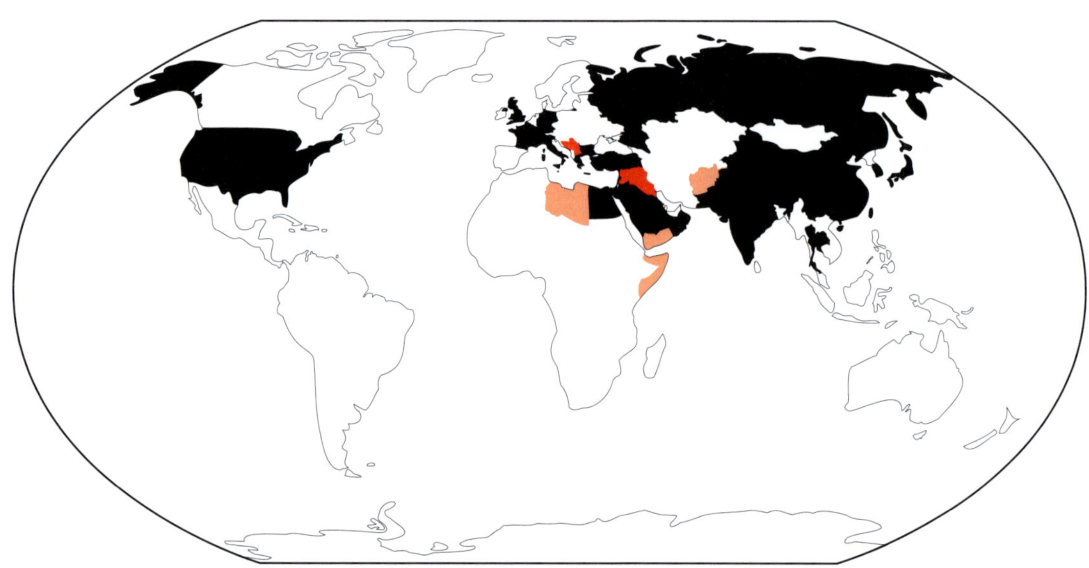

black: countries that use(d) depleted uranium (DU) weapons
red: countries where depleted uranium (DU) weapons are known to have been used
pink: countries where depleted uranium (DU) weapons have most likely been used
(2019)

Nuclear warheads today are seen as a deterrent rather than as something to be used in battle. The largest nuclear bomb, the USSR's *Tsar Bomba* (58-megaton yield),[23] is 2,760 times as powerful as those used by the USA in Japan, and could wipe out a city like New York along with its 8.419 million people. When both opponents possess the same destructive power, it makes sense that neither side pulls the trigger; the advent of nuclear weaponry has brought about a peace that is guarded by the fear of mutually assured destruction.

To bypass their very own START agreement, both Russia and the USA are building up arsenals of tactical nuclear weapons which are not curtailed by the agreement, since they are slightly less deadly than the weapons banned by START. Tactical nuclear warheads, as opposed to their strategic counterparts, commonly have a shorter range, higher accuracy, and lower explosive capacity (or yield). In short, with a tactical nuclear weapon, you won't end the war, while strategic nuclear weapons – what the general public understands as nuclear bombs – aim to cause maximum destruction in order to wipe out the enemy (both army and civilians). The concern, however, is that tactical nuclear weapons are as a result easier to pull the trigger on, and things could very rapidly escalate beyond a tipping point that provokes the use of strategic nuclear weapons, which would result in the loss of millions of lives.

A first step in that direction is the use of depleted uranium (DU) anti-tank weapons, predominantly by the US army since the 1970s. A 30 mm DU projectile penetrates a tank with three times the force of a conventional shell. On impact, a projectile made of uranium-238, a waste product of the nuclear industry, spreads radioactive and highly toxic nanodust across the battlefield, poisoning soldiers on both sides and the civilian population well after the end of the war.[24]

Yet nuclear war is not exclusive in its destructive capability. Global warming is also a threat. The Intergovernmental Panel on Climate Change (IPCC) has described tipping points in terms of temperature increases of the planet. So far, collectively, modern humans have increased the temperature of the Earth by 1.1 degrees Celsius since pre-industrial times. The IPCC warns that going beyond 2 degrees would trigger irreversible changes. It's not just a matter of rising ocean levels; ocean currents would falter, causing droughts and threatening the food supply on a global scale, and permafrost would melt, releasing further greenhouse gases into the atmosphere. At a certain point, even if humanity becomes carbon-neutral, the processes of global warming become self-amplifying.[25]

Humans today live in a mixed-threat environment. Since 2007, climate change has been a factor considered in setting the doomsday clock. More recently, synthetic biology, cyberwarfare, and artificial intelligence have been added to the list of potential threats to humankind. Each threat plays out according to its own scenario. While an all-out nuclear war would result in a rather quick end to human life, the results of climate change might finish humans off in just a few hundred years. It is also not clear how the biosphere and humans will react to the genetic modification of flora and fauna or the application of nanotechnology in the human body. Furthermore, it remains to be seen how artificial intelligence will treat human intelligence in the long run. The growing reliance on information technology (IT) poses the risk that humans will lose control and oversight of the digital world they've created. While risks are growing, humanity is lagging behind in curtailing them. It appears that humans are struggling to keep pace with the Great Acceleration they have set in motion.

Population and Urbanization

The Growth of Mankind

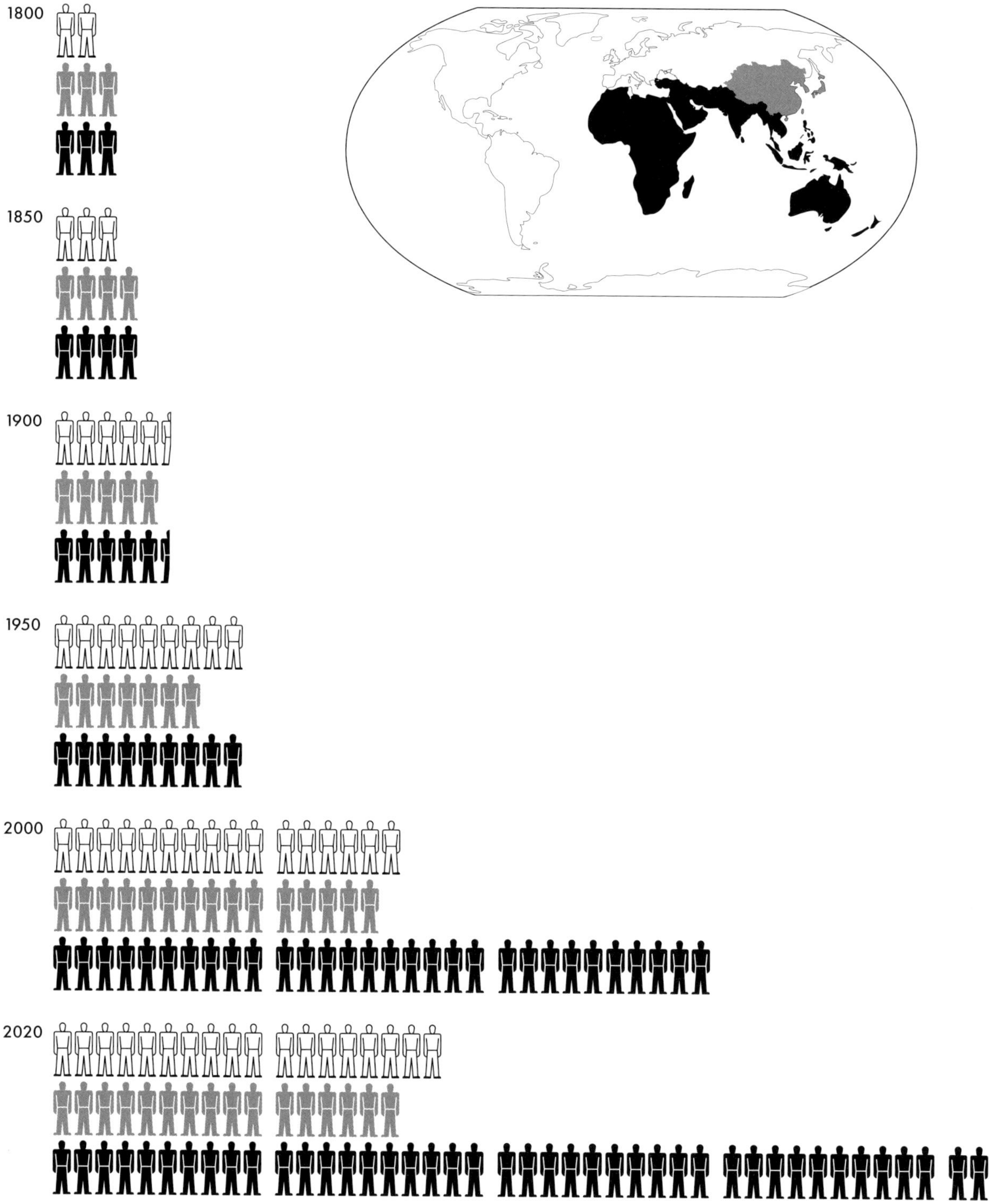

Each symbol represents 100 million humans (division of Earth based on Neurath)

white: the two Americas, Europe, the former Soviet Union
gray: China, Japan, Taiwan
black: other parts of the world

Population Growth I

The West experienced a spectacular population boom starting in the 19th century. After two devastating world wars, the baby boom of the 1950s, which led to extreme population growth and a large surplus of young men in European society, came to be seen as a threat to political stability. By the 1960s, Western policymakers identified population growth as a major hindrance to economic growth. While Western thinkers referred to the ultimately short-lived postwar baby boom, the idea of limiting population growth was picked up around the world, even in areas that had not yet experienced a population boom themselves.[1]

India was the first, yet also the most extreme, to adopt this idea. During a 21-month-long state of emergency in 1975 and 1976, known simply as "the Emergency," more than 8 million civilians were sterilized. Two thousand men died from botched operations.[2] The primary focus was on the poor, Muslim quarters of Delhi. These forced sterilizations were funded by the World Bank, the Swedish International Development Authority, and the UN Population Fund, with assistance from the Ford and Rockefeller Foundations. The World Bank president at the time, and former US secretary of defense, Robert McNamara, said proudly, "At long last, India is moving to effectively address its population problem."[3] Countries like Peru and Bangladesh had similar programs, with devastating effects on women and men, targeting the indigenous populations in the case of Peru and the poor in Bangladesh.[4]

China took a different approach. Its one child policy aimed to limit the growth of its population between 1980 and 2015. The measure was developed at the time that China's economy hit rock bottom after the disastrous "Great Leap Forward" by Mao Zedong in the 1960s. The Chinese Communist Party (CCP) justified the one child policy with prominent studies and scholarly literature like *The Limits to Growth* (1972)[5] by the Club of Rome and *The Population Bomb* (1968)[6] by Paul R. Ehrlich, which both warned about the threat of an overpopulated planet Earth.

However, it is more likely that hardcore economic reasons created the basis for the one child policy. The prevailing economic idea of the 1970s was that a population growth that exceeds economic growth results in negative economic growth.[7] Thus, if a country was not able to boost its economic growth beyond a certain threshold, the only option was to dampen its population growth. Hence, slow-growing economies in the 1970s like China, India, and Bangladesh introduced harsh measures.

Today China implements a three-child policy; however, it enforces sterilizations and abortions among its Uighur population because of the latter's desire for more autonomy. These measures, along with the Chinese Communist Party's forceful incarceration of Uighurs in reeducation camps is part of a larger ethnocide by the CCP.[8]

The threat of an overpopulated planet was not new to the 1960s. Two hundred years earlier, Hong Liangji (1746–1809)[9] and Thomas Malthus (1766–1834)[10] had discovered that increases in agricultural production might be outpaced by population growth, which would eventually lead to global famines. Both concluded correctly that land is finite, but population can grow infinitely. A devastating shortage of food would have been the case without modern farming techniques and its machinery, pesticides, and fertilizers.

Another reason the Western world was alarmed by population growth in the 1960s and '70s was its real threat to the economy. Double-digit postwar growth was waning,

Production and Unemployment in the UK

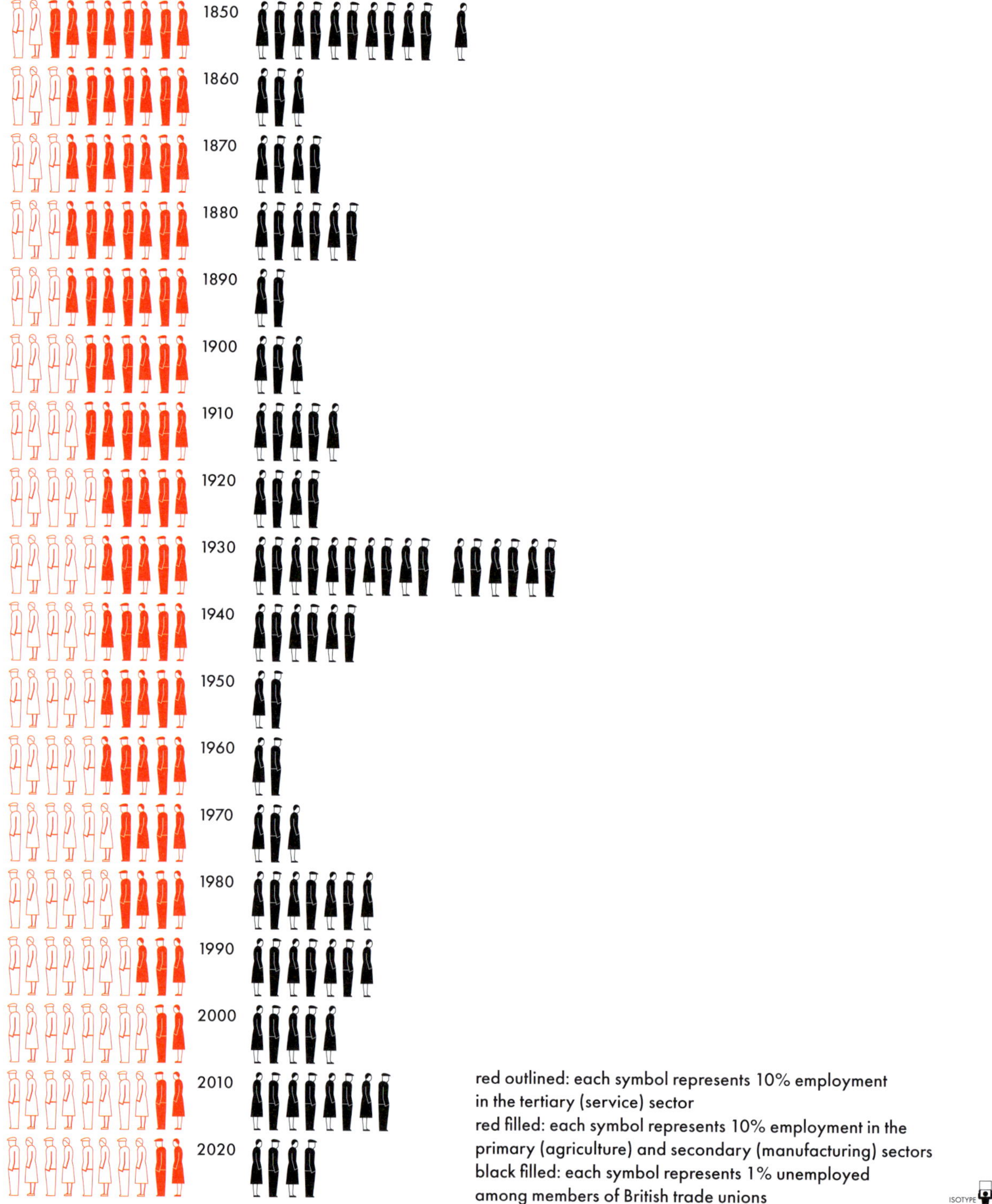

and unemployment was on the rise. Thus, more people meant more problems. The introduction and promotion of modern methods of birth control brought relief.

However, in the late 1980s, the view of population growth flipped radically with the rise of consumerism. After the West digested the shock of deindustrialization, new jobs were created in the service industry. Trading, serving, and selling, instead of producing, became the new mantra of the West's economy. Unemployment has lost its horror with the distribution of wealth, which has turned every person, productive or not, into a potential spender, viewer, and user. The economic mantra of today is "the more people, the better," since more people equals more consumers, which equals more profit.

New, but timid, criticism of population growth has been coming from people and organizations that are concerned with the state of the Earth's atmosphere and biosphere. The reasoning is very similar to the conclusions that Hong Liangji and Thomas Malthus drew some 300 years ago: planet Earth's resources are limited, but people's numbers can increase infinitely. This time the fear is not malnutrition, but a collapse of the ecosystem through pollution of the atmosphere, which could be fatal to the human race. The more people inhabit the planet, the more harm is done, especially by the people who live in the prosperous West.

Living Above Their Means

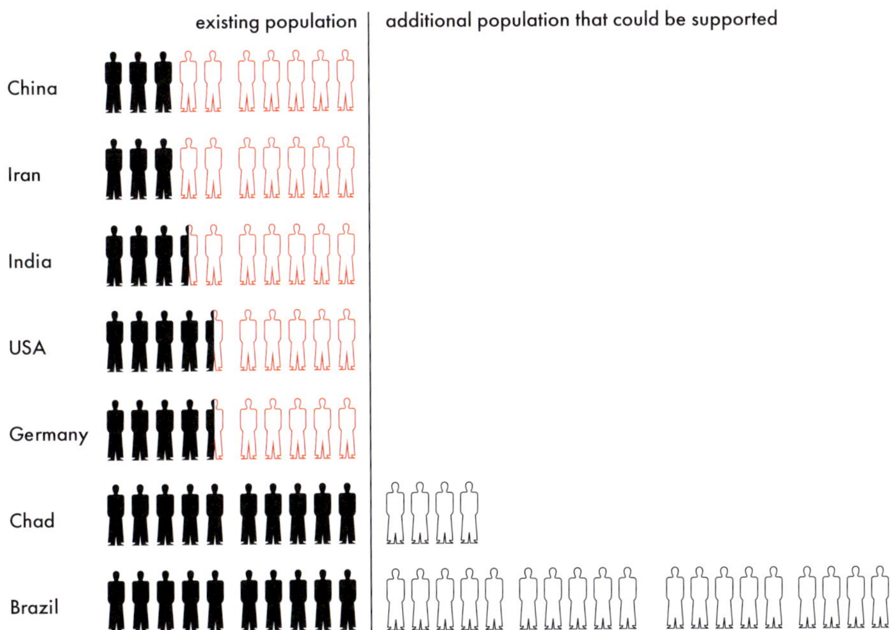

one human symbol represents 10% of the national population (2022)

black: existing population within the ecological footprint of a country
red outlined: existing population that exceeds the sustainable ecological footprint of a country
black outlined: population that could be supported within the ecological footprint of a country

The burden on the environment due to human actions can be measured using the I = PAT equation – Impact = Population × Affluence × Technology – which was developed by Barry Commoner, Paul R. Ehrlich, and John Holdren in 1970.[11] To reduce the negative impact of society on the environment, at least one of these multipliers needs to be changed.

Yet changing anything in this equation is diametrically opposite to the West's economic system of consumer capitalism. Already a stagnation in population growth or a plateau in spending capacity would threaten the entire economic system. The I = PAT formula might simplify complex matters, but it is undeniable that the affluent countries of this planet harm their environment much more extensively. And their aim is still to become more affluent. Changes in technology regarding improvements in efficiency and renewable energy sources seem to remain the only factor that could herald a change for the better in the short run. So far, no such shift is in sight.

Population Growth II

The extreme population growth at the onset of modernity in the West was triggered by better health- and childcare, lowering child mortality. As modern healthcare expanded around the globe, the population grew from 2.2 billion in the late 1930s to 7.9 billion today and is expected to increase to 11 billion by the end of the century.[12] If all goes well, this figure will mark the peak of human population.

Population growth has already started to slow down. One reason is the phenomenon of demographic transition, which describes societies' shift from high birth rates and high death rates to low birth rates and low death rates. It is believed that this transition generally goes hand in hand with advancements in technology, education, and economic development. In Europe the demographic transition precisely followed the shift from pre-industrial society to post-industrial society.

Generally, it can be concluded that the higher the income per capita and the better its people's education, the lower a country's fertility rate is. While Germany has a fertility rate of 1.5 children per woman of childbearing age, which is far below the population replacement rate, Chad scores 6.3 children per woman of childbearing age.[13]

In poorer societies with no or little social security, children are an extra helping hand in rough times and an old-age provision, thus the more kids, the tighter the social security net is woven. On the other hand, families in wealthier countries seem to make a strategic decision to have fewer children. The reasons can be manifold: private

Fertility – 1960

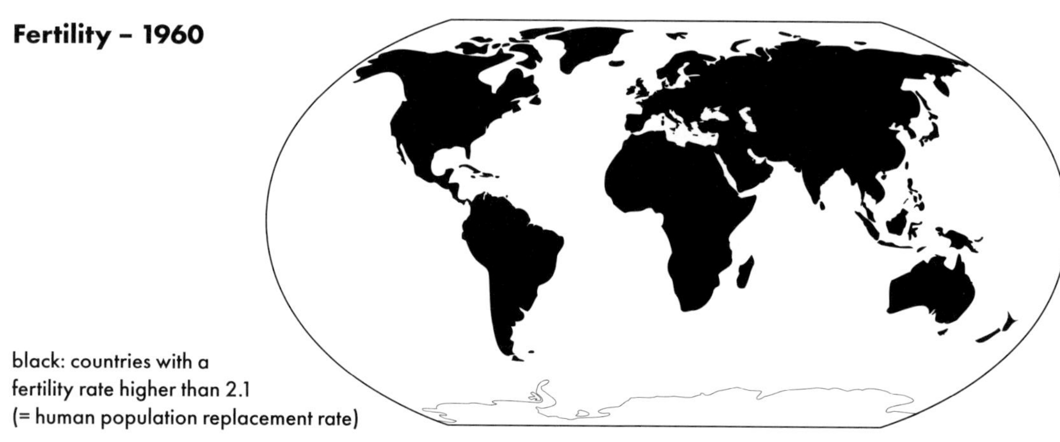

black: countries with a fertility rate higher than 2.1 (= human population replacement rate)

Fertility – 2020

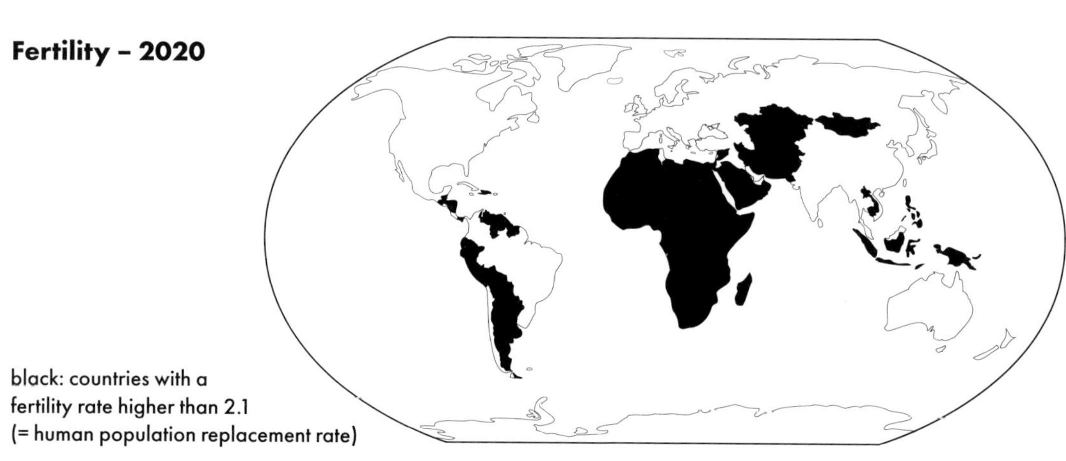

black: countries with a fertility rate higher than 2.1 (= human population replacement rate)

wealth and social security make having kids as a provision for old age less reasonable; family life is quieter with fewer kids around; and fewer of them make it possible to invest more in each child's education. It can be expensive to raise kids, especially for middle-class parents. Peer pressure forces parents to send kids to expensive private schools and finance a costly university career.

If all countries continue on the path to prosperity, fertility rates will continue to fall. The global fertility rate, which stood at 4.7 births per woman in 1960, fell to just 2.3 in 2020. In India, Earth's most populous country and home to 18% of Earth's population, the fertility rate has dropped to 2.0 children per woman, which is just below the population replacement rate of 2.1. The country experienced a steady economic growth since the beginning of the 21st century which seems to already be reflected in its declining reproduction rate.[14]

The slowing down of population growth is a prospect that is welcomed by many who care about the future of the human race and planet Earth as humanity's habitat. But what is a blessing for the planet is regarded as a blow to economic development. The high-income countries, which cause the largest environmental damage and whose decline would be the greatest blessing, are the ones that complain the most about their decreasing populations. A declining population means a declining workforce that generates less income from taxes and makes it ever more difficult to support the increasingly aging population.

Yet even worse than a declining workforce is a declining stock of consumers. The shift to an older and more conservative population hurts the economy especially badly, since the young are more eager to spend their money carelessly, while the oldies tend to hoard their assets.

Growth is the sole foundation of the current economic system of consumer capitalism. If growth reached its limits at home, it must be found elsewhere. Therefore, saturated economies are extremely receptive to countries with a growing population that is willing to spend large parts of its income. As long as the human population is increasing somewhere on the planet, and with it the stock of consumers who are able and willing to buy goods, the current economic system might endure.

Income

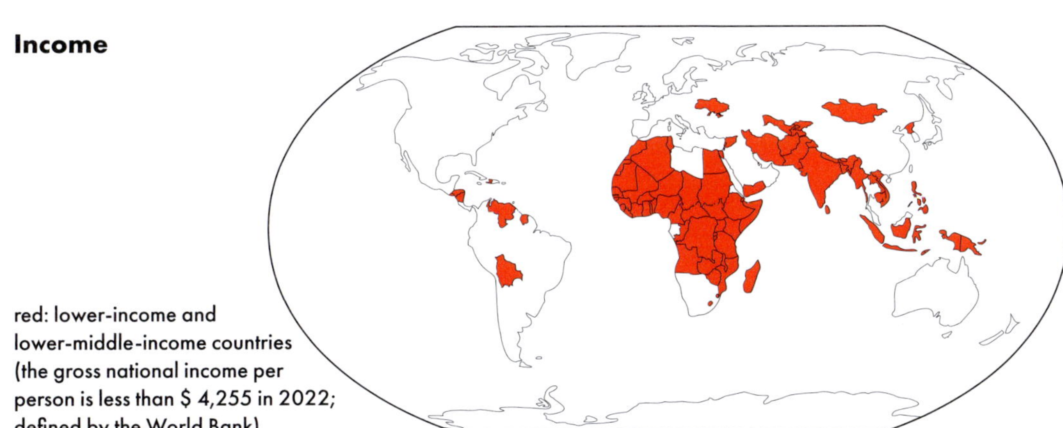

red: lower-income and lower-middle-income countries (the gross national income per person is less than $ 4,255 in 2022; defined by the World Bank)

Urbanization

Otto Neurath claimed that "urbanization is a characteristic of modernity." And he did so correctly: modernity has not come to a halt since he published the book, and neither has urbanization. Actually, human population is urbanizing at a rapid speed. While only 25% of the human population was living in urban areas in 1940,[15] this figure rose to 56% in 2020.[16] It seems that the human race is turning into an urban species, trading the farm for a flat.

Urbanization is experiencing a radical shift in its center of gravity from the northwest to the southeast. The world's urban population has risen from 570 million in 1940 to 4.4 billion in 2021, but most of this growth has occurred in Asia and especially China.[17] The urban proportion of the second most populous country grew from 16% in 1960 to 63% today, for example. In the UK, the change in this time period was from 78% to 84% and now seems to have reached a plateau.[18]

Urbanization

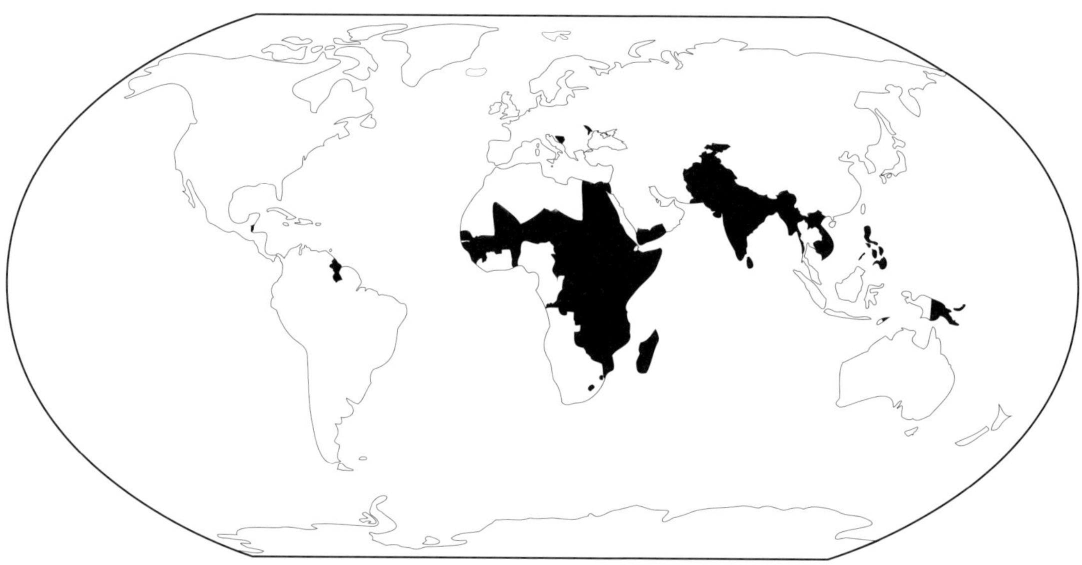

black: countries with less then 50% of their population living in urban areas (2021)

In India, whose 1.43 billion inhabitants make it the most populated country on Earth, only 35% of the people live in cities. Yet India is urbanizing fast. The urban agglomeration of Delhi, the fastest-growing city in the world and the most populous in India, expanded from 640,000 inhabitants in 1940[19] to 33 million in 2022.[20] It is estimated that Delhi will have 40 million inhabitants by 2032, becoming Earth's most populated city by overtaking Tokyo. About half of the increase in Delhi's population comes from natural growth, the other half from migration.

The example of Delhi's rapid expansion follows a general trend that points to the increase in megacities, urban agglomerations with more than 10 million inhabitants. At the same time, the population in urban areas with fewer than 300,000 people is declining. The population of cities of between 300,000 and 5 million inhabitants remained rather stable over the past 60 years.[21] The number of megacities grew from two in 1950 (New York and Tokyo) to 33 in 2020 and is expected to increase to 40 by 2030.[22]

Urban Population per City Size

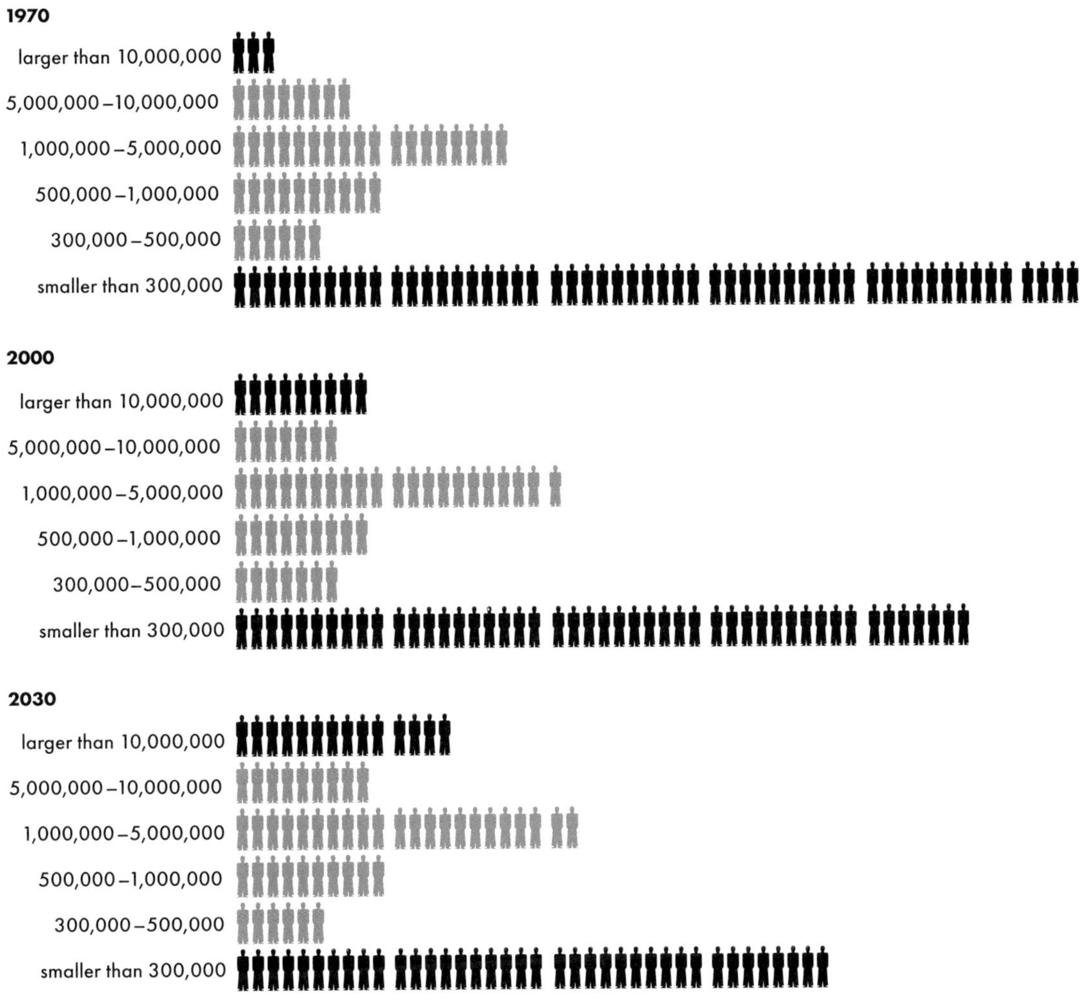

one symbol represents 1% of the global urban population

Cities need time to absorb the sudden influx of people. In 2012, Delhi counted 6,343 slums, home to about half of its population.[23] Infant mortality rates are high in India's slums: 40 deaths[24] per 1,000 live births compared to a national rate of 27 deaths per 1,000 live births.[25]

Rapid urbanization has also had its fallout in the West. In the second half of the 19th century in Europe and North America, it led to miserable living conditions in infamous slums, an example being the British cities where slums existed up until the 1970s. Strict building codes, public housing programs, and slum removal acts finally did away with inappropriate housing conditions.

If slums exist over a longer stretch of time, there is a risk of entrenchment. The overall population of Rio de Janeiro doubled between 1950 and 1980 from 2.4 to 5.2 million inhabitants, but has been growing since then at an ever slower pace, reaching 6.7 million in 2020.[26] While the city's population increased by 25% over the past 40 years, the population of its slums doubled in that same period. It is estimated that 1.2 million people now live in favelas (slums),[27] lacking access to the most basic

Urbanization, Births, and Deaths

circa 2020

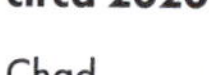

each human symbol represents 10% of the population
red: urban population

each star symbol represents 5 births per 1,000 population
each cross symbol represents 5 deaths per 1,000 population

services, like running water, education, and space for recreation. Rio de Janeiro's favela population is growing faster than the average, and there is no reverse trend in sight. This is resulting in a true risk of entrenchment, meaning that a large part of Brazil's population will remain second-class citizens just based on their area and living conditions.

The persistent appeal of cities, especially in the Global South, is based not only on the promise of attractive jobs, but more so on access to safety, better education, and better healthcare. The countryside all around the world is often not only deficient in these things, but lacking them altogether. In Chad, one of the poorest and least urbanized countries, only 24% of the population lives in cities.[28] The average death rate does not differ remarkably from that of Germany, yet what matters is not only how many people die, but the reason and at what point of their life. A shocking 46% (2015) of people in Chad die before their fifth birthday,[29] which can be seen as an indirect result of a large rural population that is facing sparse or nonexistent healthcare and maternity aid. This also affects Chad's adult population. Female and male inhabitants' life expectancy in rural areas is 1.83 times lower than in urban areas, meaning the difference between dying at the age of 38 in the countryside or 70 in the city.[30] Though this figure does not represent a general trend in Sub-Saharan Africa, it shows how great the differences can be in life expectancy and what strong forces can drive migration from the countryside to cities.

Age at Death

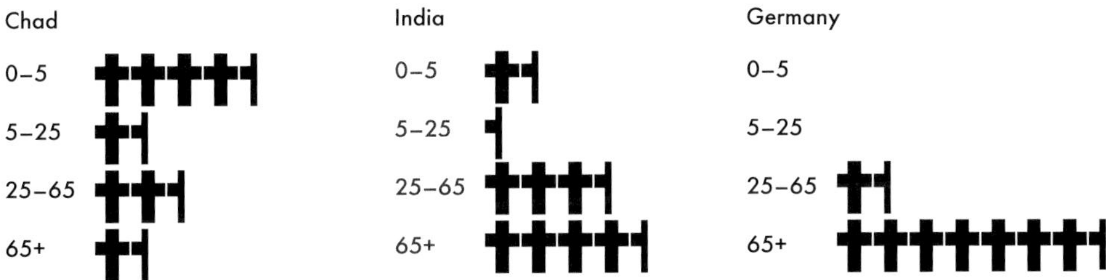

each symbol represents 10 out of 100 deaths (2017)

Various reasons are driving a migration toward cities in the Global South, the region currently modernizing and thus urbanizing at rapid speed. In 1950 more than half of the world's city-dwellers lived in high-income countries; by 2050 their share will have decreased to 20%.[31] Cities in poorer countries can invest less in public services and infrastructure, producing cities that are large in scale but highly disintegrated. The larger these urban fields become, the more difficult they are to govern and to serve through decent infrastructure.

The city of Lagos, Nigeria, home to 20 million people, opened its first 27 km long metro line in December 2022.[32] By comparison, Beijing, a city with the same number of inhabitants, has 25 lines with almost 800 km of track in total, serving 10.5 million passengers a day (2018).[33] Lagos is primarily served by minibuses, cars, and motorcycles.

On the intercity scale, the prospects look even bleaker. While Nigeria's railway was used by 15 million passengers in the 1980s, its passenger count declined to 1 million per

Urban Population and Metro Lines

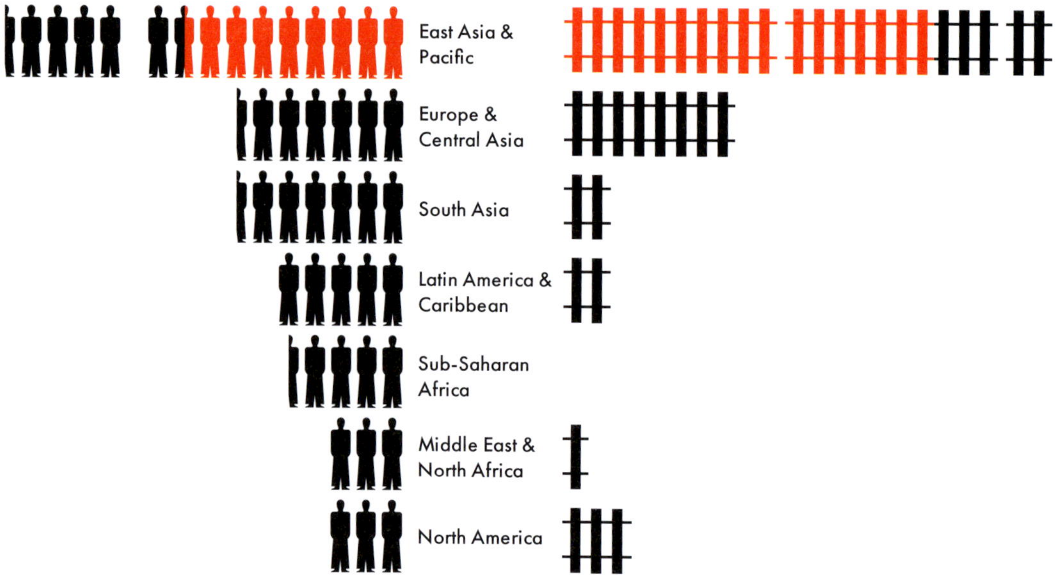

each person symbol represents 100 million people; red: China (2020)
each rail symbol represents 500 kilometers of metro network; red: China (2020)

year in the 2000s.[34] This makes movement between cities extremely difficult, results in a small migrant worker population, and fuels migratory urban growth. Unfortunately, Nigeria did not use its recent economic boom in the 2000s to improve public infrastructure – it is easier for cities to spend when money is abundant.

China has chosen a different approach. That country is using its economic boom of the past 30 years to invest extensively in urban and national rail infrastructure. There is no Chinese city with more than three million inhabitants without at least one metro line. 30 of the 45 existing metro systems have been opened in the past 10 years, and there are more to come. Shanghai's metro system first opened in 1993; today, with 800 km, it is twice as extensive as the one in London and has ten times its ridership. High-speed rail lines crisscross the country, connecting cities and providing access to the countryside. In the past 30 years, the extent of China's railways has tripled to 150,000 km, and

Megacities and Metro Lines

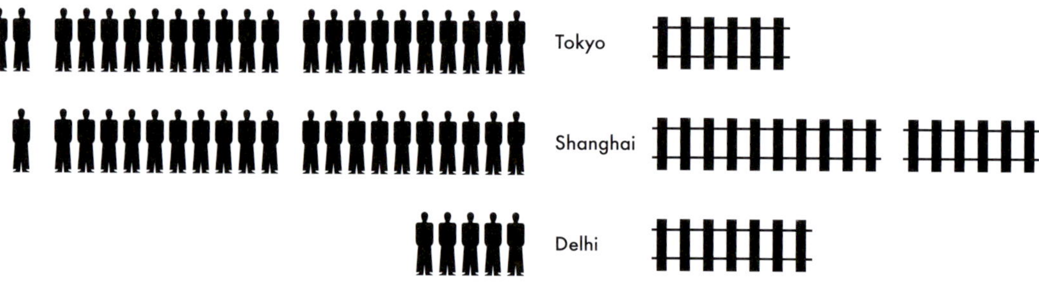

each person symbol represents 500,000 daily trips
each rail symbol represents 50 kilometers of metro network

Global Population

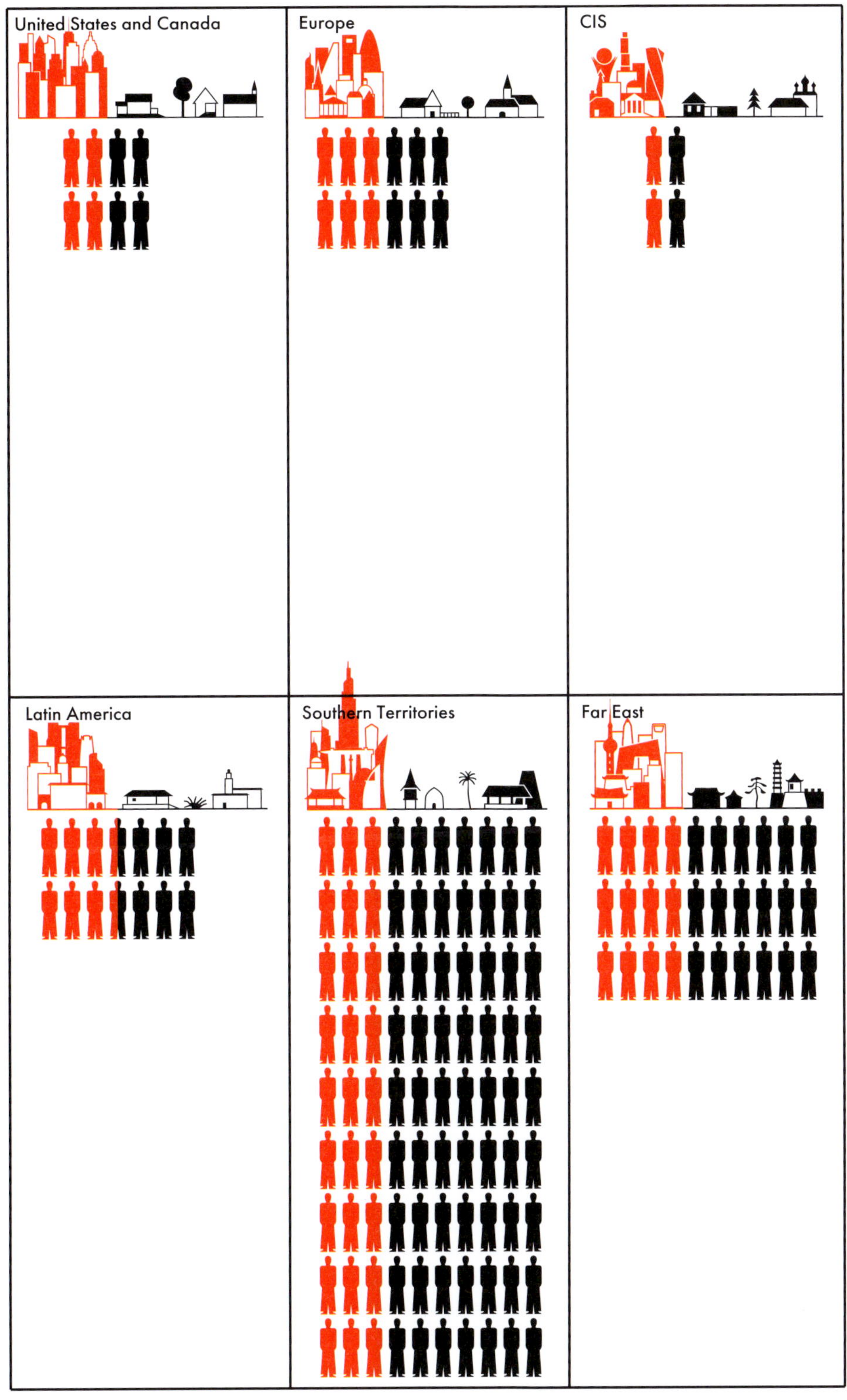

each symbol represents 50 million people (2021)
red: in cities of 100,000 or more people

ISOTYPE

in the past 13 years, a high-speed rail network of almost 40,000 km has been added. This has resulted in a highly mobile society with a large stock of migrant workers.[35]

Free of a colonial burden, China has replaced Europe in helping African states to modernize, with a third of Africa's power grid and infrastructure having been financed and constructed by Chinese state-owned companies since 2010.[36] The difference between Nigeria and China is the existence of a strong government in China, which provides transport infrastructure as well as social infrastructure. Even being non-democratic, China shows all the signs of a modern state, a state that releases its people from strong family ties to develop and address them as citizens.

The equation "more urbanization results in higher energy use" posed by Neurath holds still true across the planet. Yet there are big differences between megacities, based on the state of their development. Inadequate infrastructure might lead to chaotic cities, much to the annoyance of residents, but is a plus in terms of energy consumption. For example, the inhabitants of Lagos use about a fourth of the energy used by the average New Yorker and half that of a Beijing resident. Yet within Nigeria, the difference is stunning: a person in Lagos uses 3,750 times the energy of the average Nigerian.[37, 38]

The larger the city, the higher its energy consumption per person. In 2010, the 27 megacities then in existence housed 6.7% of the global population but used up 9% of the planet's electricity and 10% of its gasoline, and produced 13% of its solid waste. In their defense, they also produced 14.7% of the global GDP; thus, burning fossil fuels and producing waste pays off.[39]

Still, cities seem to be the best way to house all 8 billion humans who inhabit the planet. As with many modern projects, there seems to be no alternative to urban life. Yet in the shadow of extreme urban growth, the rural population is growing as well. Between 1950 and 2020, the planet's rural population doubled to 3.4 billion, which equals the entire human population in the year 1965.[40] And these people are sorely needed. The cities might be rich in capital, but they are very poor in resources. Just to sustain the construction of the buildings and infrastructure in the cities, massive amounts of cement, steel, and fossil fuels need to be produced. Billions of urban dwellers need to be fed daily with produce from rural farmlands while trucks full of wood for furniture, soybeans for vegetarian steaks, and lithium for smartphone batteries leave the countryside for the cities.

A megacity like Delhi requires about 750,000 km^2 of agricultural land, roughly equaling the area of Turkey, to feed its inhabitants.[41] While heralded for their economic clout, large cities make themselves extremely dependent on a supply chain that operates on an international and even global scale. Until now, the food supply system of large cities has not been put to a severe test. COVID-19 posed a first challenge and already resulted in (temporary) urban flight and the first discussions about the resilience of the food supply chains. To ensure the food supply and make cities more resilient to future anomalies or disasters, cities need to increase urban food production and work on shorter and more diverse supply chains, creating new and stronger connections to their immediate hinterlands.

At a time when the Earth's atmosphere and climate are endangered by atmospheric pollution, greater urbanization – which will eventually lead to higher energy usage, even in places like Lagos – sounds like a threat. Yet perhaps in the future, urbanity

Consumption of Power per Person

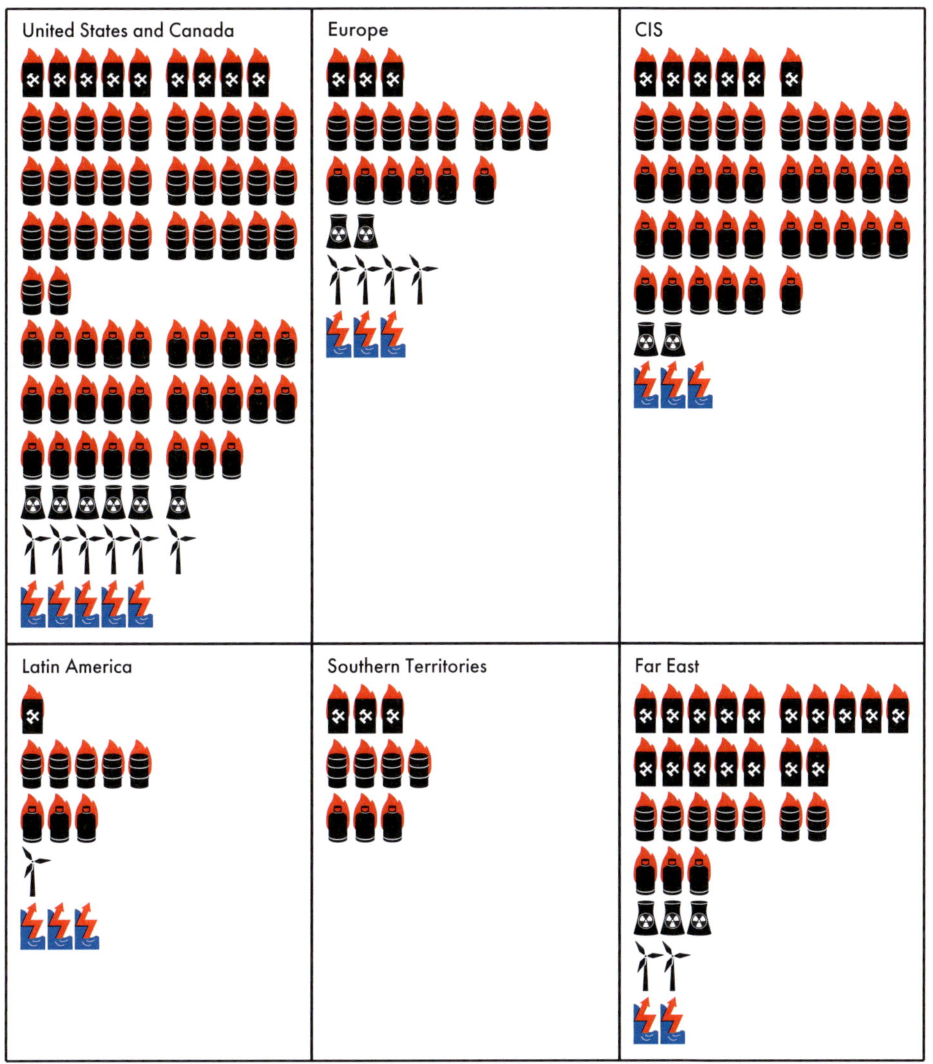

each symbol represents 1 megawatt-hour consumed per person (2021)
sources of power: coal, oil, gas, nuclear, renewables (wind, solar, & biomass) and hydroelectric

might be defined by digital connectedness and data traffic instead of by physical expansion and the number of inhabitants. Digital technology is already allowing us to spur new development in remote areas and thus soften the boundaries between the rural and the urban. With the help of digital technology, the spatial pact between city, modernity, and economy could be rewritten by including villages and towns. Public services such as education, healthcare, financial support, and even policing could be delivered virtually to rural areas already – with the precondition that electricity and the Internet are always available. The transition away from the centralized urban system of the Industrial Age, fostered by the combustion engine and fossil fuels, toward an urban network stimulated by electrification might help to render the distinction between rural and urban redundant.

Agriculture

Green Revolution

The level of employment in agriculture is an indicator of modernity not mentioned by Otto Neurath. Though already in decline before the 1930s, Neurath probably could not have imagined its marginalization today. As of 2020, only 1% of the United States population works in agriculture, as opposed to 63% in the 1840s. Manufacturing experienced an increase in the 1920s, but is down to 14% today.[1] The vast majority of Americans are working in the service sector, producing nothing physical.

Together with the US, all of the Western nations show a similar shift from a production to a service-based economy. On a global scale, the picture is very different. For example, in Chad, one of the world's poorest countries, 75% of the working population is involved in agriculture, only 2% in industries, and 23% in services, according to the World Bank.[2] This correlates with other low-income and proto-modern countries. The modern way of agriculture requires heavy initial investment. The high degree of automation and intensive use of fertilizers and concentrated feed in the West produces high yields with little manual labor, resulting in large farms that can produce food at relatively low monetary cost.

Employment per Sector in the USA

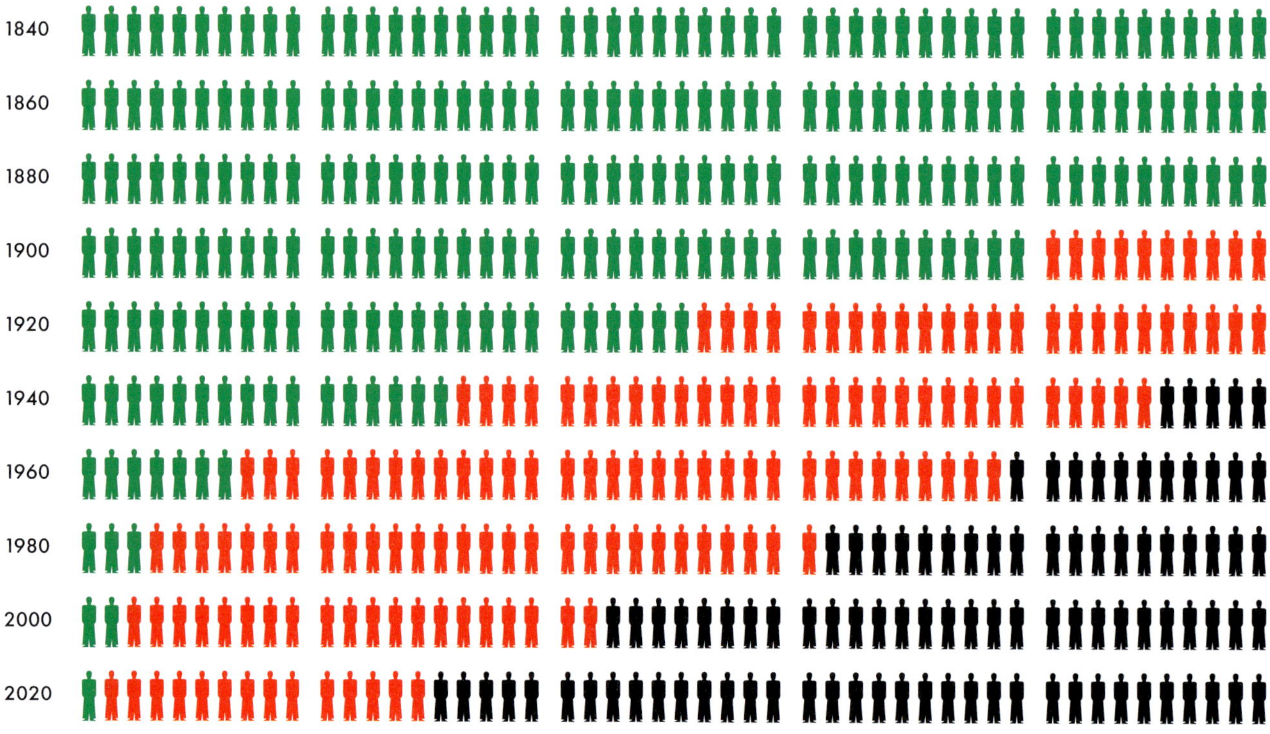

each green symbol represents 1 out of 100 engaged in agriculture
each red symbol represents 1 out of 100 engaged in manufacturing
each black symbol represents 1 out of 100 engaged in services

The high agricultural output is a result of a high fossil fuel input. Soybeans as concentrated feed for fatlings are shipped from Brazil and Indonesia to the US and Europe. Tractors, combine harvesters, and automatic feeders are run on cheap fossil fuel from the Middle East. And fertilizers made from nitrogen, phosphorus, and potassium compounds are, again, produced or mined with the use of fossil fuel. Farming in less motorized countries like Ghana means an extensive input of manual labor, reliance on local fertilizers from manure, and local animal feed, resulting in low yields at prices that have to compete on a global market. And so it happens that for locally farmed chicken meat in Ghana, people have to pay 30–40% more[3] than for imported chicken, which comes mainly from the European Union.

To stay competitive, these global price dynamics force farmers all around the globe into more mechanization, use of fertilizers, and concentrated feed.

Starting in the 1950s, the so-called "green revolution" induced a paradigm shift in agriculture. The "green" in this revolution refers to the color of the crops, while the foundation of the revolution is essentially crude oil; thus, in terms of color, this revolution

is rather black. It describes the simultaneous introduction of high-yield varieties of crops, chemical fertilizers, controlled water management, and the mechanization of agriculture. For example, in the twenty years between 1960 and 1980, crop yields in the United States doubled.[4] The number of farms shrank from a maximum of 6.4 million in 1910 to 2.4 million in 1980, and the number of farm workers declined in the same period by two-thirds, from 12.1 million to 3.3 million.[5] This was a period of extreme increase in the use of farm machinery and chemical fertilizers, while the overall amount of land used for agriculture remained unchanged.

Starting from Mexico, the "green revolution" went on a world tour via India to China and the Philippines.

Horsepower Used in Agriculture in the USA

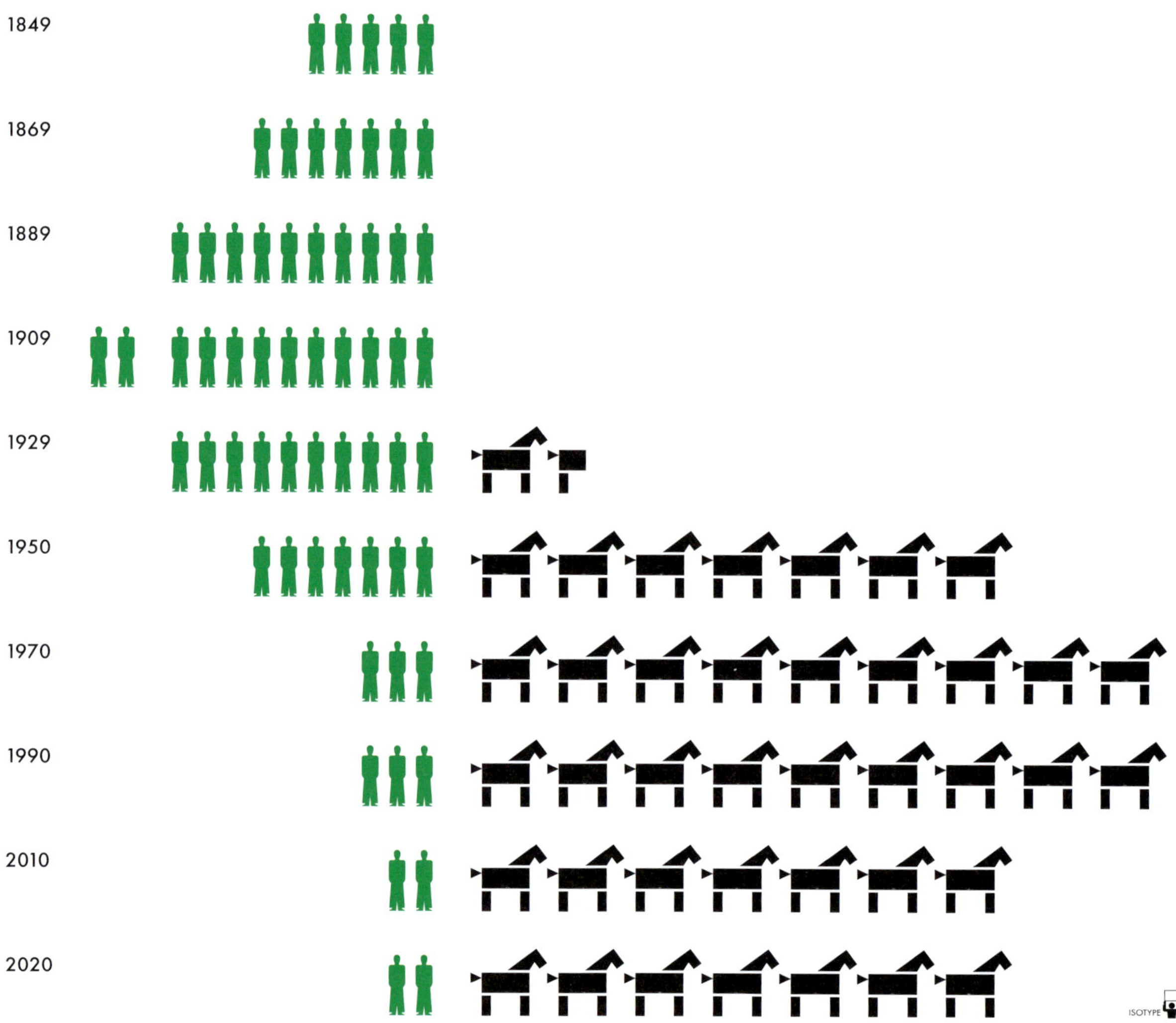

each human symbol represents 1 million people engaged in agriculture
each horse symbol represents 500,000 tractors

People Working in Agriculture Versus Energy Consumption

each person represents 2% of the population working in agriculture (2019)
each barrel represents 1,000 kg of oil equivalent per person (2014)

The godfather of the "green revolution," Norman Borlaug, who received the Nobel Peace Prize in 1971 for his work, designed a high-yielding dwarf wheat variant that doubled and sometimes even tripled the output. He tried to help the small farmers by increasing their output. Yet over the years, it became evident that the newly designed wheat variants require much more water and chemical fertilizers. The sizable investments needed for water irrigation systems and synthetic fertilizers led to a mass extinction of small farmers throughout the world and the rise of industrial megafarms.

Over the past 50 years, the population of the developing part of the world has more than doubled, while the production of cereal crops has tripled. The "green revolution" prevented the tragic famine through overpopulation which Malthus warned about.[6] While millions of human lives were probably saved from starvation due to the extraordinary increase in output from existing agricultural land, the "green revolution" has caused the suffering and even extinction of many other life forms.

Once the "green revolution" was set in motion, opposing it proved to be difficult. There was an attempt to apply similar "green revolution" methods in Africa in the 1980s, but environmental lobbyists and groups campaigned against it. As a result, foundations such as Ford and Rockefeller, alongside the World Bank, withdrew their financial support for Borlaug's Africa project. Concerned more with their own image amid a climate debate, they left the lives of millions of Africans out of the discussion. Using fossil fuel technologies to feed the wealthy West and North, and exporting excess produce at a premium to the South and East, was justified. However, letting Africa use fossil fuels for food security was a step too far.[7]

Food and Drink – 1930s

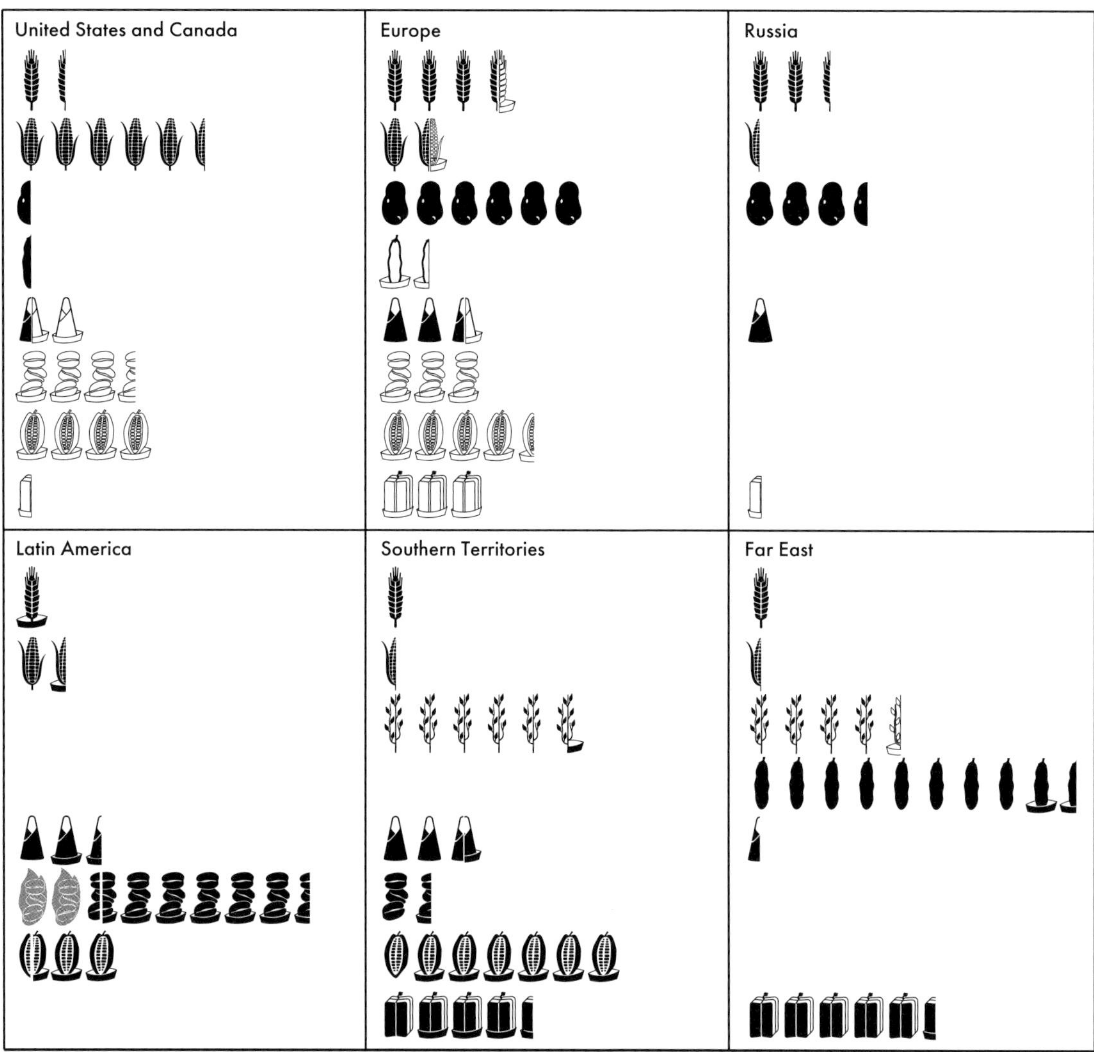

each filled symbol represents 10% of world production of wheat and rye, corn, rice, potatoes, soybeans, sugar, coffee, cocoa, tea

on ship: exported
outlined, on white ship: imported

It seems that the West regards itself as the gatekeeper of modernization while its global production capacity is waning. The West's opinion on how proto-modern regions should develop is skewed. Like parents with their kids, the West wants to protect the Global South from mistakes the West itself has made. Meanwhile, the West is not willing to change its own behavior.

As in the case of mineral resources, the West is also becoming increasingly dependent on the Global South for its food supply. The mass farming of animals in Europe is, for example, extremely reliant on imports of soybeans, which as a high-protein legume are a panacea for intensive animal feeding. Consequently, 77% of global soybean production is used as animal feed.[8]

On a global scale, the annual cereal output per hectare has increased from 1.4 tons in the 1960s to over 4.0 tons today, but higher yields come at a price.[9] The land can

Food and Drink – 2020s

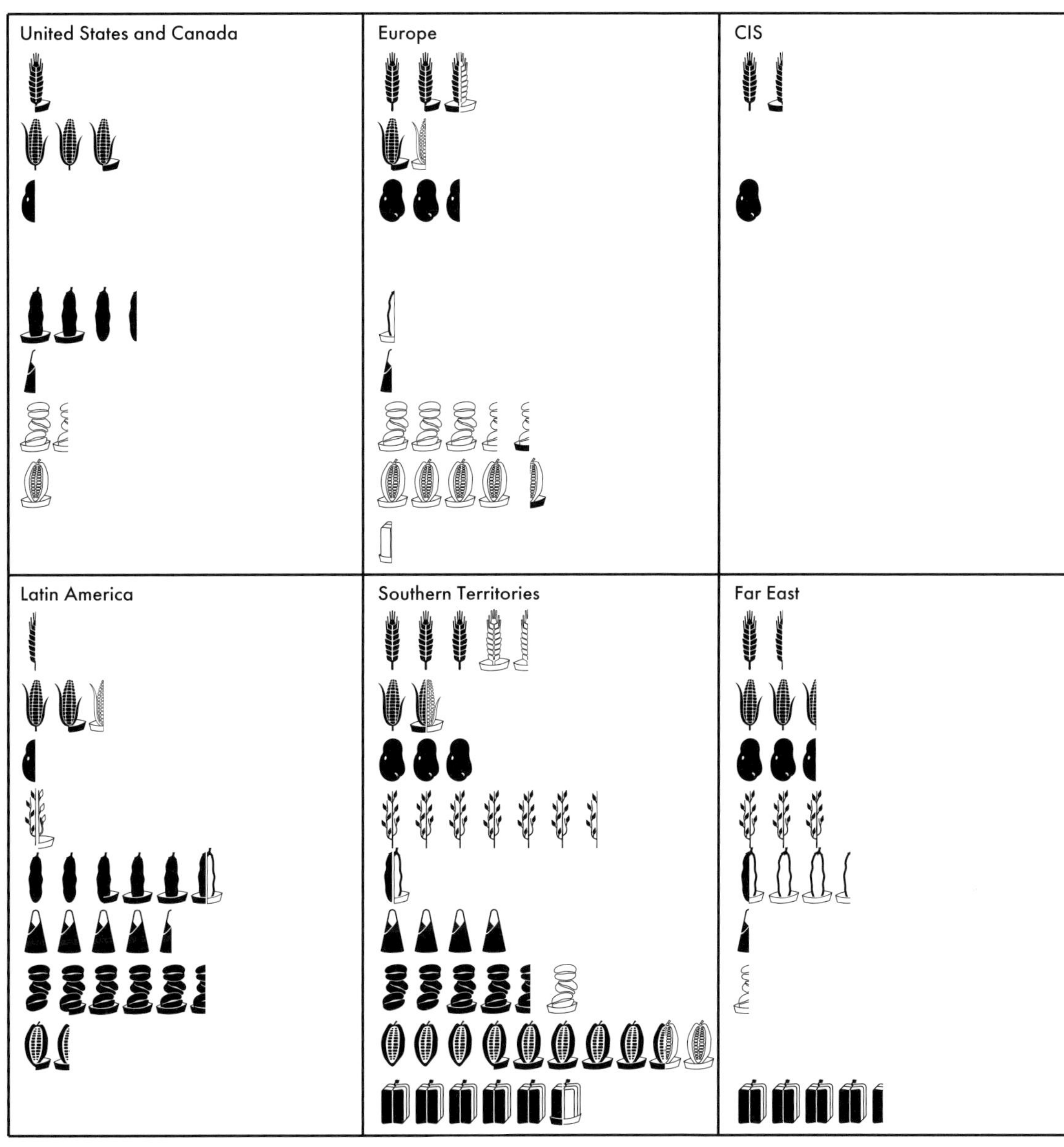

each filled symbol represents 10% of world production of wheat and rye, corn, potatoes, rice, soybeans, sugar, coffee, cocoa, tea

on black ship: produced and exported
outlined, on white ship: imported
outlined, on black ship: exported but not produced

only produce a certain output. Any additional output can only be achieved through an increase in input. In earlier times, this extra input was provided manually by adding manure and weeding. Later it was done with the help of machines and fossil fuels. The current high-yield agricultural production depends heavily on fossil fuels for the operation of agricultural machinery, the production of pesticides and nitrate fertilizers, and for food processing and transportation. To create 1 calorie of food, about 10 to 15 calories of fossil energy are used. This means that about 1,500 liters of oil equivalents are necessary to feed an American for one year (1989).[10]

The negative long-term impacts of the farming methods of the "green revolution" are tremendous, including a reduction in biodiversity and the severe contamination of groundwater through overuse of organic and non-organic fertilizers.

In particular, the use of synthetic nitrogen, which is "responsible for raising crop yields 35 to 50% over the last half century,"[11] does great harm. Unfortunately, without that rise in yield, 50% of the world's population would starve. This use was developed after World War II, when synthetic nitrogen factories switched from bomb manufacturing (nitrogen compounds are highly explosive) to agriculture. Synthetic nitrogen is lethal in all regards. Its excessive use can contribute to an increase of ground-level ozone, the emission of greenhouse gases, the thinning of the ozone layer, acid rain, polluted drinking water, and "dead zones" in oceans.

Global Agricultural Land and Yield

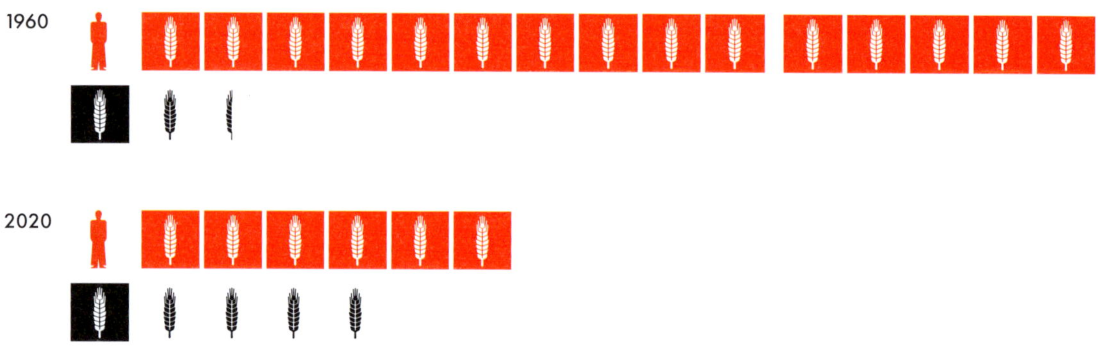

each red square represents 1,000 m^2 of agricultural land per person
each black grain symbol represents 1 tonne of cereal yield per hectare

The future of farming holds the promise of a "green revolution 2.0." With the help of satellites, drones, and robots, the land will be fertilized according to the needs of the soil. "Smart" robots will take care of sowing and harvesting as well as feeding the animals according to their needs. Crops will be genetically modified to suit the precise climatic and geological conditions and will be made resistant to all vermin, thus turning fertilizers and pesticides into relics of the past. In a nutshell: the era for a new experiment in agriculture.

This time as well, the concern remains that the hopes are high and the results are amazing at the beginning, but year by year the flaws are becoming ever clearer. The "green revolution 2.0" is another technological promise with an uncertain future. Past experience makes it ever more difficult for people to become enthusiastic about the new, about modernity. Humans want to survive, as individuals but also as a species.

Meat Production

A rather new sector of agriculture is the mass production of meat. The discovery of antibiotics and vaccines allowed larger numbers of livestock to be raised without the threat of disease. Processing and preservation techniques facilitated the slaughtering and storage of large quantities of meat. A third factor that made the mass production of meat possible is the development of concentrated feed from energy-rich resources. Global trade in the energy-rich soybean in particular allowed the upscaling of the meat industry.

The increase in meat production over the past 100 years is stunning, and so is its impact on land, animals, and people. Livestock takes up nearly 80% of global agricultural land, while producing fewer than 20% of the calories in the human diet.[12] Thus, meat production is highly inefficient in terms of the use of land and resources. For example, 60% of the agricultural land in Germany[13] is used for the production of

Global Animals, Feed, and Fields per Person

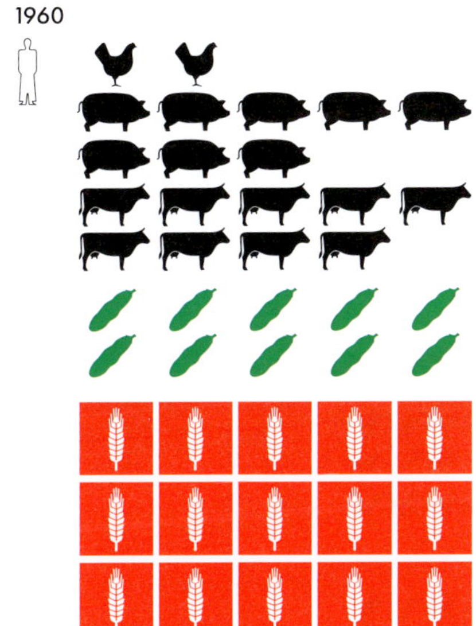

each animal symbol represents 1 kg of meat per person
each soybean symbol represents 1 kg of beans per person
each red square represents 1,000 m² of agricultural land per person

livestock, and on a global scale 78% of agricultural land is reserved for holding and feeding animals.[14] The amount of agricultural land that could be reclaimed by removing meat from our diet would be enormous.

Cattle meat production is particularly environmentally damaging for two reasons. Cows require the greatest land area and the most water per kilocalorie of meat.[15] At the same time, cows are the largest water polluters through their feces and the largest producers of greenhouse gases through their digestion. The average cow produces 250–500 liters of methane a day.[16] By producing 14.5% of all greenhouse gases, farm animals pollute the atmosphere as much as the entire fossil fuel-based transportation sector.[17]

On top of all of that, cows are very inefficient producers of meat. Most of the food spent on cows translates into bones, the hide, and internal organs. A live steer weighing about 450 kg equates to about 200 kg of beef, which means that more than half of its weight is not used for direct human food production. Thus, most of the environmental damage described above is done for waste.

Annual Chicken Consumption

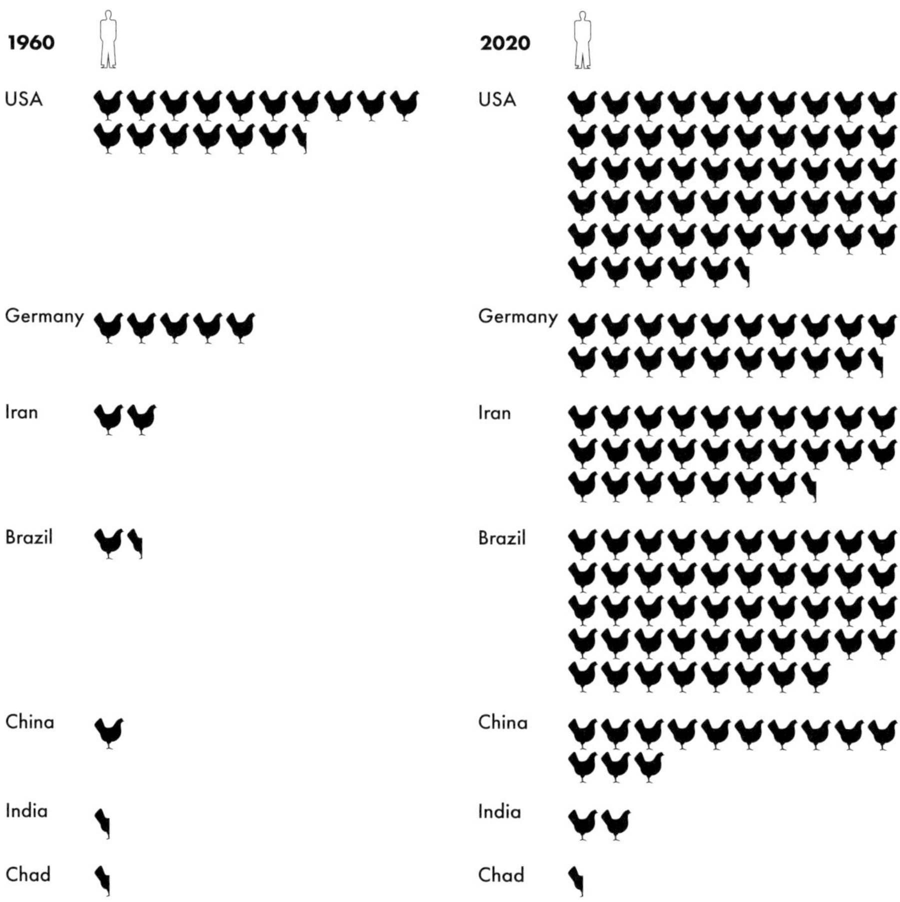

each symbol represents 1 kg of chicken (~1 chicken) consumed per person per year

Chickens Killed per Second – 1960 and 2020

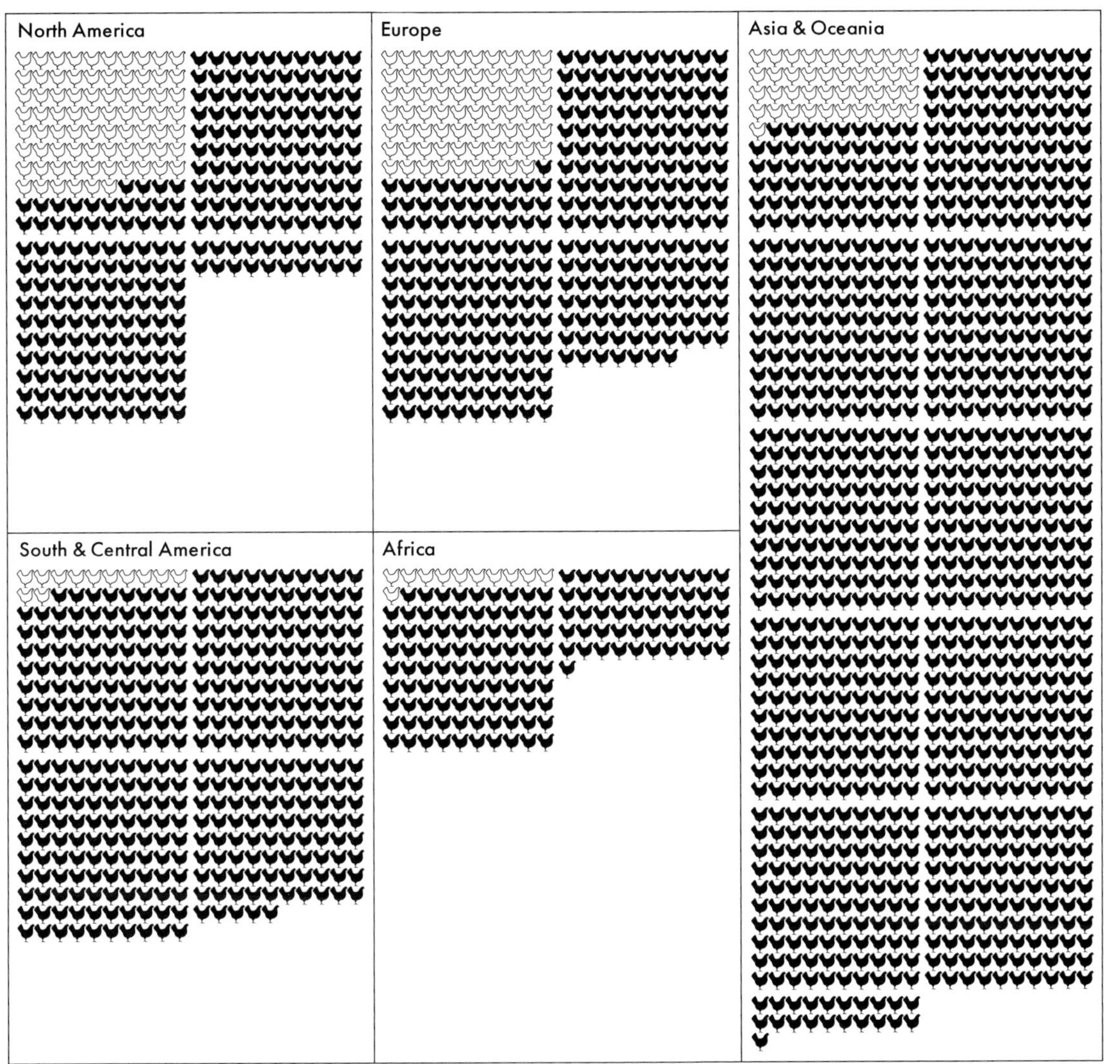

white symbols represent chickens killed in 1960
white plus black symbols represent chickens killed in 2020

Compared to beef production, the production of chicken meat is okay. What is shocking about chicken farming, however, is the tremendous growth it has seen over the past 80 years, as it has grown from about 7 million tons in 1960 to around 122 million tons in 2021.[18] On a global scale, chicken meat is the most popular meat, since it sidesteps religious objections to pork and beef and can be produced rather cheaply: industrially produced chickens grow extremely fast and can be slaughtered after two months.

The mass meat production industry has had some blowback. Primarily in the late 1980s, Britain was hit by bovine spongiform encephalopathy (BSE), more commonly known as mad cow disease. One possible cause of this disease was the use of protein supplements from meat and bone meal which was widespread in Europe prior to the late 1980s.[19] Animal remains were fed to cattle in a practice adopted in the UK as early as 1926, creating a rather sick diet for herbivores that are used to eating grass. 229 people in 12 countries died of a disease that exhibits neurological symptoms similar to those detected in the infected cows; it was called a new variant of Creutzfeldt–Jakob disease (CJD).[20] BSE is still diagnosed in cows, but major outbreaks of CJD have been avoided ever since.

The fear that BSE was causing CJD in humans was present as early as 1990. Still, in 1996, Health Secretary Stephen Dorrell told the British public that there was no risk from eating UK beef. Mere months later, the UK government released a statement confirming that consumption of BSE cattle was the most likely cause of the lethal disease CJD. A ban was placed on the export of British beef products, and 4.4 million cows were slaughtered in an attempt to eradicate the disease. The difficulty in detecting CJD is the 4- to 5-year dormancy period in its host. The disease resides not only in the brain, but also in the blood, which complicates blood transfusions.[21]

At the same time, the poultry industry must contend with bird flu, an influenza caused by viruses that adapted to birds. Between 2003 and 2021, 456 people died of the H5N1 variant, with most of the cases appearing in Asia.[22] Not to forget the third of the three largest meat-providing animals, the pig. Its industry is combating the classical swine fever (CSF), a virological infectious disease. In 2020 the African variant of African swine fever virus (ASFV) was detected in wild hogs in the north of Germany and in Denmark. By the end of 2021, Denmark had killed all its wild hogs and had erected a 70 km long and 1.5 m high fence along its entire border with Germany to protect its industrial pig meat production from possible infectious animals from Germany.[23]

The human population is growing, and slowly but steadily it is also becoming more affluent. All over the planet, a meat-based diet is a sign of prosperity. Thus, meat consumption is doomed to increase. The annual meat consumption of a person in the United States is 150 kg, while a person from India munches on just 10 kg of meat per year.[24] Thus, in the eyes of the global meat industry, there is still room for growth.

As an alternative, the industry is working on cultured meat, which is produced by in vitro cultures of animal cells. This method makes it possible to grow meat without animals. Cultured meat holds the promise of reducing pressure on farmland, preventing the killing of billions of animals per year, and making meat production more efficient, since energy would not be wasted on bones, hide, and internal organs. Again, it is technology that seems to bring redemption. The impact of this new industry, eventually working on the massive scale the meat industry does at the moment, is not foreseeable. And again the once bitten, twice shy modern human remains skeptical.

On the other hand, detaching food production entirely from the landscape seems to be just the next step in a development that began in modern times with greenhouses and megabarns. Cheap and easily available mechanically processed food is the foundation of modern civilization. It liberated and still liberates humans from harsh manual farm labor as a full-time occupation. Just as the modern human is determined to remain skeptical of modernity, s/he remains addicted to it.

Confirmed Cases of Variant Creutzfeldt-Jakob Disease (Mad Cow Disease) up to 2021

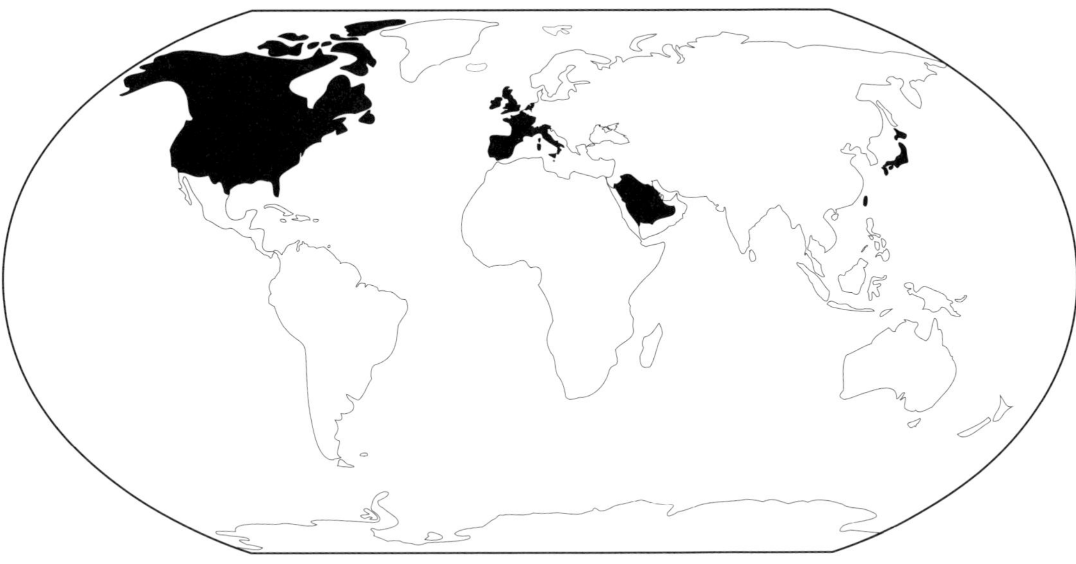

black: countries in which there have been confirmed human cases of variant Creutzfeldt-Jakob Disease

Human Cases of Avian Influenza (H5N1 variant), 2003–2021

black: countries in which there have been confirmed human cases of avian influenza (H5N1 variant)

Land Grab

For the time being, crops and livestock need land to grow and be fed, but agricultural land is divided unevenly among nations. Countries like Russia and Canada have plenty of land to feed their people, while others, like Saudi Arabia and the United Arab Emirates (UAE), have almost no fertile land at all.

Since the early 2000s, economic liberalization, global transport and communication networks, and global demand for food, energy, and commodities have encouraged large-scale acquisitions of land by transnational companies, governments, and individuals.[25] The aim is to seek access to large areas of fertile land for the cultivation of food crops and biofuel feedstocks. One of the key drivers was a global crisis in food prices in 2007.[26] This was caused by a variety of factors, such as higher demand from a rapidly growing middle class in China, and initial experiments with maize-based biofuels in the US. In order for companies to secure production and costs, a land grab occurred.

Large Land Acquisitions by Singapore

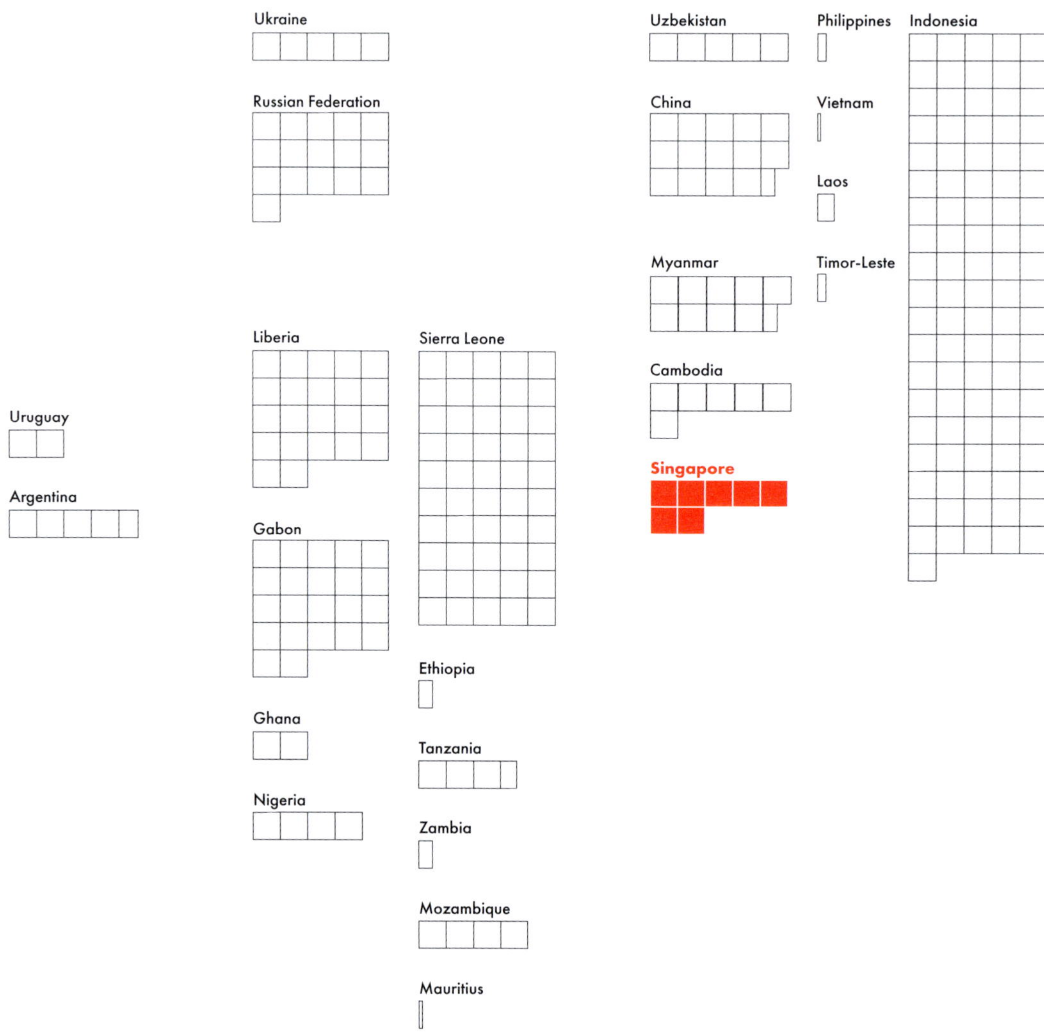

each square represents 100 km² owned or rented by Singapore (2023)
red shows the land area of Singapore itself

The demand for more land to produce goods in faraway countries had been accompanied by the displacement of indigenous communities, deforestation, and damage to the natural environment by the introduction of industrial agriculture.

Africa in particular has become an attractive destination for land investments because of its relatively low population density. Millions of hectares are bought or leased by nations or private companies based outside Africa, as well as by more wealthy countries on the continent such as Libya and Egypt.[27] In 2009 the United Arab Emirates struck a land acquisition deal for 16,800 km² – an area as large as one-fifth of the UAE, or the size of Kuwait – in what is now South Sudan for a period of 50 years.[28] Singapore has the goal of producing 30% of its own food by 2030 in order to avoid a disruption in supply. To achieve this goal, the country has made large-scale land acquisitions in places like Argentina, Sierra Leone, Russia, and Indonesia that amount to a total of 26,900 km², which is 37 times its own area.[29]

Area per Person – 1960 and 2020

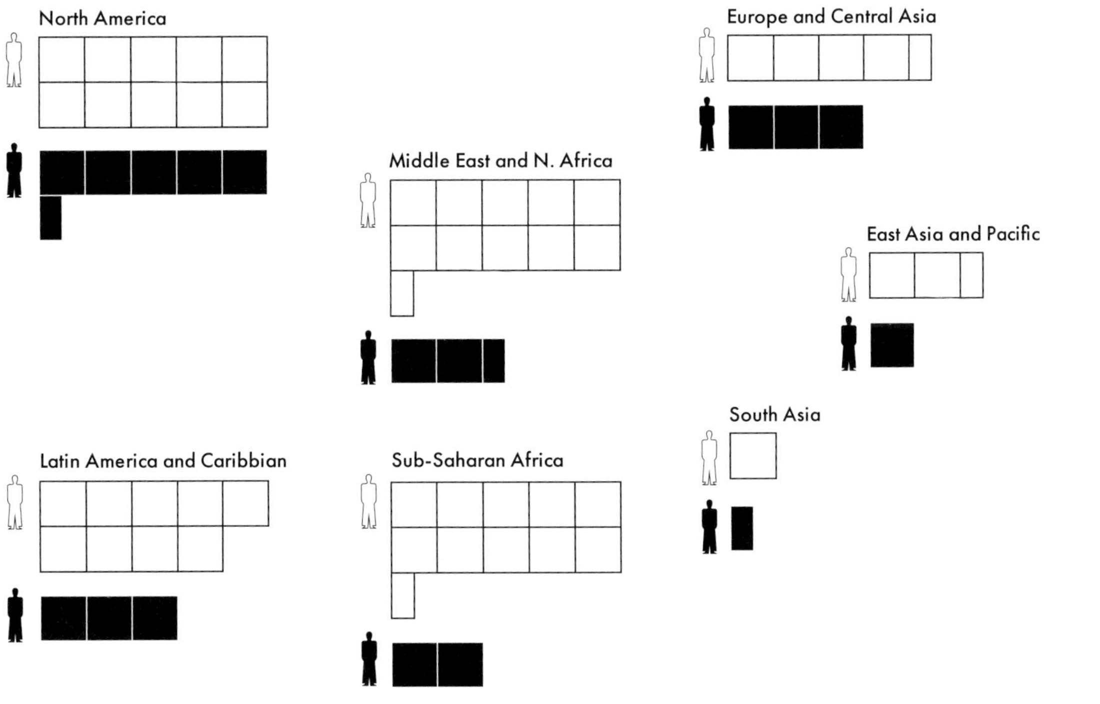

each white square represents 10 km² per person in 1960
each black square represents 10 km² per person in 2020

The struggle for land is only ever intensifying, since the land area per person is decreasing. Therefore agricultural land per person is declining every year, especially in the Global South, following the Malthusian dilemma that land is finite, but the population can grow infinitely. Until now, the industry has managed to squeeze out a greater and greater yield per hectare, but the soil is already showing signs of exhaustion. Information from the United Nations indicates that up to 40% of the world's land is now degraded,[30] mainly by intensive farming for food production and textile fibers.

Land Use

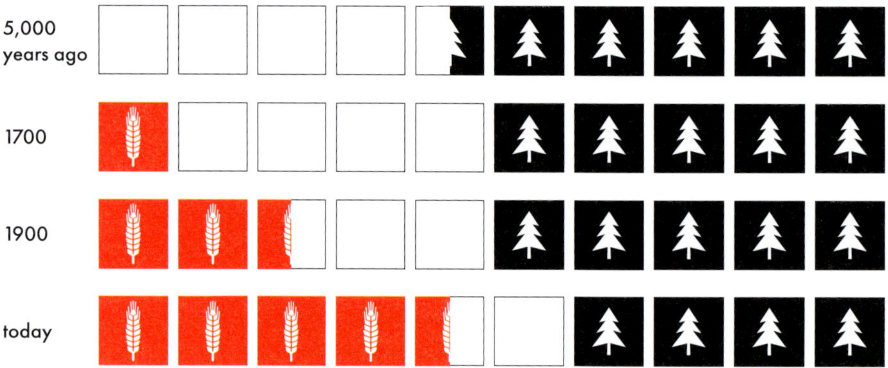

each square represents 1 billion hectares or 10% of Earth's exploitable surface (without deserts, glaciers, mountains, or other barren land)
white with black outline: wild grassland and shrubs
red: land used for crops and pasture
black: forests

Simultaneously, the clearing of unused land for cropland is coming to an end. There is simply no unused land in the future. Cutting trees only accelerates climate change, and as a result of this, valuable agricultural land is being depleted.

Thus, getting hold of agricultural land has become part of the survival strategy of some countries, and their approach is becoming ever more cunning. Old-school colonization, by which a more powerful nation-state controls and exploits the people and natural resources of another nation-state, is no longer found anywhere on the globe (at least not in its formal construct of the settler/exploitation/trading colonies of western Europe from the 1400s to the second half of the 1900s). The system has shown its flaws, since owning a country also meant owning its problems. Neocolonialism, as it's called today, is much more efficient in exploiting resources and human labor very specifically from a remote distance. Colonizers don't even have to set foot in foreign countries; they can still exploit them with the help of contemporary communication and surveillance methods. By generating a dependence of the often developing nation on wealthier, former colonizing countries, these wealthier nations benefit economically and at times politically from an uneven balance of power. The raw materials of the South are mined and farmed on the cheap and introduced into wealthier economies. Manual labor and the primary and secondary economic sectors are especially favored for outsourcing since there is little added value and profit margins are small.

Manufacturing

Economic Scheme – 1930s

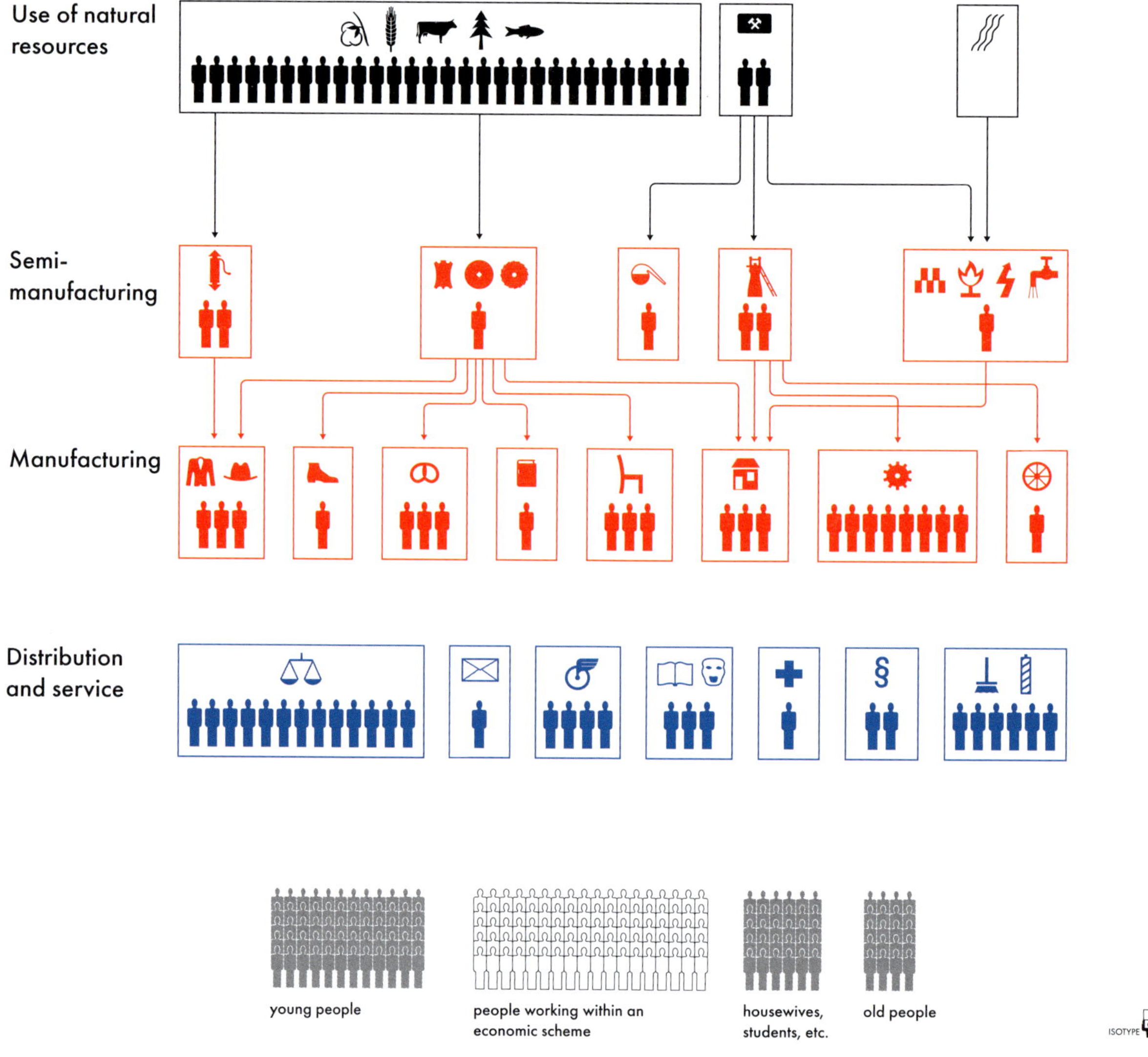

each human symbol represents 5 per thousand of the total population

In charting the economic scheme of his time, Neurath implied that the economic scheme of a single country represented all the countries in the world, saying: "The general scheme remains the same." This was neither correct in his time, nor is it today. Neurath's scheme represented the economic model of the Western countries, as does its updated version.

Economic Scheme – 2020s

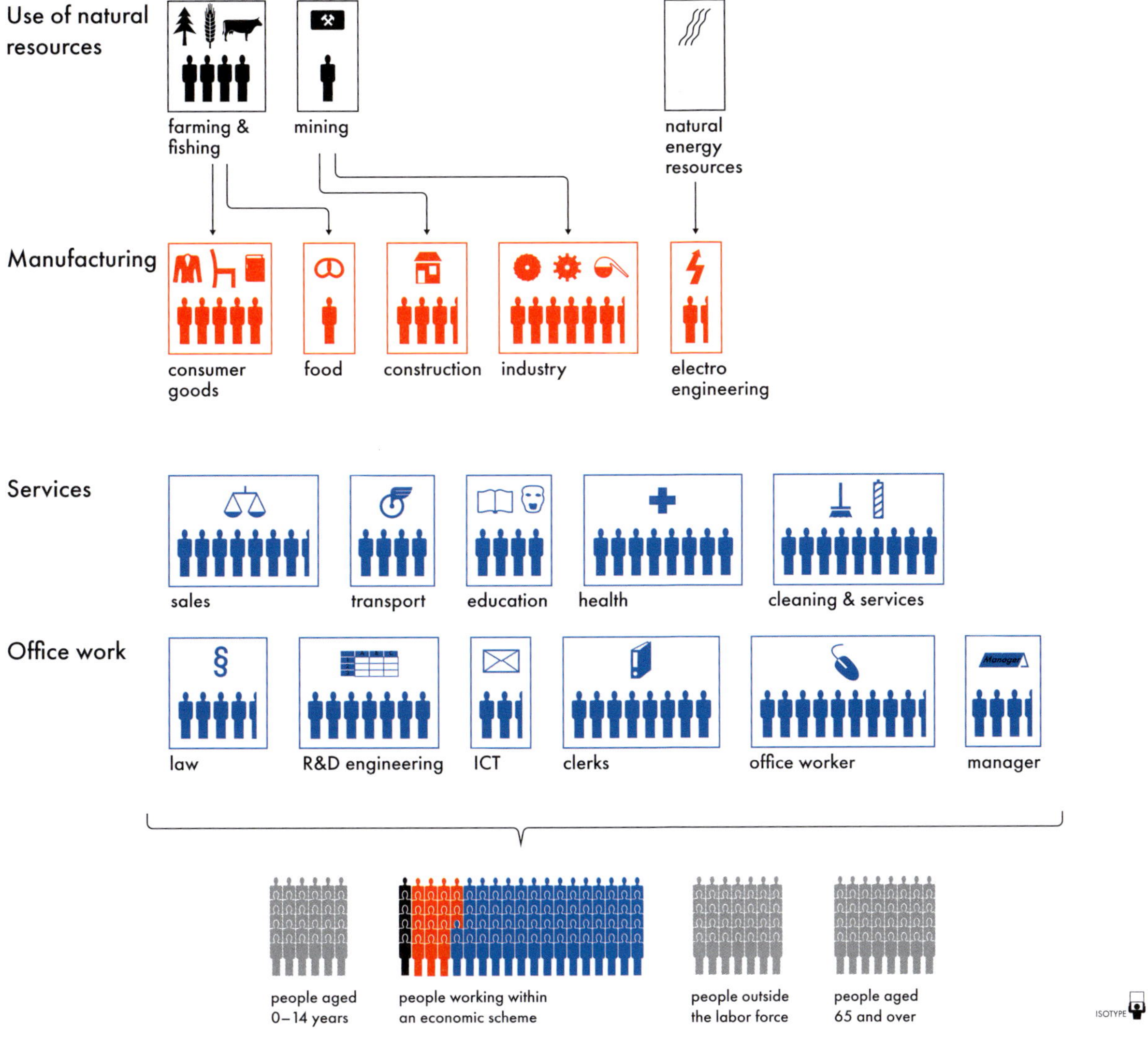

each human symbol represents 5 per thousand of the total population

Nevertheless, the shift from a manufacturing to a service-based economy, mentioned in the preceding chapters, can be studied here in detail. Further automation and mechanization are steadily increasing the number of people working in the service sector. Yet to keep an economy and a country running and to maintain its structure, a certain number of manual workers, especially in the construction sector, is essential.

Production

Moving from the field to the factory, away from agriculture and toward manufacturing, was the basis of modern society. The "modern man" described by Neurath was the factory worker, a kind of human who simply did not exist in the 18th century. While this transformation is coming to an end in the West, it is in full swing across large parts of the globe, with China its undisputed champion in the 21st century. In 1980, 87% of China's population was still working in the primary and secondary sector.[1] Today that number is around 50% and is declining with every year, showing a clear trend toward a service-based economy.[2]

Starting in 1979 with Deng Xiaoping's "reform and opening," a radical change of direction for the future of China, the country established itself as the world's workbench. Watching the British colony of Hong Kong booming on its doorstep in the 1970s, China created hospitable conditions for cheap manufacturing in designated "Special Economic Zones" in the 1980s. Within these zones, China enticed foreign investors with the industrial production of goods at a much cheaper rate, thanks to an inexpensive and vast labor force. The rich countries of the West were quick to embrace this system.

The US and many European countries, spoiled by a booming economy in the 1950s and 60s with repeatedly double-digit growth figures, got nervous when the GDP growth and productivity stopped to increase throughout the 1970s and '80s.[3] In the US, labor as share of national income fell from 65% in the 1970 to 55% in the 2010s, while capital as share of income did the opposite in the same time frame.[4] Thus labor and especially low wage jobs added ever less to economic growth, meaning in vernacular terms: "working hard won't make you rich" anymore; but gaining and trading assets will. The strategy to stabilize the GDP growth figures or even raise them, and with

Global Motor Vehicle Production

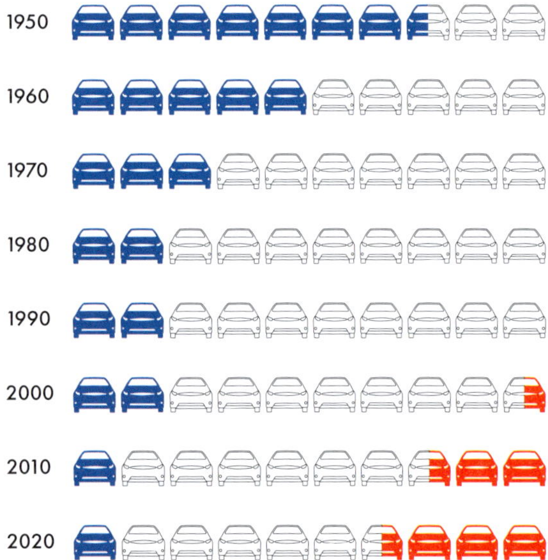

each blue symbol represents one motor vehicle per 10 people produced in the USA
each red symbol represents one motor vehicle per 10 people produced in China
each outlined black symbol represents one motor vehicle per 10 people produced in other countries

Minimum Wage Versus Textile Price, USA

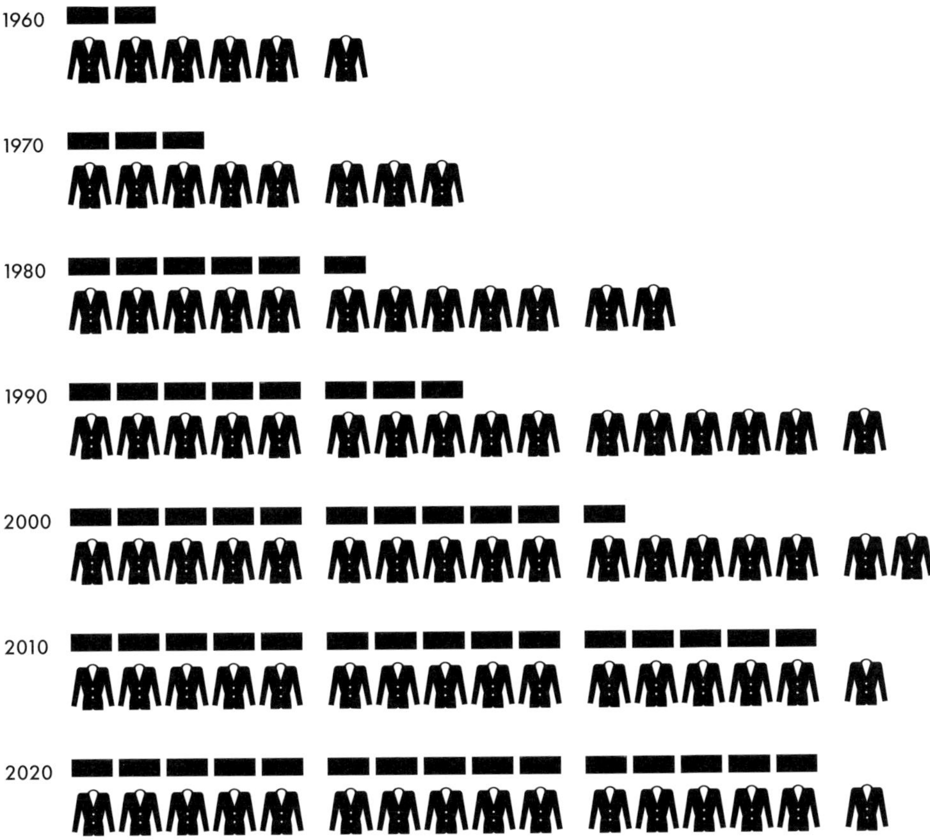

green: each bar represents $ 1,000 of annual minimum wage
black: each symbol represents $ 10 as price for apparel (adjusted for inflation)

it the standard of living, was to keep high earning jobs and outsource the production that that requires low earning mundane jobs overseas. The focus "at home" should be predominantly on trade and the development of new technologies. While in the United States, the minimum wage seemed to have increase from about $1 to about $7 between the 1960s and the 2020s, it has been roughly stagnant if adjusted for inflation in this period.[5] The almost zero gain in income was compensated by reducing expenses.

Outsourcing manufacturing to low-wage countries in Southeast Asia subsequently led to a halt in prices of consumer goods. By outsourcing manufacturing to low-wage countries, the West began to live under the illusion of ever cheaper consumer goods, which was indulged in and led to an unprecedented increase in consumption. At the start of the new century, this resulted in a halt to pay raises – affluence was generated not by earning more, but by paying less.

Slowly, production costs in China are rising as well, due to growing income and a more affluent population. High labor costs naturally lead to the development of nonhuman, thus robotic, production processes. But still there will remain enough manufacturing processes that are difficult to automate, and Chinese factories will move

Power Consumption per Capita

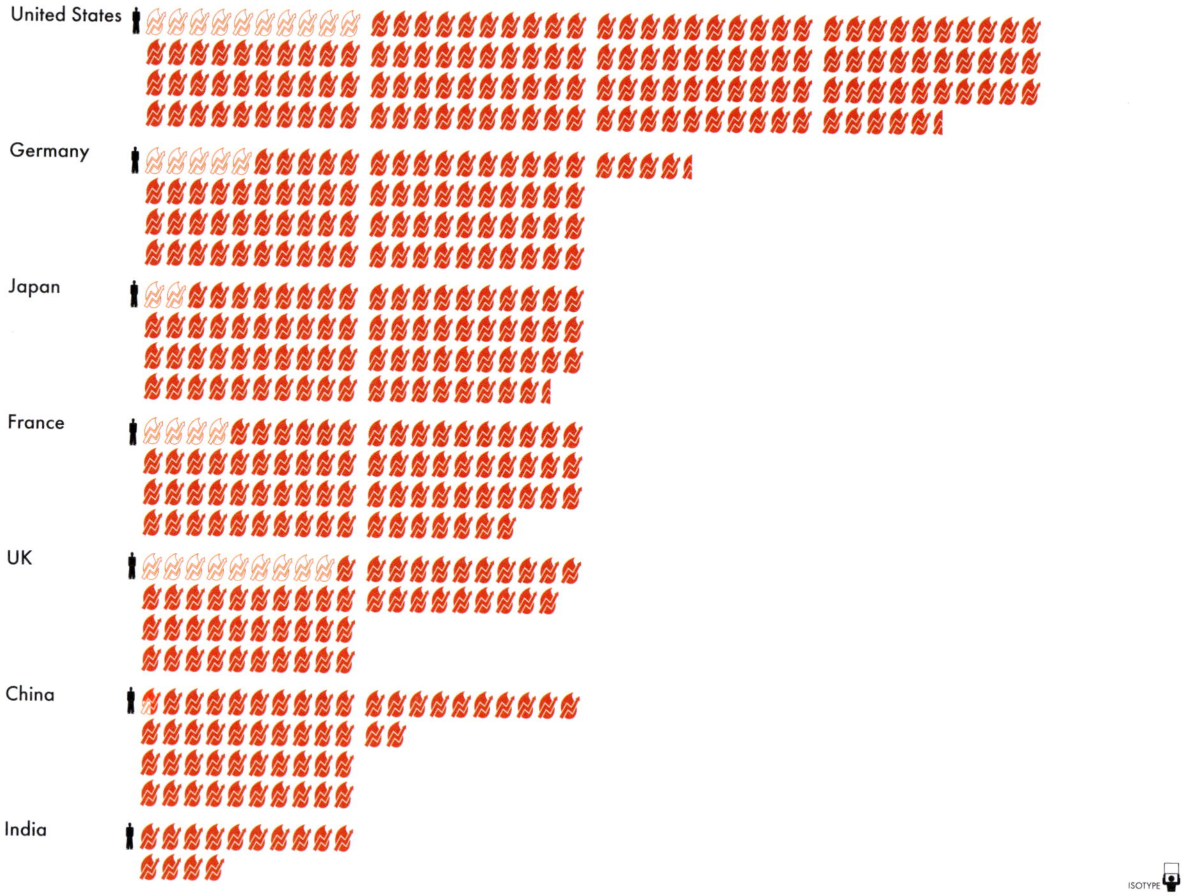

each outlined red symbol represents 500 kilowatt-hours in 1936
produced annually from coal, petroleum, and hydropower

each outlined and filled red symbol represents 500 kilowatt-hours in 2021
produced annually from coal, oil, gas, nuclear plants, renewables, and hydropower

to low-wage countries. In some sectors this is happening already, making Vietnam the new low-cost production floor. Yet if China and India, with their 2.8 billion inhabitants, start to consume at the pace seen in the US, for example, no country or region on Earth could keep up with the demand. Not even the entire continent of Africa houses a workforce large enough to produce for the West, China, and India. The only way out would be full-scale automation.

Of the "Big Seven,"[6] meaning the seven richest nations on the globe, mentioned by Otto Neurath, five are still in the ranking. As Italy and Russia (Soviet Union) have fallen off the list, China and India have joined. Ranked according to their wealth, the list today reads as follows: United States, China, Japan, Germany, United Kingdom, India, France. The two newcomers China and India show very different patterns of development. While India's economic clout is currently based on its large population, China is the world's manufacturing powerhouse, with 28.7% (2019) of global manufacturing output.[7] That is almost as much as all six other countries combined. India accounts for only 3%.[8]

Strikingly, the USA consumes almost two and a half times the power of the equally developed and industrialized United Kingdom. Both countries generate about 20%[9] of their GDP from industry, the economic sector with the greatest need for energy.

Looking at the energy intensity (a measure that compares the amount of energy expended to generate one unit of GDP) of the seven countries, the inefficiency of the US economy becomes evident. To gain $ 1, the US uses three times the amount of energy as the UK.

India even expends 6 times the energy of the UK to gain $ 1.[10] Low energy prices and easy access to fossil fuels are certainly one reason for this difference. Countries with low energy prices simply have less incentive to become more efficient. India in particular, which generates only 26% of its GDP from industry (while China's figure is 40%), burns a lot of fuel for little cash.[11]

Low energy costs are often artificial, since the energy sector is heavily subsidized in India, reaching an equivalent of US$ 7.8 billion in 2020.[12] The low energy costs keep old gas-guzzling engines in place, resulting in bad air quality, especially in urban areas.

The air quality in Delhi is, according to a WHO survey of 1,650 cities, the worst of any major city on Earth.[13] Not even the low rate of car ownership is providing much relief to Delhi's problem with smog. Only 6 out of 100 people in India own a car, while in the US almost 90 do.[14]

However, for automobile producers, the figures for China and India sound like bells in heaven, or the ring of a cash register. Two countries, each with a large population dreaming about owning their first car, hold great promise for future revenue.

Power to Generate $ 1 | **Electricity Prices**

India

China

United States

France

Japan

Germany

UK

each flame symbol represents 1 kWh produced in order to generate $ 1.00 of GDP (2021)

each coin symbol represents $ 0.01 per kWh of electricity for households (2021)

Motor Vehicle Ownership

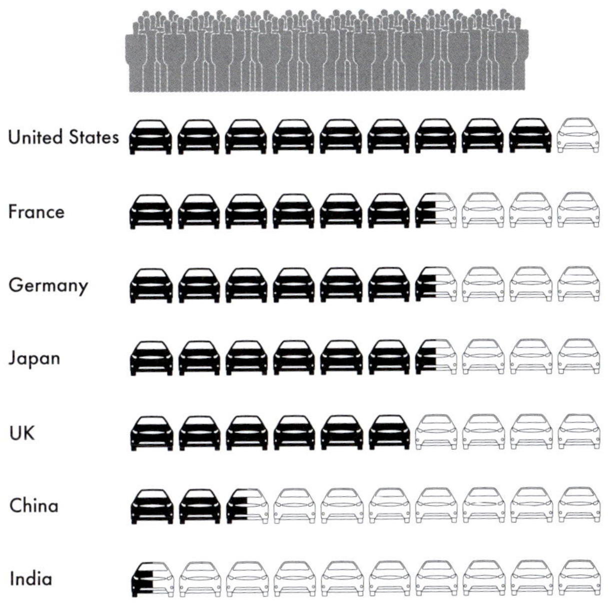

each filled black symbol represents one registered vehicle per 10 people (2020)

Home and Factory Weaving

In the late 19th century, large-scale manufacturing in factories was replacing small-scale home production centers. Neurath illustrated this shift by comparing home and factory weavers. In many areas of manufacturing, this trend continued after World War II, and the automated manufacturing of consumer goods became ever more elaborate, demanding less and less human labor with every step of development.

Yet the labor-intensive and difficult-to-automate garment industry resisted and serves as a perfect example for the shift of manufacturing from West to East. Britain's textile industry, which employed almost 600,000 people[15] in the 1920s, is now down to 60,000.[16]

Today the textile industry is dominated by Southeast Asia, and Bangladesh in particular. If Britain's textile industry declined rapidly, Bangladesh's industry emerged at an even faster speed. In 1990, about 300,000 garment workers produced textiles worth $ 624.0 million. Thirty years later, 4.2 million people worked in an industry that exported $ 31 billion worth of clothing.[17] Accounting for 80% of the country's exports, the garment business is the number-one industry in Bangladesh.[18] On the one hand, it is the abundance of cheap labor that makes the country attractive for garment production; on the other hand, it is the absence of laws that regulate workers' rights, environmental harm, and factory construction. Lax rules allow cheaper production, but expose the people involved to higher risks. In 2013, the collapse of the Rana Plaza factory building in Dhaka, Bangladesh killed at least 1,132 people and injured more than 2,500. The factory had manufactured textiles for brands that included Benetton, Prada, Gucci, Versace, Moncler, the Children's Place, Mango, Primark, and Walmart. As of 2023, the murder trial against owner Sohel Rana is still in infancy after six years.[19]

Garment Workers and Exports in Bangladesh

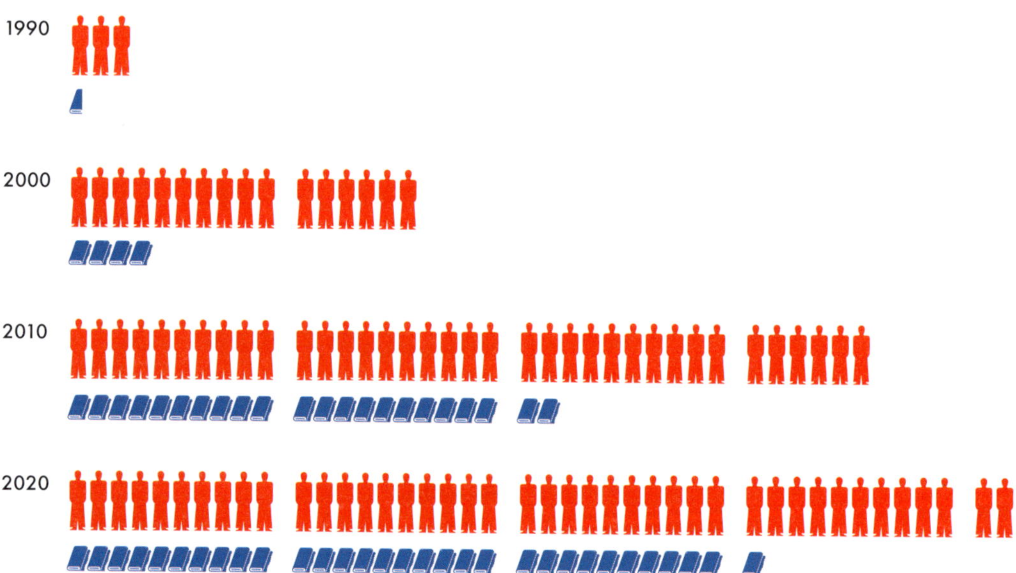

each red symbol represents 100,000 workers in the garment industry
each blue symbol represents 1 billion US $ of garment exports

Largest Textile Exporters in 1928

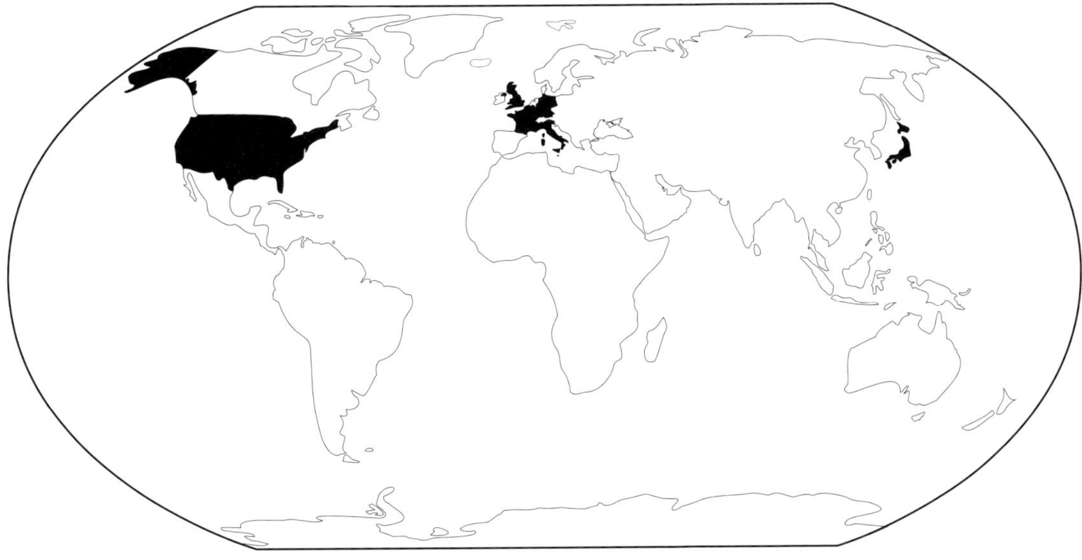

black: countries which share more than 5% of world textile exports

Largest Textile Exporters in 2020

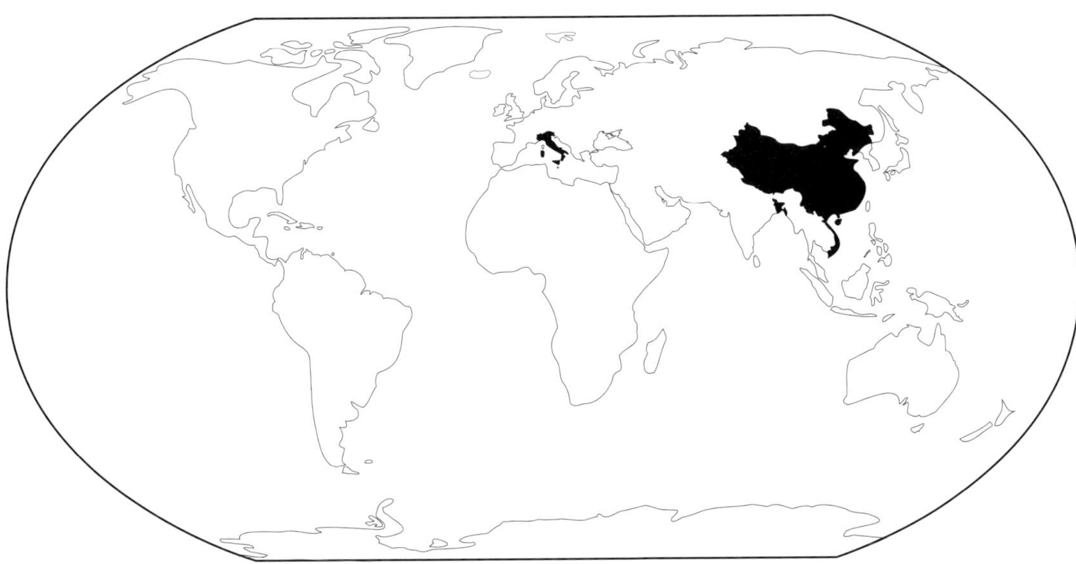

black: countries which share more than 5% of world textile exports

The good news is that working conditions are steadily improving, wages are rising, and poverty is declining rapidly. Bangladesh, one of the world's poorest nations in the 1970s, has risen to lower-middle-income status in 2015 and is today on par with countries like India and Nigeria.

The minimum wage of a garment industry worker in Bangladesh is 5,300 taka, equivalent to € 55, per month.[20] A minimum-wage earner in the UK will earn this in approximately 5 hours.[21] Thus, between the West and the East there is still enough asymmetry to promise large profit margins for decades to come. The huge difference in income, along with cheap transportation, makes it possible for the Earth's wealthiest people to be flush with the Earth's cheapest clothes.

Global Consumption of Major Textile Fibers

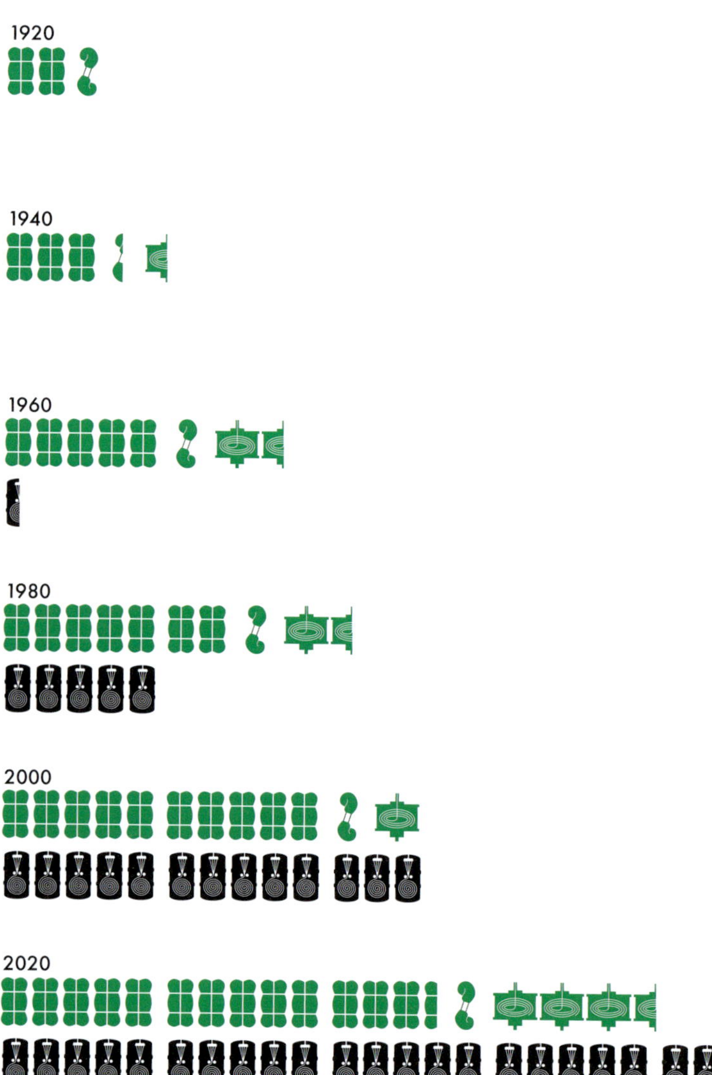

each green symbol represents 2 million metric tonnes of fiber from renewable resources; cotton, wool, rayon/viscose
each black symbol represents 2 million metric tonnes of fiber from fossil-based synthetic fibers; acrylics, polyester, nylon, etc.

Next to low wages, living conditions in Bangladesh are dire. Its weaving factories, predominantly situated in cities, are a big attractor for people from the countryside. As a result, the country rapidly urbanized and 52% (2020) of its urban population is living in slums.[22] Over the course of 50 years, the entire structure of a society changed from rural to urban, from field to factory, and from time management by the sun to time management by the clock.

Annual working hours per worker are among the highest in the world and are increasing (against the international trend), social security is poor, and workers' rights are regularly shunned. By exporting modernity to countries like Bangladesh, the West ought to take on the responsibility of exporting its benefits to the people. The garment workers of Bangladesh also want to go on vacation, go skiing in the Himalayas or lie in the sun on the beach, choose from a limitless supply of clothes, and spend their disposable income on unnecessary luxuries like the modern consumers of the West. While these luxuries are a given for the workers in the West, their colleagues in Southeast Asia don't dare to dream about such a lifestyle, not even for their kids.

As the location of manufacturing changed, so did the very materials used by the garment industry for the very same reason: cheaper production costs. Nylon and polyester were introduced in the 1940s as the first synthetic fibers based on fossil resources. While in the 1960s there were barely any oil-based synthetic clothes on the market and at the turn of the millennium it was still 50/50, today two-thirds of all clothes are made from non-renewable (fossil) resources.[23]

Viscose (rayon), a semi-synthetic fiber made from natural sources such as wood and other agricultural products, was developed in the late 19th century. This natural-based alternative is cheaper but unfortunately relies on a more toxic method of production. Therefore, its production is often outsourced to countries where emission control and labor laws are lax, so workers are exposed to toxic carbon disulfide or emissions go unchecked. China is its biggest exporter.

Environmental concerns led to the innovation of Lyocell,[24] a green production method, in the 1980s. Lyocell production is growing, but is still considered too expensive for many. Even still, rayon is found to decompose faster than cotton, and if regulations were strictly implemented, these fibers would offer a solution to the problem of fossil fuel-based clothing and plastic waste.

Overall, the green movement, which has lobbied and fought against the usage of fossil fuel resources since the mid-1970s, has lost the battle big-time. The focus seems to have moved to recycling clothes. As industries invest in recycling plants and the narrative of synthetic fiber recycling, factories and jobs are created that depend on a continuous influx of synthetic textile waste. In the long run, this endorses synthetic fiber creation and its industry at large.

To start manufacturing, raw material is needed. While synthetic fibers are drawn entirely from fossil fuel resources and therefore don't require any natural land area, cotton, the second most frequently used textile fiber, is growing in fields. Its production has shifted, as has its further refinement, from the West – predominantly the US – to the East – predominantly China and India.

Global Cotton Production

Other Countries and United States

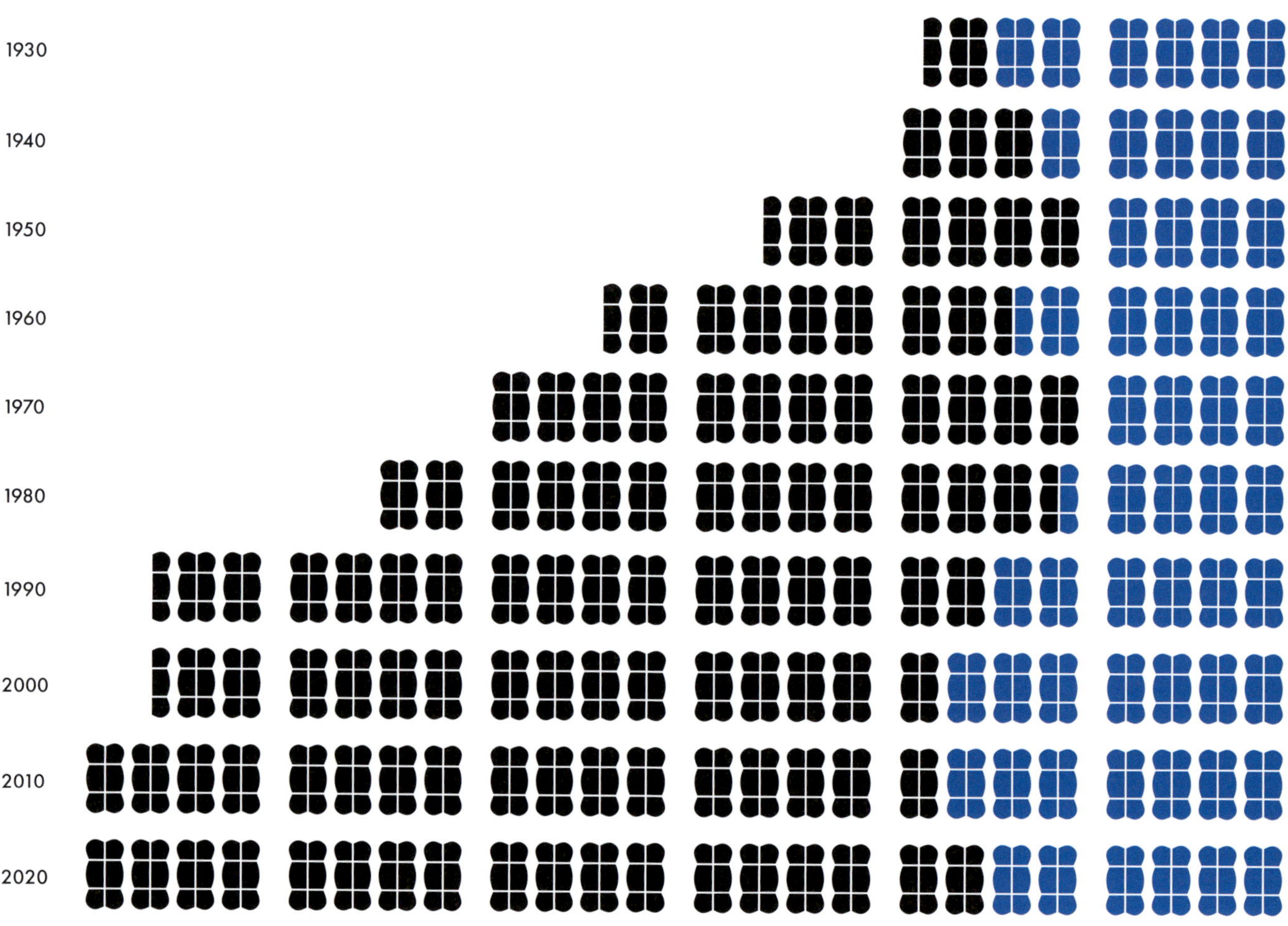

each symbol represents 2.5 million bales of cotton
black: other countries
blue: United States
red filled: China
red outlined: India

China and India

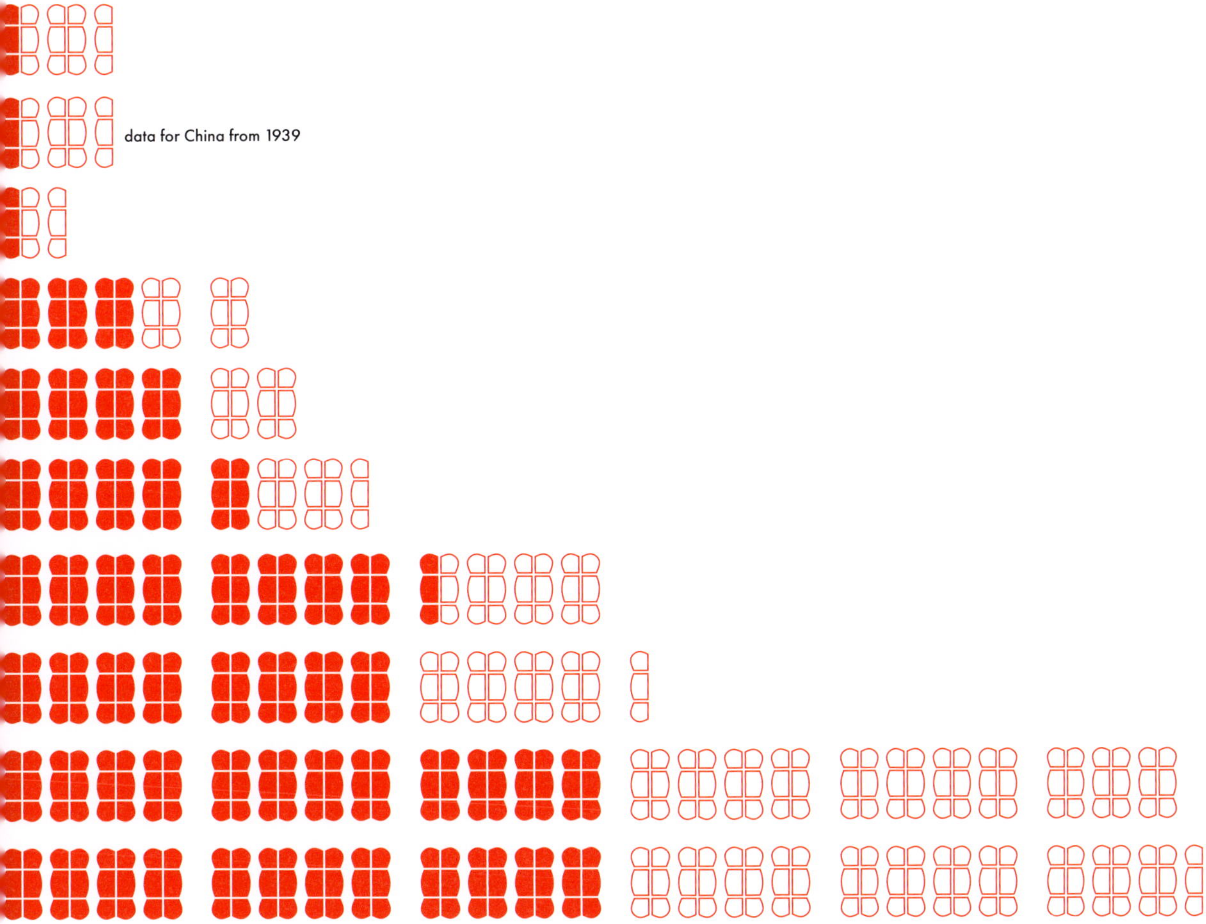

data for China from 1939

ISOTYPE

Raw Materials

Resources

In his book, Otto Neurath posed the question: "How is it possible to increase production of food and drink, shelter and recreation, the building of houses, schools, and theaters and to reduce working hours, the number of accidents, disease, and other burdens?" These noble aims resonated in the Western world in the first half of the 20th century, when heavy industry was still very much present as an economic factor.

Today, sites of production and consumption have moved far away from each other, so that working conditions in mines and factories neither affect consumers nor are noticed by them. Prior to the 1960s, when production and consumption still occurred in close proximity, goods reflected the pride or suffering of the workers in the house or next door. Workers' strikes happened in front of department stores displaying goods that the striking workers had produced some weeks before. As most of the manufacturing has been moved to low-wage countries, the lax labor laws, long working hours, frequent accidents and other burdens of laborers are unknown to the affluent consumers of the West.

The same goes for air pollution. The 1961 campaign promise by Willy Brandt, who became the German chancellor in 1969, that "Der Himmel über dem Ruhrgebiet muss wieder blau werden"[1] ("The sky above the Ruhr Valley must turn blue again") came true, but only by darkening the skies over the cities in Liaoning, China.

Distribution of Raw Materials – 1930s

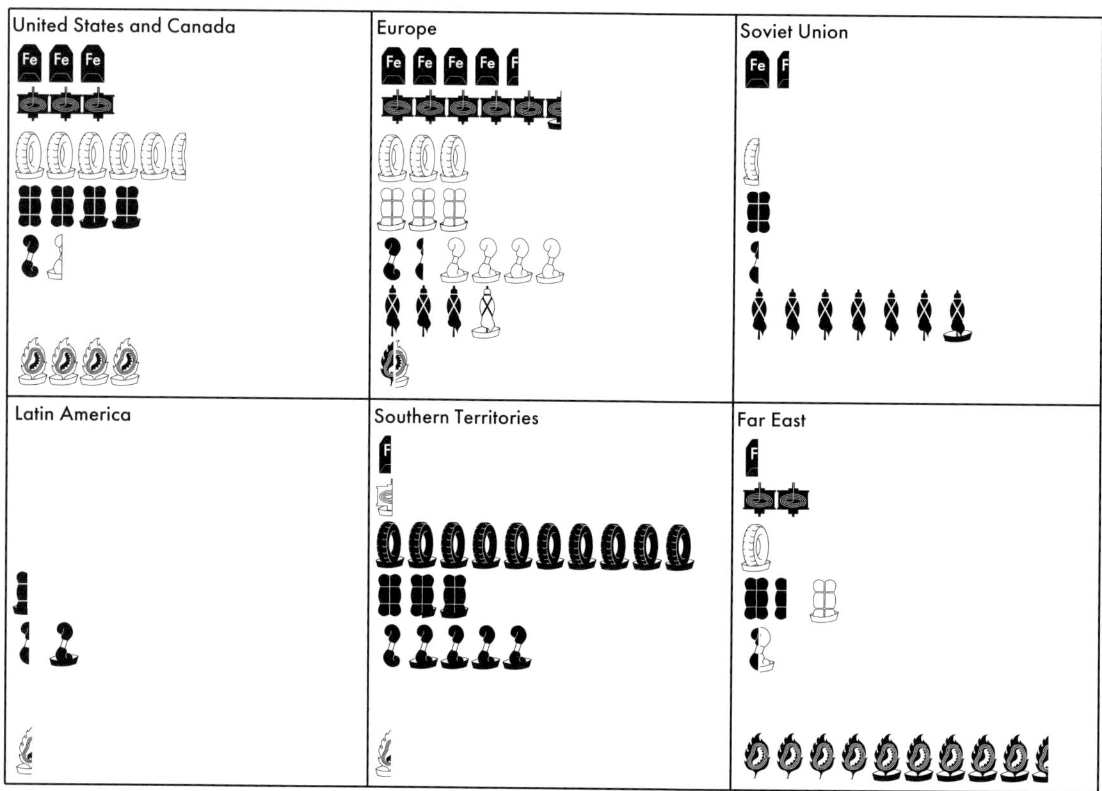

each filled symbol represents 10% of global production
of pig iron, rayon, rubber, cotton, wool, linen, silk

on ship: exported
outlined, on white ship: imported

The shift away from agriculture and manufacturing to the service industry is reflected in the production of raw materials. Compared to the 1930s, the West is hardly producing any raw materials. Europe stands out in the production of linen, but considering that linen's market share is less than 1% of the global textile fiber market, this is a small victory. The global distribution of raw material production shows again that the manufacturing of today's goods is concentrated in the Global South and especially Southeast Asia.

The West loves to think of itself as an innovator and developer and thus entitled to set global standards. Little does it realize that this way of thinking does not differ much from the mindset of the 19th century. To colonize the world of today, it is not necessary to physically conquer a country. It suffices to generate and export desires while simultaneously setting new standards. By setting new standards and creating dependencies, one can dominate and dictate. Setting the standard for containers dictates the layout of the world's container ports; setting the standard for the Internet protocol dictates the coding language for all; and setting the standard for human interaction, e.g., human rights, dictates the way humans interact with each other.

Distribution of Raw Materials – 2020s

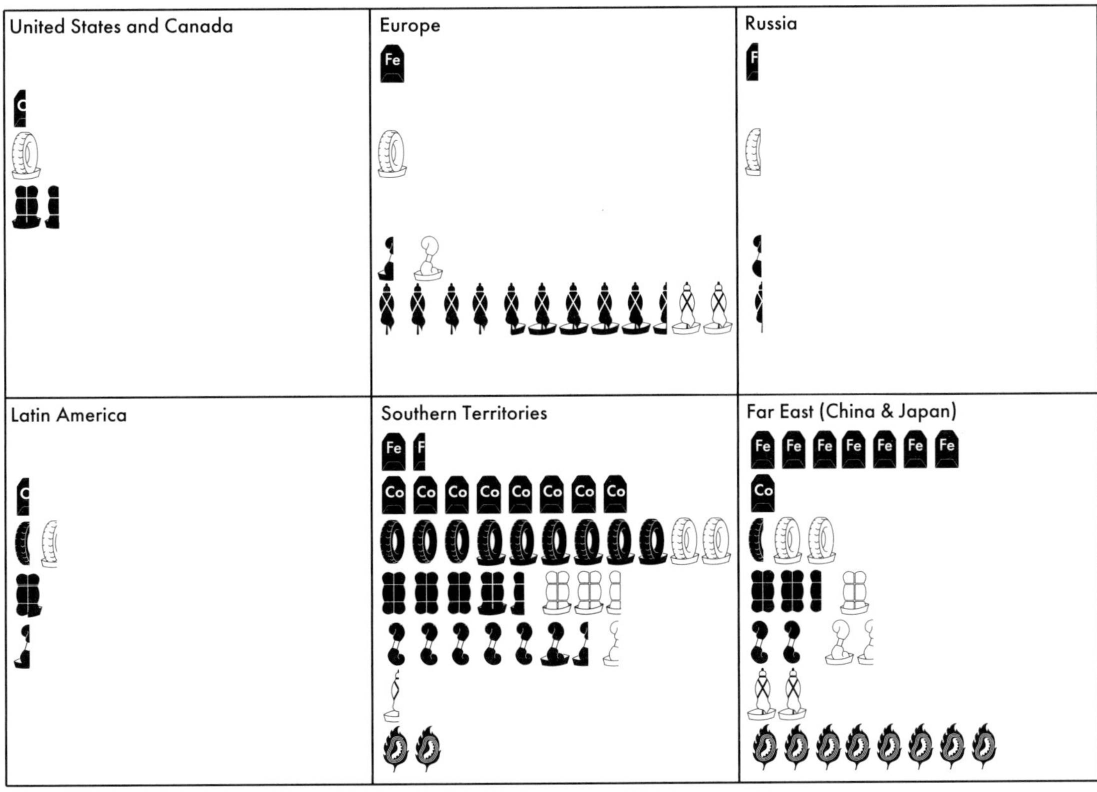

each filled symbol represents 10% of global production of pig iron, cobalt, rubber, cotton, wool, linen, silk

on ship: exported
outlined, on white ship: imported

While European families plan weekend trips to visit former coal mines and steel mills to get an idea of a sooty and smoky past, most Chinese experience this as their normal course of life. The international division of labor had the big advantage for the West that the pollution from heavy industry, and the health risks it entails, moved far away and out of sight. Yet outsourcing the dirty parts of the global factory floor to China is not changing the planet's overall air quality. Today's pig iron production might be happening on the other side of the globe, but it is still happening inside the same atmosphere.

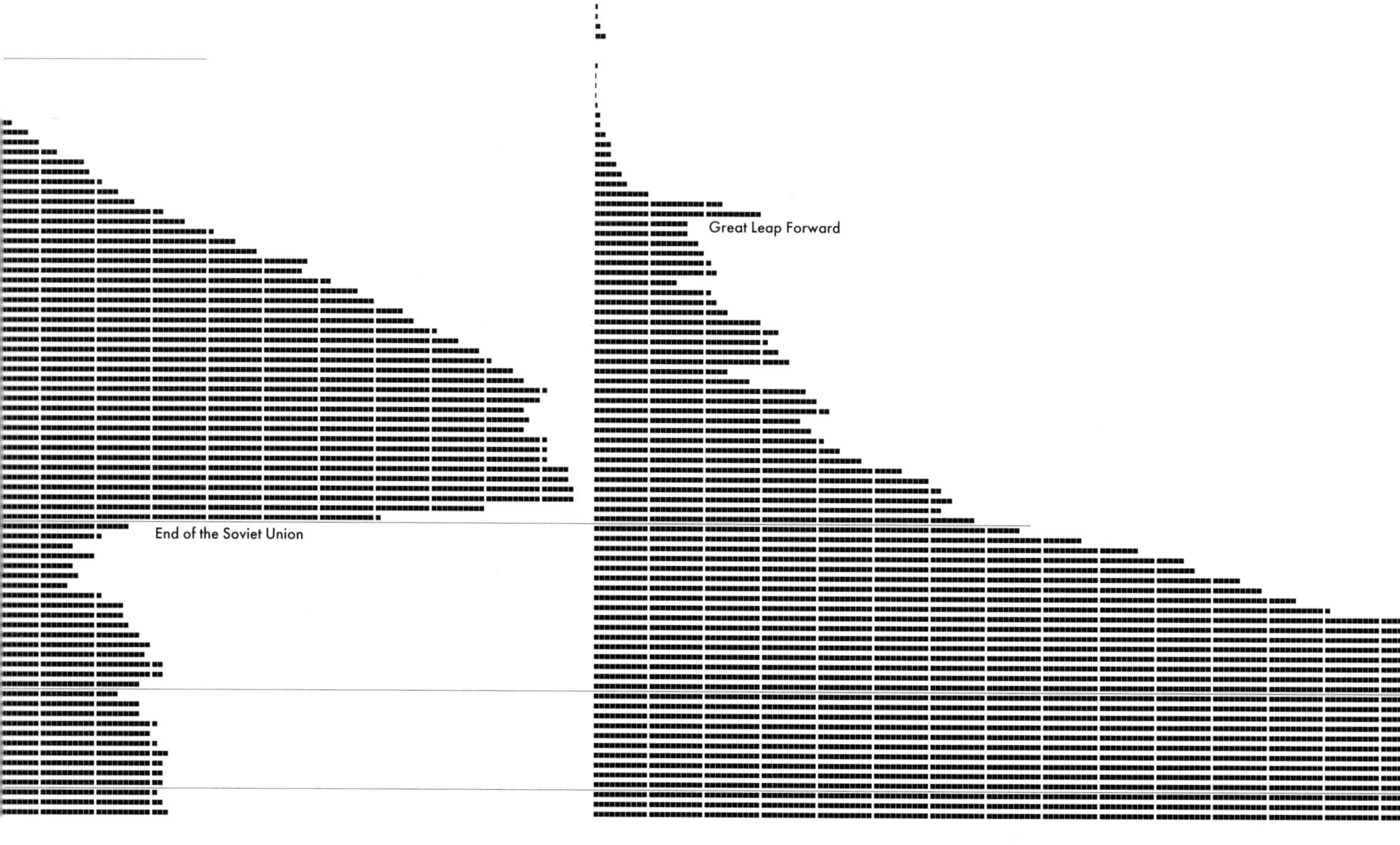

Pig Iron Production

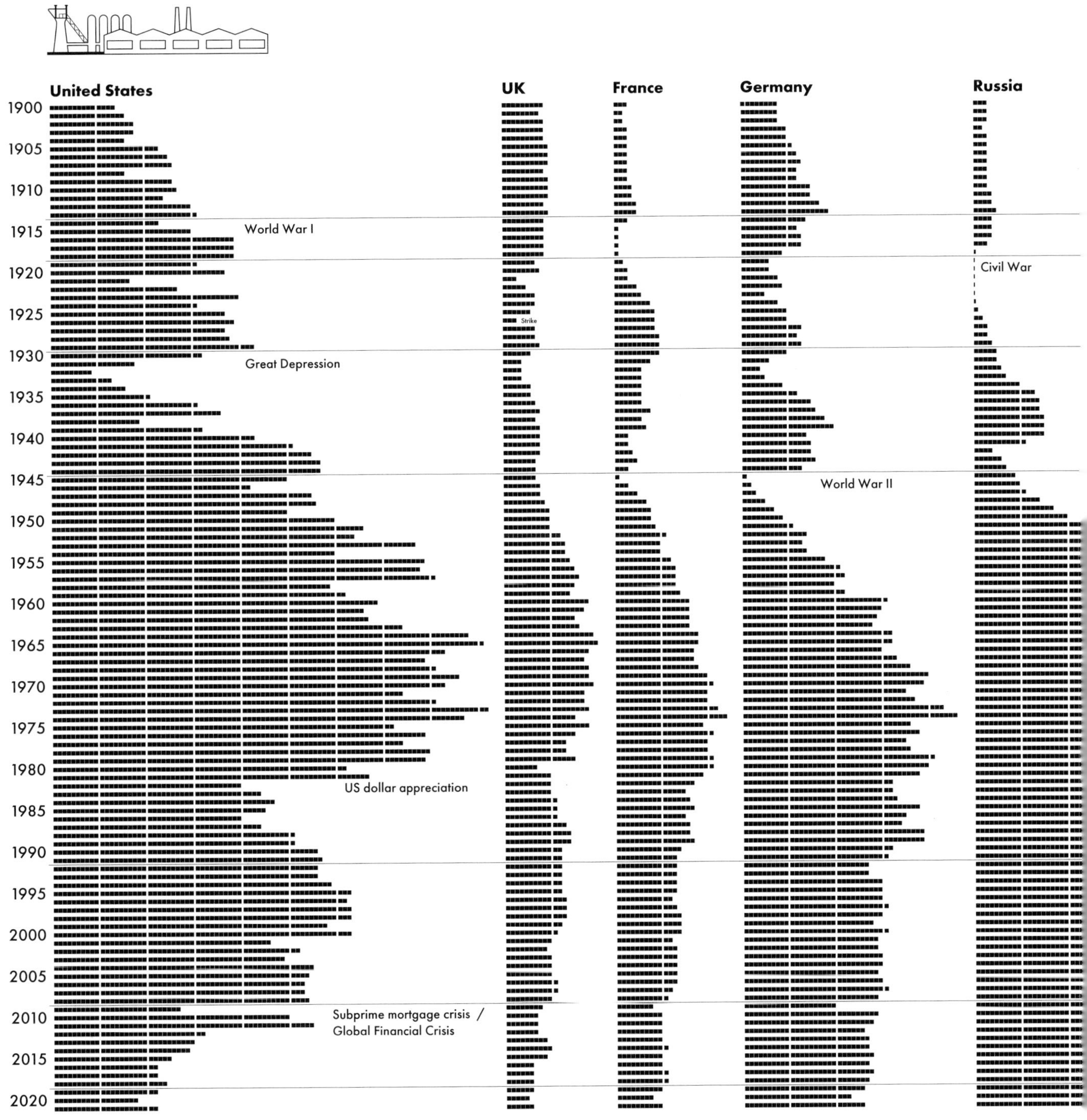

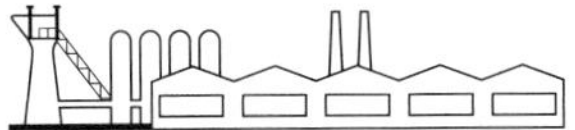

United States | UK | France | Germany | Russia

1900
1905
1910
1915
1920
1925
1930
1935
1940
1945
1950
1955
1960
1965
1970
1975
1980
1985
1990
1995
2000
2005
2010
2015
2020

World War I

Civil War

Strike

Great Depression

World War II

US dollar appreciation

Subprime mortgage crisis / Global Financial Crisis

each unit represents 1 million long tons

Iron Production

While plastics (synthetic materials made from fossil fuels) are on the rise, metals, and specifically iron, are still the core material of industrial production, putting them at the center of modern life. 90% of all metal that is refined today is iron.[2] As reinforcement for concrete, a use discovered by French gardener Joseph Monier in the mid-19th century, iron laid the groundwork for modern architecture. In the form of steel or in combination with other materials, iron is the main material used in contemporary skyscrapers, cars, rockets, and desktop computers.

In the early 20th century, abundant iron production was the sign of a great nation, with the US taking a strong lead. If this is still true, then China is the greatest nation, producing about 67% of the world's pig iron in 2022. The development of pig iron production illustrates very impressively how the West outsourced its heavy industry to China throughout the past 35 years.[3]

One of the most symbolic acts was the disposal of the Westfalenhütte by ThyssenKrupp to the Chinese steelmaker Jiangsu Shagang in 2001. The entire steel mill – 250,000 tons, complete with furnaces, casting plants, and roll mills – was dismantled, then shipped from Dortmund, Germany to Zhangjiagang, China, where it was rebuilt to continue producing steel.[4] Cheerful articles in German newspapers and magazines at the time celebrated the end of a dirty page in that European country's history books.

This trend was global. The modern strategy of division of labor was upscaled to the strategy of international division of labor. It was all planned out very neatly: a planet that runs as smoothly as a factory. Resources come from the poor South; the dirty, labor-intensive production process is carried out in Southeast Asia (predominantly China); and the management, financing, and innovation happen in the West. Needless to say, it was the West that came up with this scheme, and it relies on other regions consistently lagging behind. This global division brings with it dependencies on a huge scale and relies on logistics that keep the factory running. The high-seas shipping industry played the role of Earth's conveyer belt.

For about 25 years, with a brief interruption by the global financial crisis of 2008, this system functioned pretty well. But it seems that China has had enough of it. That country is developing its own system of management, finance, and innovation. At the same time, China realizes how dependent the rest of the world has become on its manufacturing. And interestingly it is exactly the mundane elements of early industrialization and modernization like iron ore, household goods, and accessories that hurt the Western customer the most when they are not available.

The former site of the Westfalenhütte steel furnace in Dortmund is now home to logistics centers for Amazon, Decathlon, and DB Schenker.[5] Next to it, a new factory emerged that focuses on the processing of high-end and high-quality steel for the German car industry. These are beacons of the new economy; smoking chimneys are long gone. The start of the 21st century saw efforts to enhance the industrial image of the Ruhrgebiet through culture and tourism. The Zollverein Coal Mine became a World Heritage Site and the area's flagship for its successful transformation. It is part of the European Route of Industrial Heritage, a tourist route connecting the continent's industrial heritage sites.

1900
1905
1910
1915
1920
1925
1930
1935
1940
1945
1950
1955
1960
1965
1970
1975
1980
1985
1990
1995
2000
2005
2010
2015
2020

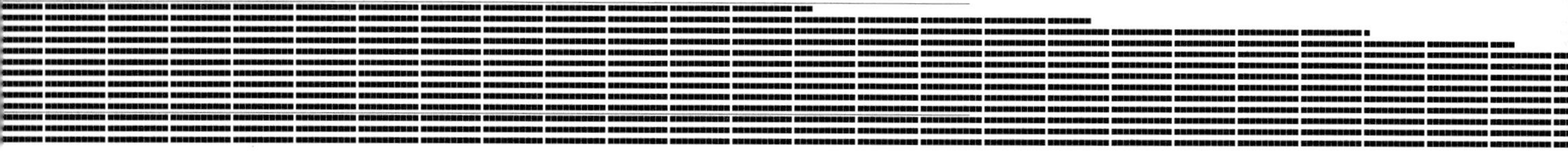

Pig Iron Production

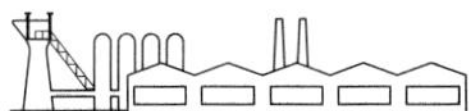

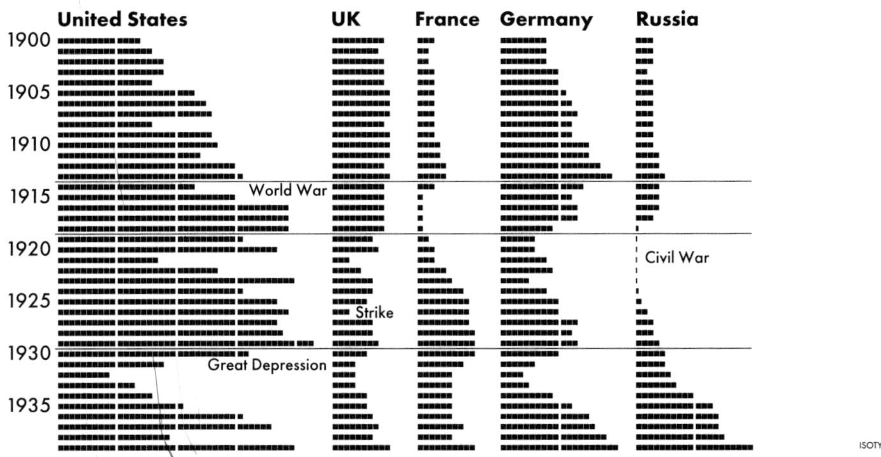

each unit represents 1 million long tons

diagram as presented in the book *Modern Man in the Making*, here as a scale comparison.

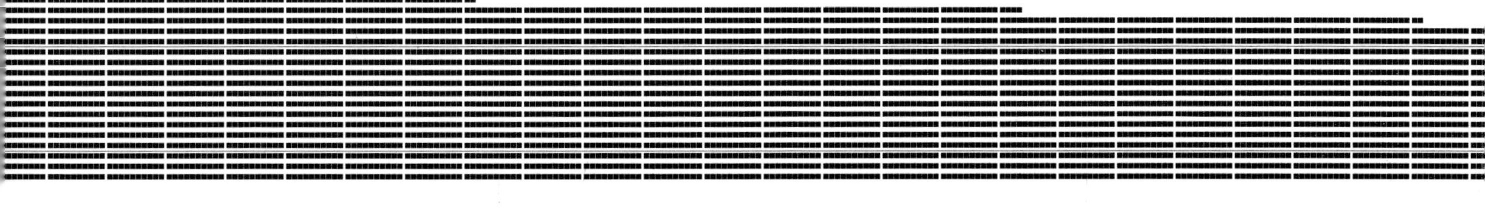

Innovation

The West is obsessed with innovation. Combine that with the words "start-up," "design," and "target group," and you have the perfect recipe for a future "unicorn," a privately held start-up company valued at over US$ 1 billion. Yet most innovations result in a demand for resources. Mobile phones need rare earth minerals; batteries need lithium, cobalt, and nickel; and appliances need plastics for their casing. Most of these resources are not available in the countries where the ideas emerged. Thus, with its innovations, the West schedules resources it does not own and has no right to use. At a very early stage, land, people, and cultures are included in an equation they are not aware of until investors show up. Only very strong communities and well-organized nations can resist the big money promised by mining companies and their shareholders.

One example is Greenland, which resisted the lure of a mining contract for uranium and rare earths proposed by an Australian mining company whose top shareholder is a Chinese company. In 2021 Greenland's parliament passed legislation to ban uranium and rare earth mining in one of the Earth's biggest deposits.[6] Less well-governed countries can't resist, and crucially often can't afford to resist. While Greenland's GDP per capita in 2020 sits comfortably at US$ 54,570, that of Namibia (with the largest uranium deposit in the world) is a rather meager US$ 4,250.[7] Regulations are few and corruption is frequent, and thus the earthly resources are mined under the most terrible conditions.

The recent shift to electrification fueled the demand for cobalt, since it is an essential ingredient in lithium-ion batteries. 48% of the world's cobalt reserves are in the Democratic Republic of Congo.[8] In its cobalt mines, child labor is common, workers' rights are often nonexistent, and safety is very poor. The sites of these mines are very different from the shiny flagship smartphone stores and the high-end electric cars in the Western world.

Cobalt

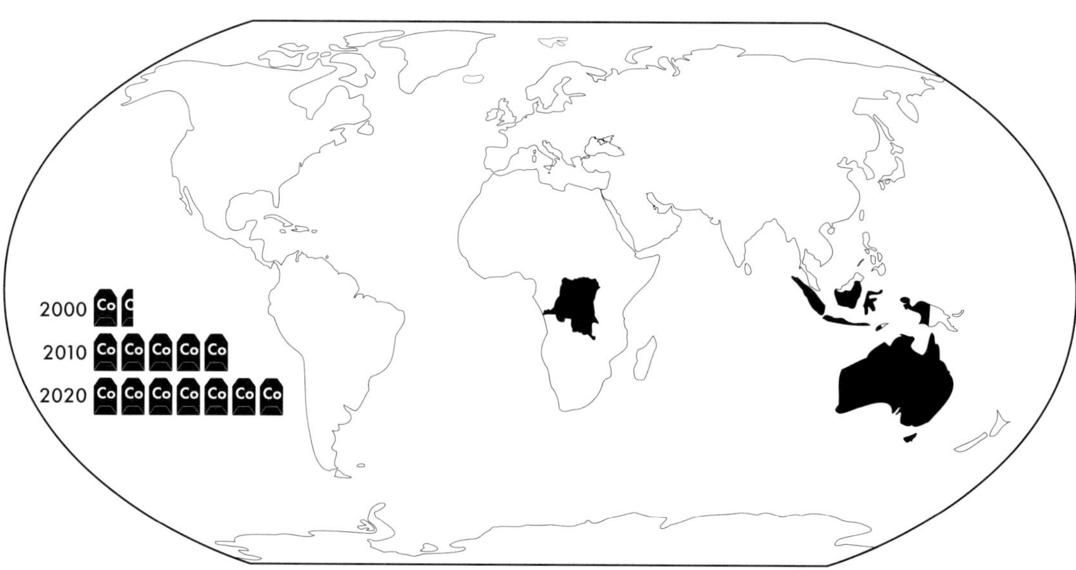

the three countries shaded in black account for 73% of global cobalt reserves (2022)
each bar represents 2,000 tons of cobalt mined globally in the specific year

In Neurath's time, most of Asia and Africa was firmly in the grip of European colonizers. Instead of today's 203 countries, there were only 80 countries. Eighty years later, the political map has changed radically, yet one thing has not: "The Southern world has to provide the Western world with much raw material for industrial centers and with foodstuffs, leaving the masses of population in the South at a low subsistence level."[9]

Lithium

the three countries shaded in black account for 70% of global lithium reserves (2022)
each bar represents 2,000 tons of lithium mined globally in the specific year

Nickel

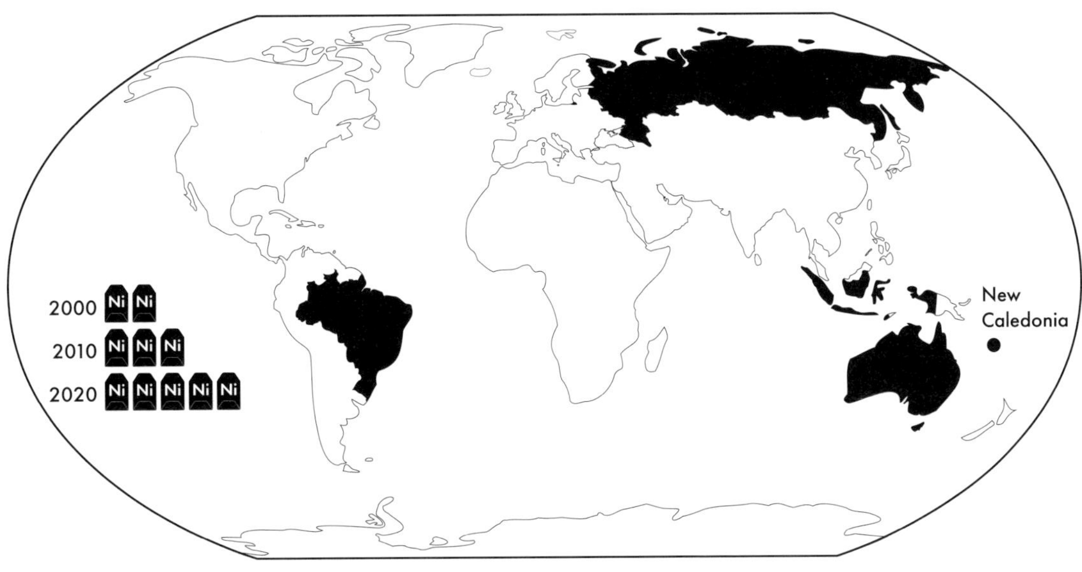

the five countries shaded in black account for 73% of global nickel reserves (2022)
each bar represents 500,000 tons of nickel mined globally in the specific year

The supposedly innovative thinking has yet to take into account the land and the people who actually own the resources. The thoughts are instead adjusted along the profit chain. If everyone along the production line has a reasonable monetary profit with the highest profit at the trading company, the product is worth capitalizing on a global market. This means that as cobalt in Congo is mined cheaply (by over 40% Chinese-owned mining companies) due to minimal regulation, and sold at ever higher prices along the chain, the Congolese are bled of their resources while Mercedes-Benz sells their luxury electric cars made in Germany for a pretty penny. The Congolese don't profit beyond the miners' salary of € 3.50 per day and whatever the mining companies pay to the government for mining permissions.[10, 11]

Congo (Kinshasa), Indonesia, and Australia together are home to 73% of the world's cobalt resources.[12] Two-thirds of global cobalt mining is in the hands of three companies: the Anglo-Swiss company Glencore and the Chinese firms Huayou Cobalt and China Moly.[13]

Reserves of High-Impact Minerals and Fossil Fuels

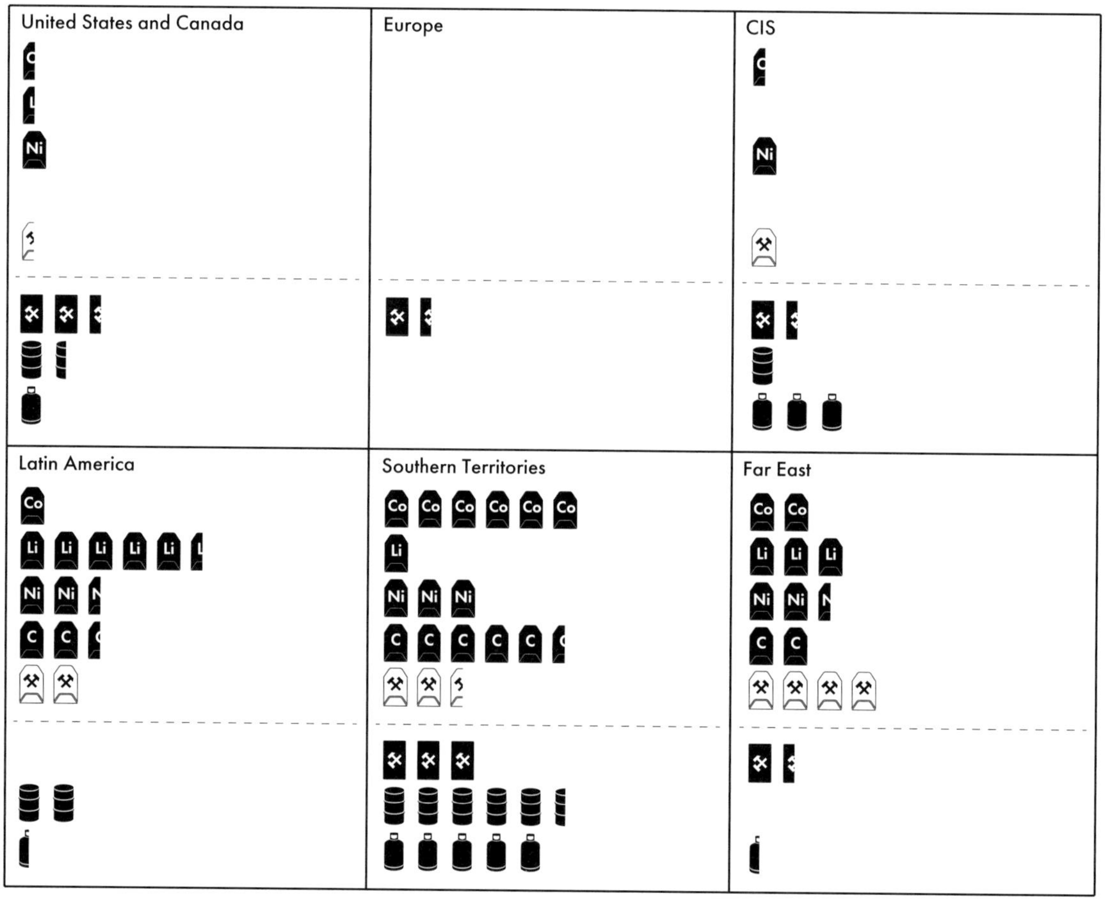

each symbol represents 10% of the known reserves on planet Earth

high-impact minerals: cobalt, lithium, nickel, graphite, rare earths (white bars) (2021)
fossil fuels: coal, oil, gas (2020)

Chile, Australia, and Argentina sit on 70% of the world's lithium reserves[14] and Indonesia, Australia, Brazil, Russia, and New Caledonia (France) possess about 73% of the world's nickel reserves.[15] The three main resources needed for car batteries are thus spread unequally across the globe. The global dependencies on these countries will increase with the growing demand for these resources. Global economics and, consequently, social stability will depend on the political stability of these specific countries.

Global Lithium Supply Chain

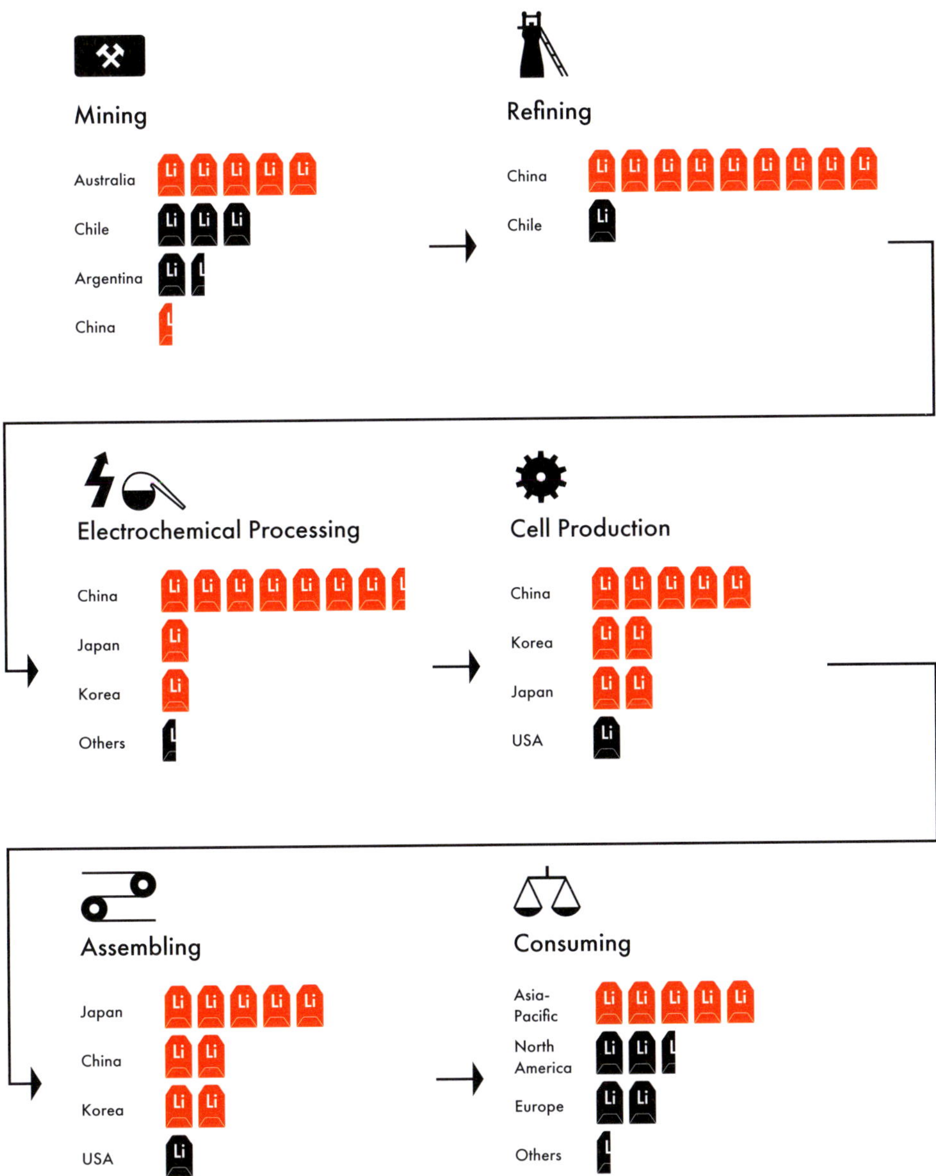

each symbol represents 10% share of the lithium supply chain
red symbols represent the East Asian and Asia-Pacific share

"High-impact" minerals only feature in a small number of technologies, but their future demand is significantly greater than today. One example is lithium, which will only be used in energy storage, but must ramp up its production by 488% to meet demand. Cobalt and graphite fall into the same category.[16]

To make large profits, a first and important step along the supply chain is to make sure that the raw material is exported quickly from the mines to the home market, where the refinement can be done and added value can be generated. Mining is labor-intensive, dirty, and risky – work that is left to the people of the Global South. The refinement of resources is capital-intensive, since it relies on expensive machinery and refined logistics, which the Western world does not want to give out of hand.

The example of the lithium supply chain shows that China is a quick learner. With almost no lithium mines of its own, it has managed to get hold of almost 90% of the raw material refining, even from a highly developed country like Australia.[17] By doing so, China transformed itself into a major player in global battery production.

This example reflects the current way of thinking and at the same time the current worries. The Western world knows of its growing dependency and is trying to gain ground against China. Yet how the countries and people who own the natural resources can be included better and how they can move up the supply chain is still not part of the discussion. True and holistic innovations would include social, environmental, and political responsibility along the entire supply chain. With these, modernity would take its next leap forward.

Whenever promises of salvation are made in the name of modernity and progress, caution is advised. From the very beginning, modernity has been built on the promise of abundance – in fact, modernity is the fulfilled medieval dream of Cockaigne, the land of plenty. Remarkably, modernity's abundance always seems to come from the riches of the Earth. Columbus promised a land of gold, gold promised immediate wealth, coal and oil promised easily transportable and cheap energy for all, uranium promised clean energy through nuclear power, and finally lithium, cobalt, and nickel are promising clean and safe energy through electricity.

Each promise is built on finite resources and mostly resources that belonged to others. The current phase of modernity that dreams about the electrification of everything, which should result in an ecological modern lifestyle, is prone to the same illusion as the fossil phase or the nuclear phase of modernity. Living in such an illusion is a characteristic feature of modernity. Thus the good news is that we are certainly living a modern life; the bad news is that we have not moved one inch closer toward making modern life sustainable.

Fossil Fuel

Oil

Fossil resources serve as the perfect example for explaining our dependence on the treasures of the soil for development. Countries that have been at the forefront of industrialization, thus modernity, were in possession of coal, the natural resource this progress was based on. It might have even been the easy availability of coal in the UK that instigated technological progress in the first place. Other countries that followed, such as the USA, Germany, Russia, and France, all possessed coal reserves of their own. The international dependency of these leading nations of early industrialization was minimal. After World War I, the large coal reserves in the Ruhrgebiet in Germany led to a conflict with neighboring France, which had comparatively small coal reserves and occupied the area. It was coal and not oil that was the basis of the foundation of the European Union after World War II, in the form of the European Coal and Steel Community (ECSC) to regulate a peaceful trade of resources particularly between the two squabblers, Germany and France. The rise of European powers in the 18th and 19th centuries had largely been due to coal, and for lack of oil reserves, Europe had to continue to bet on coal.

In fact, the lack of oil reserves was one of the major reasons Nazi Germany lost World War II. It was the first full "war of the machines,"[1] with tanks, airplanes, and warships growing hungry for gasoline. The US, sitting on large quantities of oil and at a safe distance from the war, supplied the Allied forces with 6 of the 7 billion barrels of oil used by the Allied forces.[2] Coal was surpassed by oil, and with it, Europe was surpassed by the USA as the new global power.

The transformed global order after World War II left the European countries with little access to the 20th century's main fuel supply. Europe's own oil deposits in the North Sea were discovered rather late in the 20th century. At the start of the 20th century, it was above all the United Kingdom that had an advantage through its colonial protectorates in the Middle East, where the world's largest oil fields were discovered.

Coal Reserves

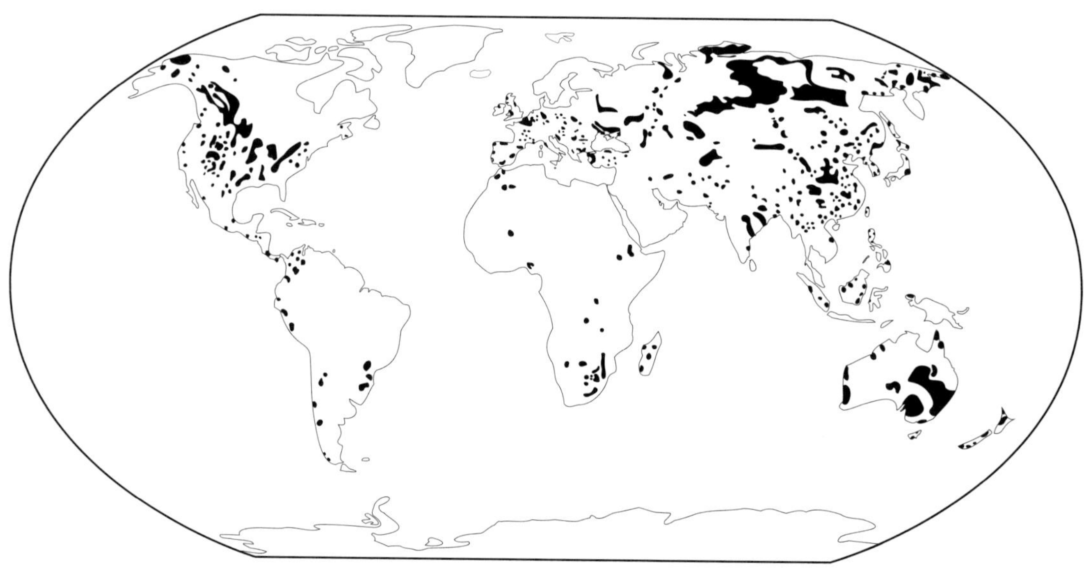

black: coal reserves – anthracite, bituminous, and lignite (2020)

The British Petroleum Company, founded in 1909, originated in the oil fields of Iran (Persia) and had no domestic production until 1965.[3] A geological roulette blessed a few sparsely populated Middle Eastern countries with large quantities of oil, a substance the rest of the world became addicted to.

In 1960 the Organization of the Petroleum Exporting Countries (OPEC) was formed by Iran, Iraq, Kuwait, Saudi Arabia, and Venezuela at a time when the oil market was dominated by the "Seven Sisters" (today: "Big Oil"), the world's seven largest private oil companies, headquartered in the US, UK, and the Netherlands.[4] Founding OPEC was a move to decolonize the oil market and gain greater control over oil prices by coordinating domestic production. As in October 1973, OPEC members unilaterally declared significant production cuts and an oil embargo against the US and other industrialized nations that supported Israel in the Yom Kippur War, the globe was sent into its first major oil crisis. High oil prices resulted in various measurements, like car free Sundays, fuel economy standards for vehicles, vacation for schools in winter to save on energy for heating, and the creation of the International Energy Agency.[5]

Today, the 13 members of OPEC produce about 36% of the world's oil and have access to 73% of the globe's proven oil reserves. 11 of these 13 countries are rated "not free" by the American watchdog Freedom House, and the remaining two (Kuwait and Nigeria) are considered only "partly free." And so it happens that the world is put in the precarious position of being reliant on autocratic systems, giving them authority over the stuff the modern world is built upon.

Crude Oil Reserves

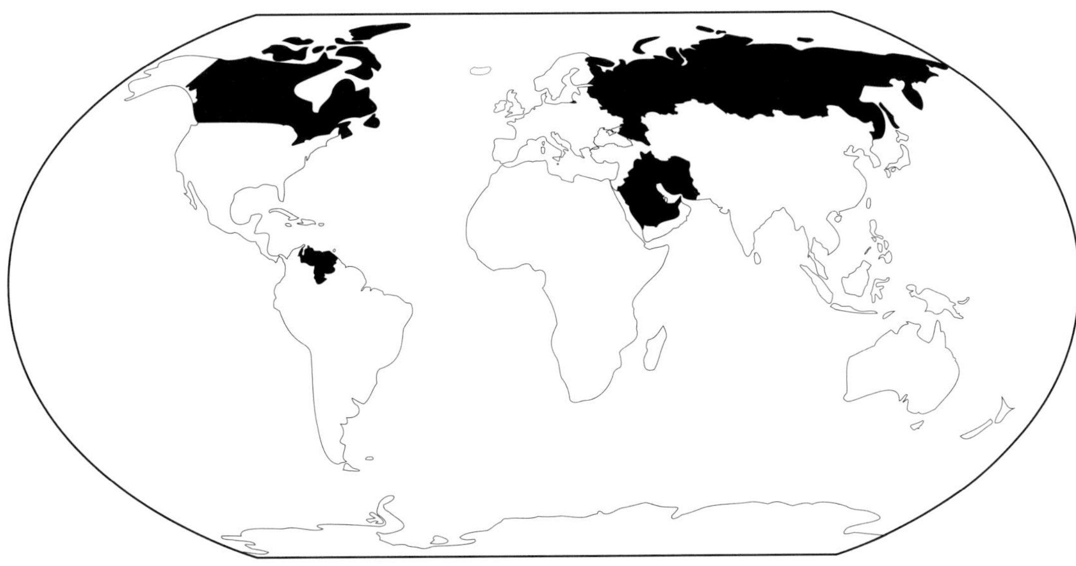

black: countries with 80% of the world's proven oil reserves larger than 100,000 million barrels (2020)

Nowadays the use of fossil fuels is ubiquitous. As mentioned in the previous chapters, modern food production thrives on fossil fuels through the use of fertilizers and machinery – thus humans eat oil. Most of today's textile fibers are synthetic, thus made from fossil oil – so humans wear it; and oil plays a vital role in the construction industry – thus humans live in it.

The introduction of nuclear energy was the first attempt to cut the ties with fossil resources. Several severe accidents and the fact that there is still no permanent storage site for nuclear waste leaves this option in limbo. However, the fragility of the EU is revealing itself amid the Russo-Ukraine war, exposing its dependency on autocratic regimes of the Middle East for oil and Russia for natural gas. Nuclear power might be the clearest way forward. The current push to clean energy by wind, sun, and hydropower appears to be a better option, but is still in its infancy.

Global Energy Consumption

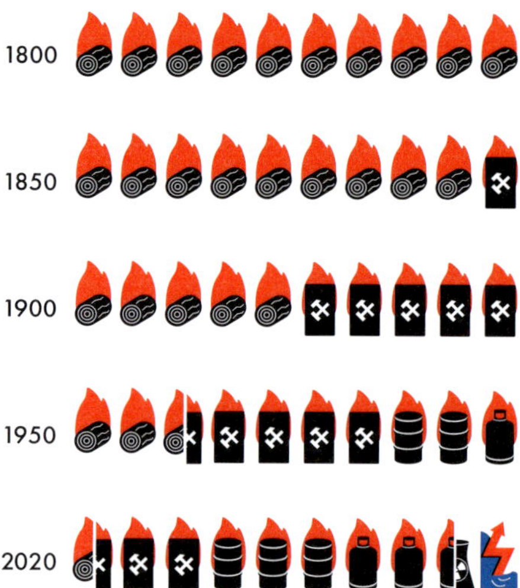

each symbol represents 10% of global energy consumption
sources of power: traditional biomass (wood), coal, oil, natural gas, nuclear, renewables

Unfortunately, sun and wind are rather uneven in their output, and energy storage on a large scale is still problematic. Transforming peak sun and wind energy production into hydrogen seems to be the most feasible option at the moment. The resources for batteries, photovoltaic panels, transformers, and other appliances still need to come from diverse destinations, and most of them from below ground in the Global South.

Specific periods of modernity can be defined according to their main drivers: the 19th-century coal modernity, the 20th-century oil modernity, and a possible 21st-century oil/nuclear/sun/wind modernity. While the carbon-based energy sources are physical substances that can be stored in barns and tanks rather easily and their energy released rather easily, the new sources of energy are more abstract and less immediate.

Wood is tangible, can be collected in individual pieces, and is rather light, while it inherits a large amount of energy: it has a high energy density. Nomads can carry it with them to overcome stretches of desert or barren land. The big advantage of fossil fuels is their higher energy density. That of oil and gas is about three times that of wood. This means that one kilogram of gasoline equals 3 kg of wood. A full tank of a car containing 70 liters of gasoline (1.0 l = 0.75 kg) equals about 160 kg of wood, or the weight of about two passengers.[6] The difficulty in the electrification of an individual means of transportation lies precisely in the low energy density of batteries. The advantage is that the batteries themselves are not the fuel; they don't disappear, but can be recharged many times. New technology is developing batteries with a higher energy density, and maybe someday they will carry as much energy per kilogram as wood.

Energy Density per Source

each flash symbol represents one megajoule per kg of power source: natural gas, gasoline, coal, wood, battery

The changing relationship between humans and energy concerning the ever-higher degree of abstraction of the energy source will create the biggest challenge for the modern human. A foundational element of modernity is the security of an energy source and the individual independence it provides. If the experiment of a fossil-free future is to succeed, it is essential to ensure this. In the future, dependencies might only grow by relying on photovoltaic panels and batteries.

Sources of Power

Not only the source, but also the amount, of power produced since the 1930s has changed radically. Today the Far East and the Southern Territories, predominantly China, consume more oil than the rest of the world put together. Yet, in times of 8,000 km long gas pipelines between Russia and China and a fleet of 600,000 oil tankers[7] that are capable of carrying up to 560,000 tons of crude oil, energy consumption can occur far away from the places where energy sources are produced.

Upcoming and rapidly growing countries like China resort to well-established methods of generating power. Today, China operates almost half of the world's coal-fired power plants. These plants are comparably cheap and easy to switch on and off on demand and therefore guarantee a steady energy output that can match demand. In the next ten years, China plans to add another 300 gigawatts of coal power plants to its existing 1,000 gigawatts.[8] For human health, coal-fired power plants are a

Crude Oil Consumption

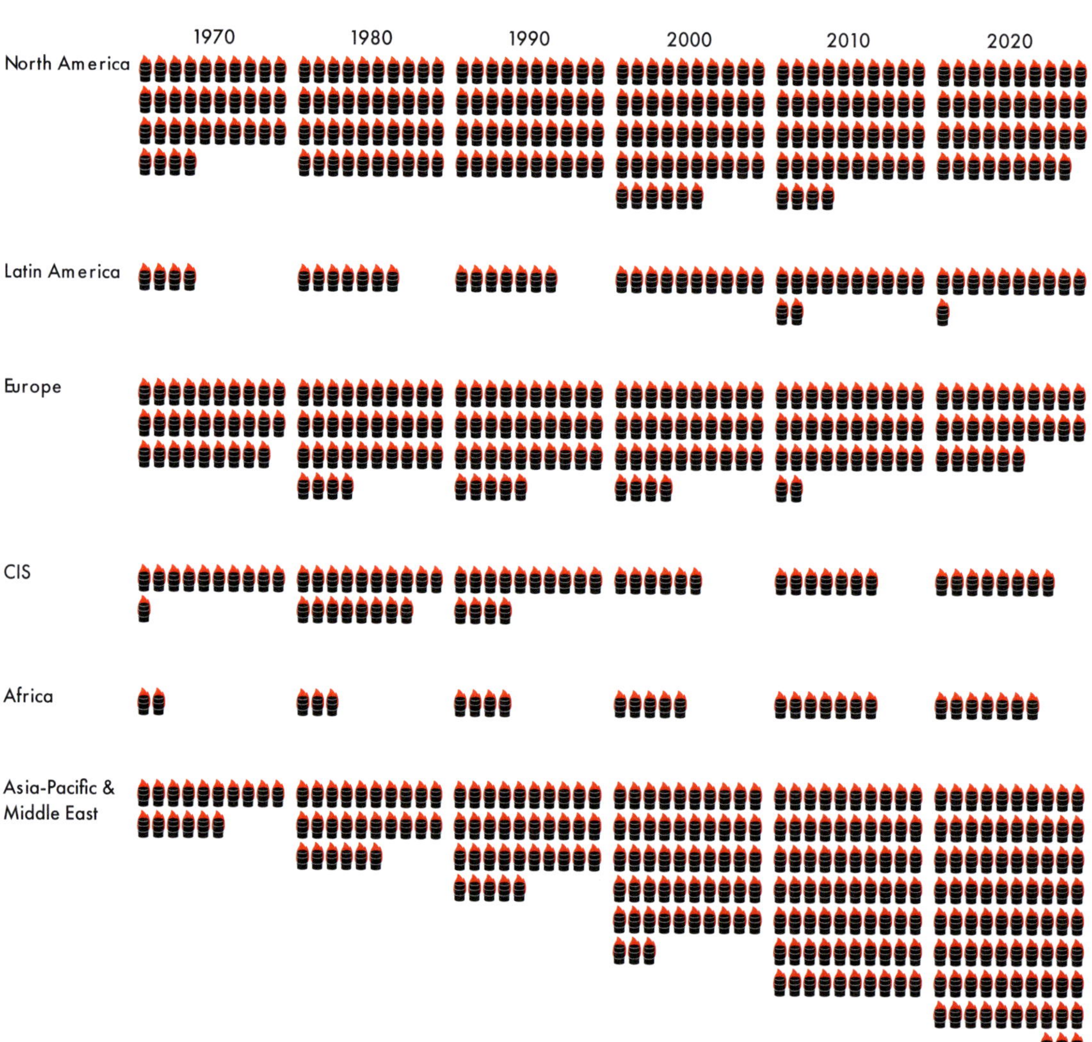

Coal-Fired Power Plants

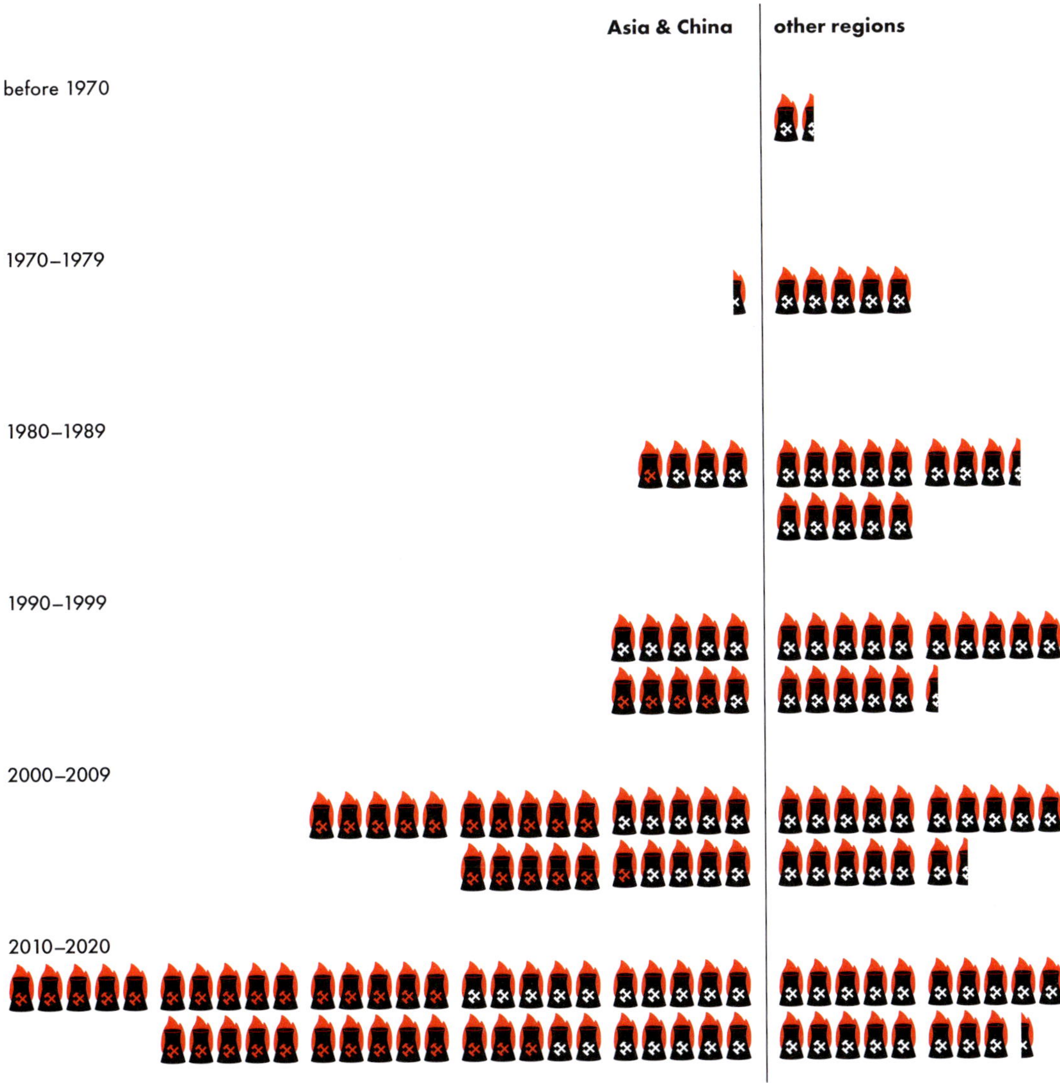

each symbol represents 100 coal-fired power plants
red hammer: China

disaster. They are causing air pollution which can lead to asthma, brain damage, heart problems, and cancer. At the same time, coal is the single biggest CO_2 contributor, thus adding massively to the warming of the atmosphere. But energy security has priority for now.

The extravagance of North America becomes evident when looking at power consumption per person. The equally developed Europeans are using about half that amount of energy. Citizens of the US in particular are used to a modern lifestyle that involves a rather careless provision of private cars, air conditioners, and other energy-consuming appliances. Since it is very difficult to change people's habits, all hope is set on the switch to sustainable energy sources.

Sources of Power

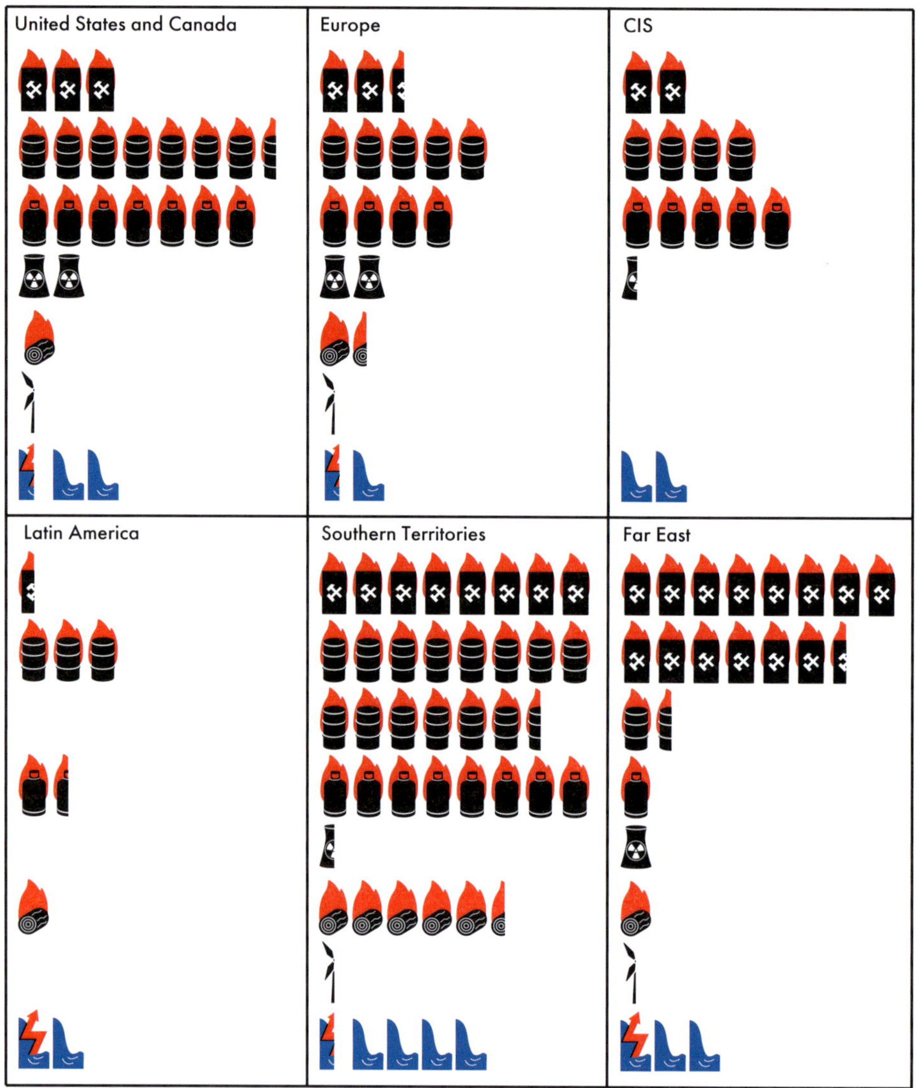

each symbol represents 1,500,000 million kWh produced annually (2020)

sources of power: coal, oil, gas, biofuel, wind & solar, and hydropower
water with lightning bolt: hydropower is being used; water without lightning bolt: a potential energy source yet unused

The oil crisis of the 1970s, the Fukushima Daiichi Nuclear Power Plant disaster in 2011, and recent disruptions in the energy delivery system due to the COVID-19 pandemic and the Russo-Ukrainian war in 2022 provide additional evidence that the diversification of energy sources and an exit from fossil fuels and nuclear energy are necessary for humanity's future.

Today the CIS (Commonwealth of Independent States) countries, the USA, and Canada rely on fossil fuels and nuclear energy for 90% of their energy consumption, while in Latin America that figure is just over 70%. In comparison to Europe, which still relies quite heavily on nuclear energy, Latin America is, with 28% hydroelectric and renewable energy, the most advanced region in terms of clean energy consumption and is therefore also rather independent of fossil and mineral resources.[9]

Currently 2.5% of all energy consumed on the planet is hydroelectric and another 11% is from renewable resources. The long-term aim is to turn this 13.5% into 100% and have the planet run entirely on sustainable energy.[10]

This is a tough call, especially for developing countries that have struggled for decades to establish a stable and reliable energy supply and that lack the infrastructure to integrate such systems. Bangladesh experiences a power outage on 249 days of every year,[11] a phenomenon unthinkable to many residents of the Western world. It seems that while the West dreams of a fossil-free energy supply all around the planet, many inhabitants of this planet reduce this dream to simply: an energy supply.

Days of Power Outages per Year

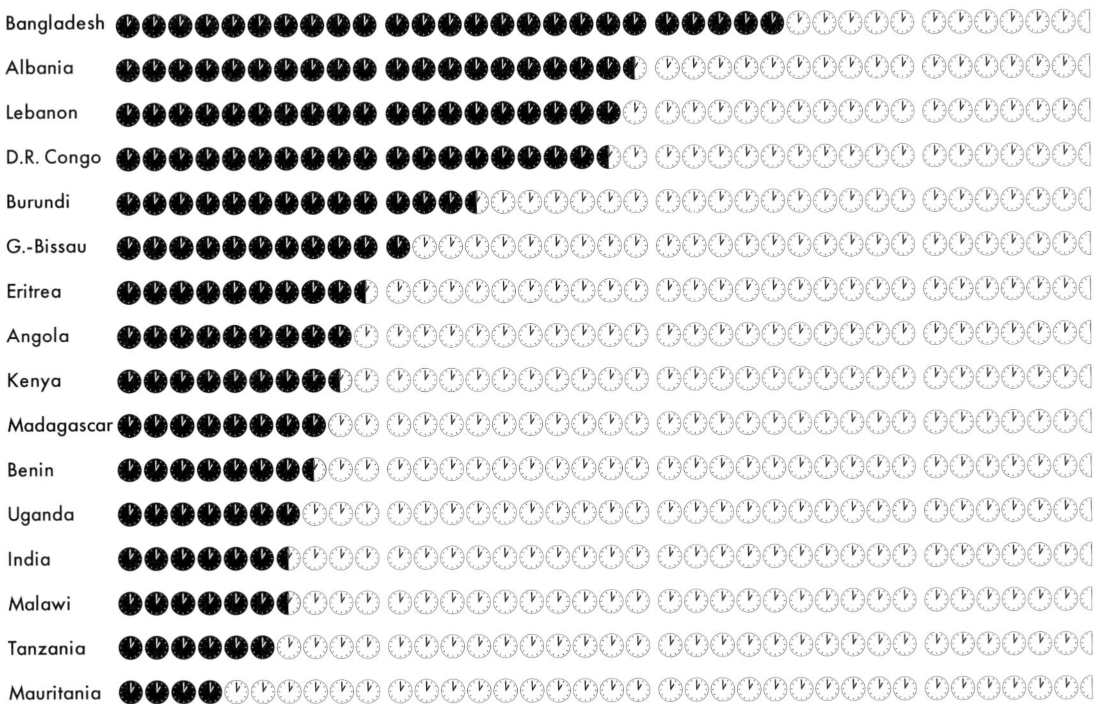

each clock represents 10 days per year (2020s)

black clock: average number of days per year that establishments experience power outages or surges from the public grid

The Car

One of the single biggest causes for private fossil fuel consumption is the automobile. The introduction of the private car was only possible with the development of relatively cheap gasoline. The car provided masses of people the freedom to travel individually. While the twenty-mule team,[12] a carriage drawn by 20 mules or horses, was the maximum capacity of any vehicle in the 19th century, a private car today can easily be equipped with a 200-horsepower engine, gulping gasoline instead of water. If all horses captured in motor vehicle engines were released as real horses in flesh and bone, 160 planet Earths would be needed to feed them.

Today, car ownership serves as an excellent indicator of the wealth of a nation. A high car ownership rate hints not only at a high level of personal income, but also at the existence of a dense and well-maintained highway network throughout a country. Consequently, this implies a small rural-urban income and service gap. In addition to the road and highway grid, a dense network of gas stations and mechanics must be in place to allow a smooth ride.

Within the group of wealthy nations, a country's size and rate of urbanization have an influence on car ownership. Larger and less urbanized rich countries generally have a higher rate of car ownership, since their population depends much more on individual transportation.

Considering its size and income level, China still has a rather low rate of car ownership. What is currently a blessing for the environment might change very soon. If China caught up and reached US ownership rates, it would add 940 million cars to its streets and to the world. This would increase the total amount of cars on planet Earth from

Main Second-Hand Vehicle Exporters to Africa

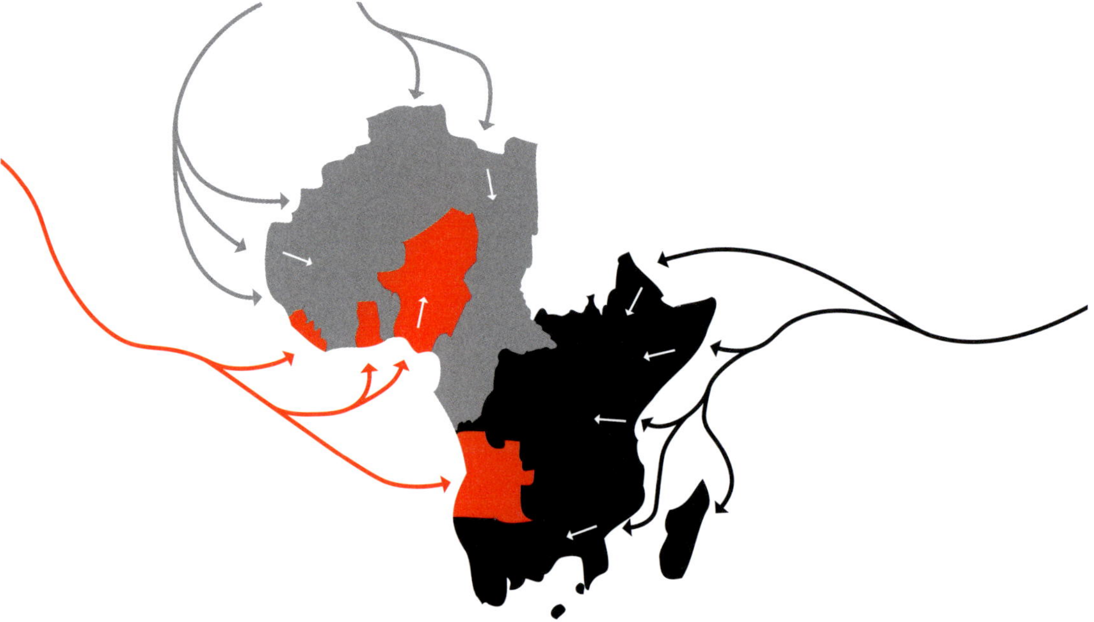

red: United States
gray: European Union
black: Japan (via UAE)
(2017)

the current 1.4 billion to 2.3 billion. And this is only China. If India follows the same path, another 950 million cars would be added and the current car stock would more than double to 3.1 billion vehicles.[13] These figures sound like a death blow to all ambitions that are set up to reduce humans' impact on Earth's natural environment. Yet the very fair question is: Why should the Chinese, the Indians, and all other not-yet-so-rich people on Earth be forbidden from enjoying their own ride just because they were late to the party and now all the booze is gone?

The current shift away from the combustion engine toward the electrical engine in automobiles might be the right exit from the toxic highway. It holds the promise of individual transportation, free of fossil fuels and thus free of toxic exhaust. Yet this shift still bears some unanswered questions for the future. The resources for batteries are an especially large concern. The natural deposits and therefore the mines of bauxite and lithium, two fundamental ingredients in batteries, are in the Global South.

Damage is already being done in the form of the unjust exploitation of local communities and the environmental harm to indigenous land. And even if working conditions were improved and social and environmental justice performed, the question remains if there are enough natural resources to replace the current fleet of 1.4 billion cars, or the expected 3.0 billion cars that will cruise the planet's roads by 2050.[14] The final, most pressing, question is reusability. What will happen to all these billions of electric cars and their highly toxic batteries?

The current strategy for getting rid of used cars is to ship them to the South. African nations with no or low emission standards are the final destination for some 40% of all used light vehicles.[15] Used cars are handed down the income ladder, first among

Age Restrictions for Importing Vehicles to Africa

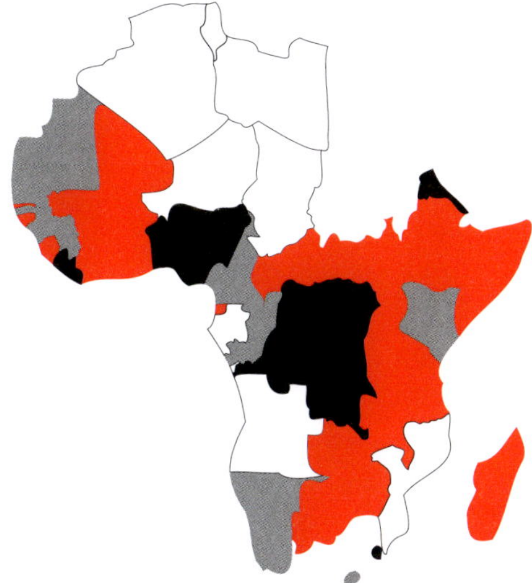

red: import cars have no age limit
black: import cars have an age limit of 10 years or more
gray: import cars have an age limit of less than 10 years
white: import cars have an age limit of 5 years or less

Egypt, Morocco, South Africa, and Sudan: ban on used vehicle imports (2019)

the affluent countries of the West and at the end of their life span to the Southern Hemisphere. In Kenya, for example, more than 95% of cars that are currently added to the existing fleet are used cars, imported mainly from Japan.[16] Although Kenya is approximately the size of France, it has a paved highway network of a meager 14,000 km,[17] compared to France's 1 million kilometers. At the same time, in Kenya only 6 out of 100 people own a car.[18] One factor constrains the other, but mainly low income does not allow a higher car ownership rate.

The West's view of car ownership in countries like Kenya is twofold. To the car companies, the future seems bright. Kenyans' growing personal income could mean a growing number of car owners and thus a booming market for new cars in the future. Contrary to that is the ecological view, which is more in favor of the status quo of a low rate of car ownership. Once again, future economic development and equal rights for all people clash with the future of the planet. Achieving the humanitarian goal of eradicating poverty and making all the world prosperous would result in billions more cars. No matter if they are combustion or electrically powered, it is doubtful that humans would survive this ride.

Modernity is extremely good at adding new ideas for consumer goods and devices that make the lives of humans more convenient, but it has few answers for the afterlife of these very ideas, the goods, and the devices. Modernity's dependency on natural resources puts a "natural" expiration date on its very existence. Only by overcoming this dependency can the modern human survive.

Global Trade

Merchant Vessels

The international division of labor was only possible thanks to cheap transportation over long distances. For example, raw materials from Africa need to be shipped to factories in China, where they are turned into consumer goods that have to be shipped to retailers in the US and Europe. *Homo sapiens* had been separated by the oceans since it moved out of Africa 70,000–120,000 years ago.[1] Modern ships transformed the oceans from dividers into connectors that are plied by large vessels, interlinking individual participants to form a global economy. Today, approximately 90% of the

Merchant Vessels Launched per Year

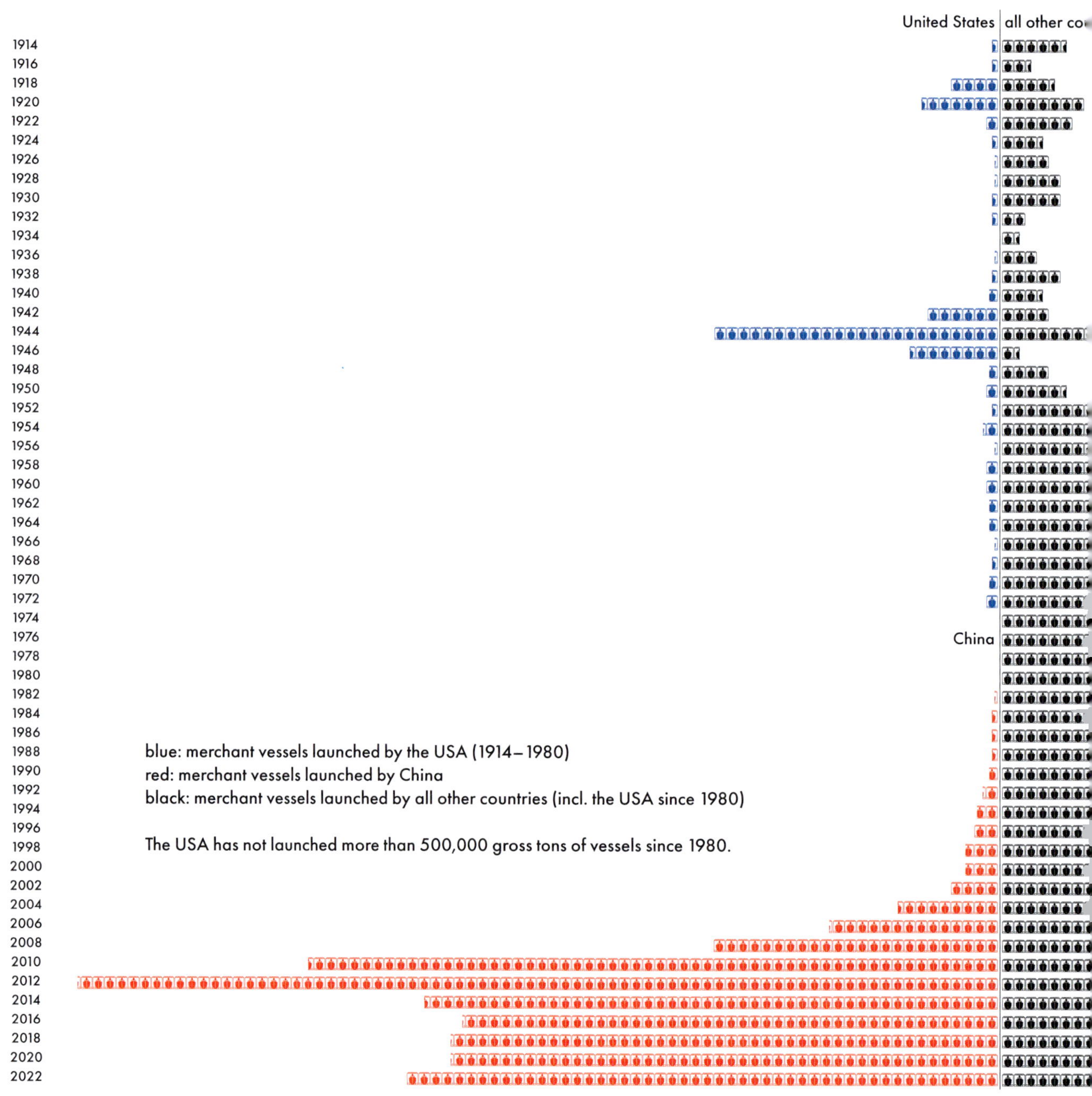

each symbol represents 500,000 gross tons (vessels of 100 gross tons and over)

world's traded goods are carried on the seas and with increasing demand – the traded volume is expected to triple by 2050.[2]

The merchant vessel infrastructure of the high seas is functioning as the conveyer belt of the global economy. The first signs of imminent weakness in the system of global trade appeared when a strong demand hit the world economy after a sharp decline due to the COVID-19 pandemic. The global chain of supply and demand was so out of order that shortages appeared in the Western world, the final destination of the supply chain.

This was the first time that the global division of production itself showed flaws, since earlier disruptions had been caused by natural disasters, war, or technical failures. The disruptions in the global supply chain are so severe that "just-in-time production" as the basic principle of globalization is now in doubt.

ISOTYPE 

The Container

The power of modernity has a lot to do with standardization. Standardization allows people from all around the world to join a larger and often globe-spanning project. Packaging as well, no matter if it concerns goods or data, thrives on standardization. What containers are to global trade, data packets are to digital networks.

Containers make it possible to secure a specific amount of goods in a single box. This box has the perfect size to fit on trucks, ships, trains, and even airplanes. The magic of the container is the ease with which it can hop on and hop off from one mode of transportation to the other, from the site of production to the site of consumption, no matter where that might be. Ideally, the goods arrive right at the doorstep of the consumer.

Since their introduction in the mid-1950s, shipping containers have revolutionized world trade. They made transport so cheap that manufacturing could be located basically anywhere on the planet. It was to a large extent the container that paved the way for the international division of labor and for Asia becoming the world's workshop.

As early as the 1930s, the international standardization of containers had been established to accommodate transport between European countries.

Malcolm McLean, a partner in a trucking company, decided to attempt to use the containers commercially in the early 1950s. As a trucker, he was concerned with the time-consuming process of transferring goods between trucks and ships. On Thursday, April 26, 1956, the ship SS *Ideal-X* was loaded and sailed from the Port Newark-Elizabeth Marine Terminal in New Jersey for the Port of Houston in Texas. Carrying 58 "trailer vans," which were later called containers, the converted World War II oil tanker was the world's first operating container vessel.[3] Before containerization, ships were usually loaded and unloaded manually by longshoremen with break-bulk cargo. Ships often spent more time in harbor than at sea. The arrival of container shipping changed global trade, and with it the entire shipping industry. It emptied out formerly busy wharfs and docks since it made "nineteen in every twenty men redundant."[4] Since containers are weatherproof, they killed warehouses, leaving docklands abandoned as ports expanded elsewhere.

Evolution of Container Ships

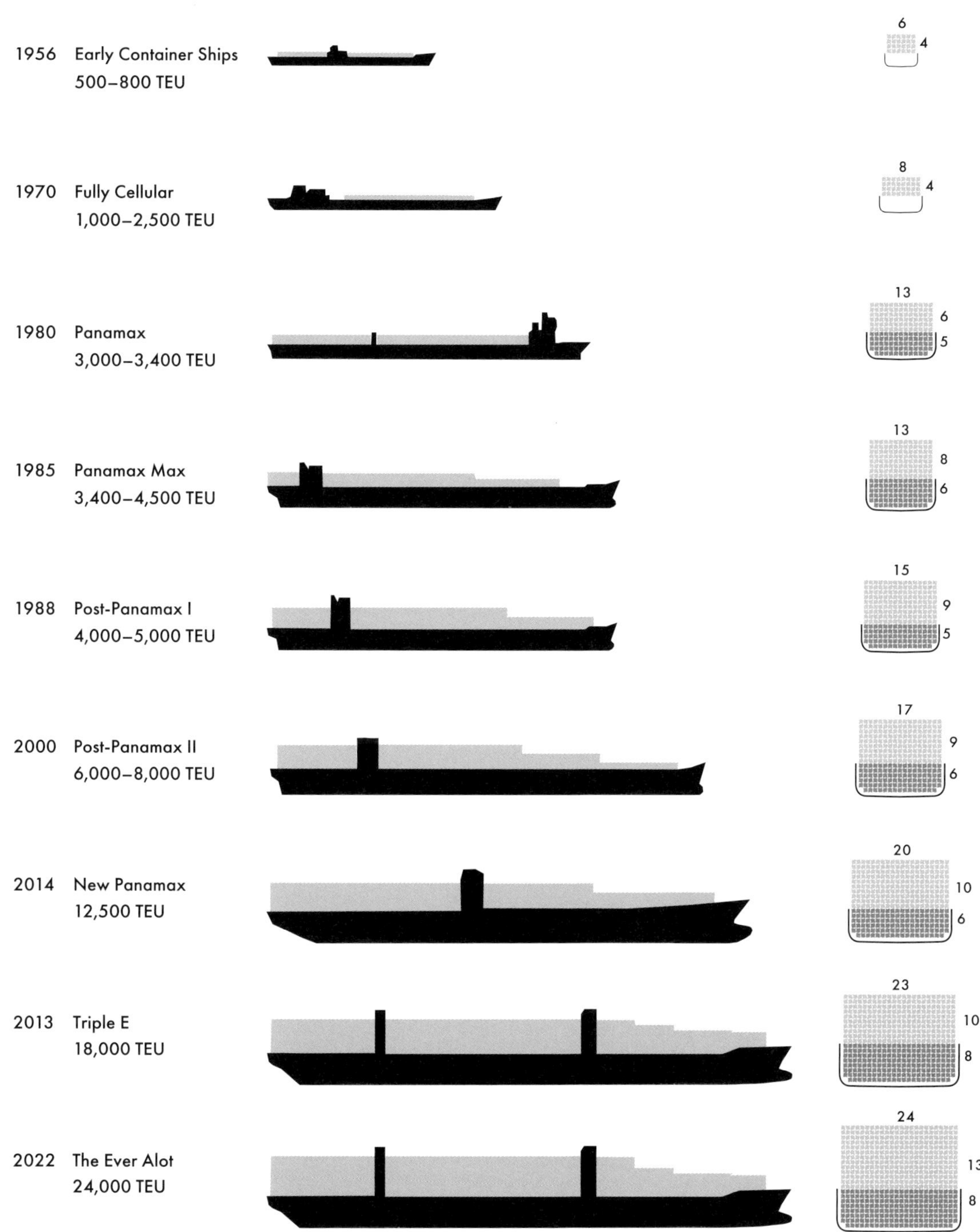

TEU = Twenty-foot Equivalent Unit; based on the volume of a 20-foot-long (6.1 meter) intermodal container

Global Container Ships and Container Capacity

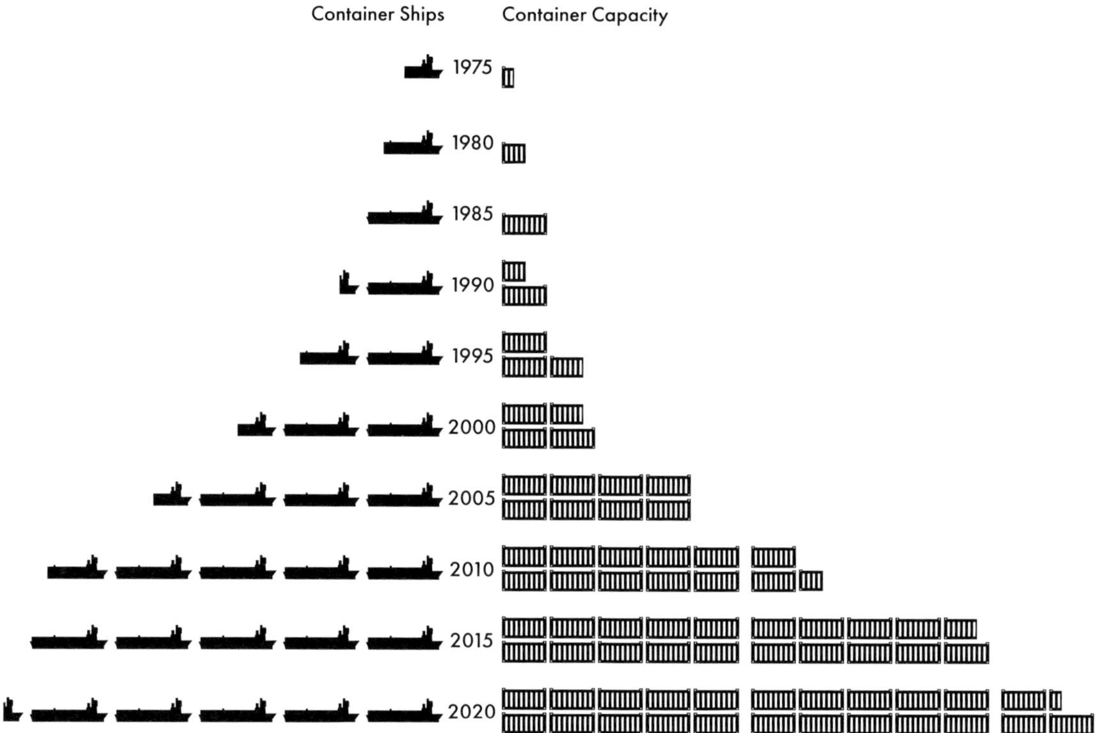

From the 1960s onward, the use of containers expanded mightily. In Rotterdam, Europe's largest harbor, the number of container transshipments rose steadily from 150,000 Twenty-foot Equivalent Units (TEU) to 1,107,000 TEU between 1968 and 1974.[5] Around that time, international negotiations were held to arrive at a global dimension for containers that would fit all road, rail, and maritime transportation. In the late 1960s, ISO standards for containers were published by the International Maritime Organization, resulting in "one box for the world."[6]

Today, there are six standard sizes of containers circulating around the globe: 20 ft, 40 ft, 40 ft high-cube, 45 ft high-cube, 48 ft, and 53 ft, while only the 20 ft and 40 ft containers are used for shipping. The volume of containers is measured internationally in TEU, an abbreviation for "Twenty-foot Equivalent Units," i.e., the 20 ft ISO container.[7]

The container symbolizes the success of global human cooperation. With the container, mankind has achieved something that it has failed to do in other areas, such as measuring length (meters/feet) or weight (kilos/pounds). Its width is adjusted to the width of Earth's roads and its height is made to fit Earth's tunnels, while its length again is suited to fit road traffic. Currently about 40 million containers are in use all over the planet.[8]

Containers made shipping incredibly cheap by cutting out almost all labor costs from the dock workers. A 20 ft container costs only € 600 for its 28-day journey from

Earth's 20 Largest Container Ports

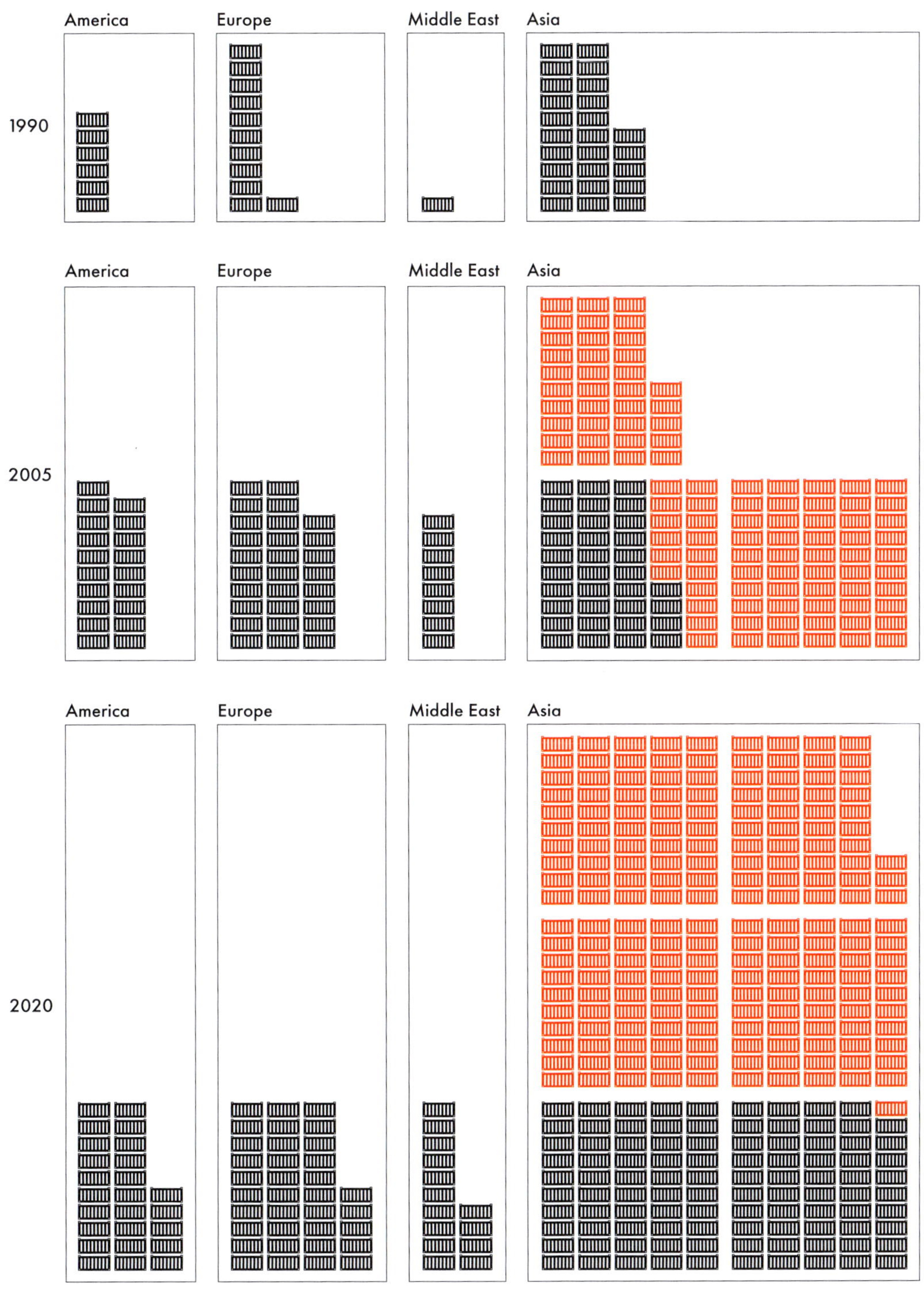

each symbol represents 10,000 TEU containers of cargo throughput in ports per region
red: Chinese ports

Container Port Logistics

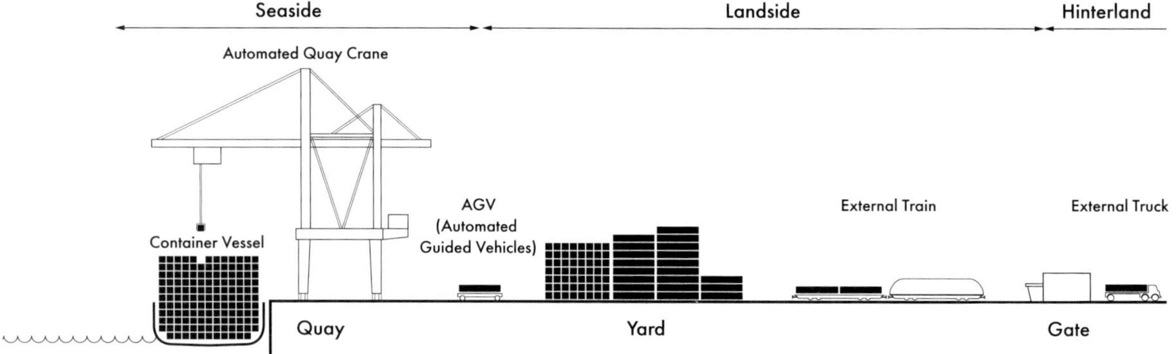

China to the Netherlands.[9] If one considers that about 3,675 iPads would fit into this container, the shipping costs add only € 0.16 to the purchase price of an iPad. Container ships lug around a quarter of the world's traded goods by volume and three-fifths by value.[10] As with all great achievements, however, the simple act of putting so many eggs in one basket means that when ships experience rough weather or humans become overconfident in their capacity and loading, containers go overboard. In 1997, a ship lost 62 containers to the depths of the ocean. Twenty-three years later, millions of multicolored pieces of Lego are still turning up on the beaches of Cornwall.[11]

The ocean itself is not the only hazard to the shipping industry. Pirates have made a business of capturing ships and holding the crew hostage until a huge ransom is paid. Piracy off the coast of Somalia began as a result of the civil war in Somalia. With no military control over its waters, international ships began trawling and depriving local fishermen of their food supply. To counter this, local militias were formed; the lucrative industry of piracy was discovered and grew to become an industry that in turn improved local economies and towns. In 2009 the *Maran Centaurus*, carrying 2 million barrels of oil and an international crew of 28, was captured and released for US$ 5.5–7 million.[12] At its peak in 2011, Somali piracy alone was estimated to have cost up to US$ 6.9 billion.[13] Since 2018, the coast of Somalia has been almost entirely peaceful, thanks to heavy international military intervention.

Panamax

While the size of containers is the result of restrictions given by road and railway infrastructure such as bridges, tunnels, and roadways, the ships themselves are restricted by similar parameters. A few bottlenecks in the global shipping network place a limit on ever-increasing vessel sizes.

The allowable size of ships passing through the Panama Canal is limited by the width and length of the available lock chambers, by the depth of water in the canal, and by the height of the Bridge of the Americas since that bridge's construction. The realization of a third set of locks in 2016 led to the design of a larger generation of container ships called post-Panamax or super-Panamax. The expansion doubled the Canal's total capacity.

Other restrictions on the dimensions of container ships are the Suez Canal ("Suezmax"), the Straits of Malacca ("Malaccamax"), and the Saint Lawrence Seaway ("Seaway-max"). All have different specifications for ships to pass.

In 2021, the *Ever Given*, a "post-Suezmax" container ship with a capacity of 20,124 TEU and a crew of 24, ran aground in the Suez Canal, obstructing the canal for about six days and holding up nearly $ 60 billion in trade.[14] The 18,300 containers on the *Ever Given* contained goods like IKEA furniture, microchips, pillowcases, barbecue grills, swimwear, camping equipment, and bikes. All produced in China, these goods were destined to be sold on the European market. Though the reason for running aground was a sandstorm, the event shows that ever-larger container ships and ever more traffic on the seas test the existing infrastructure to the max.

The *Ever Given* is a perfect example of the complexity in the shipping industry today. At the time of the accident, the ship was owned by Shoei Kisen Kaisha (a Japanese ship-owning and leasing company), chartered and operated by the container transportation and shipping company Evergreen Marine (Taiwan),

Maximum Ship Dimensions per Route

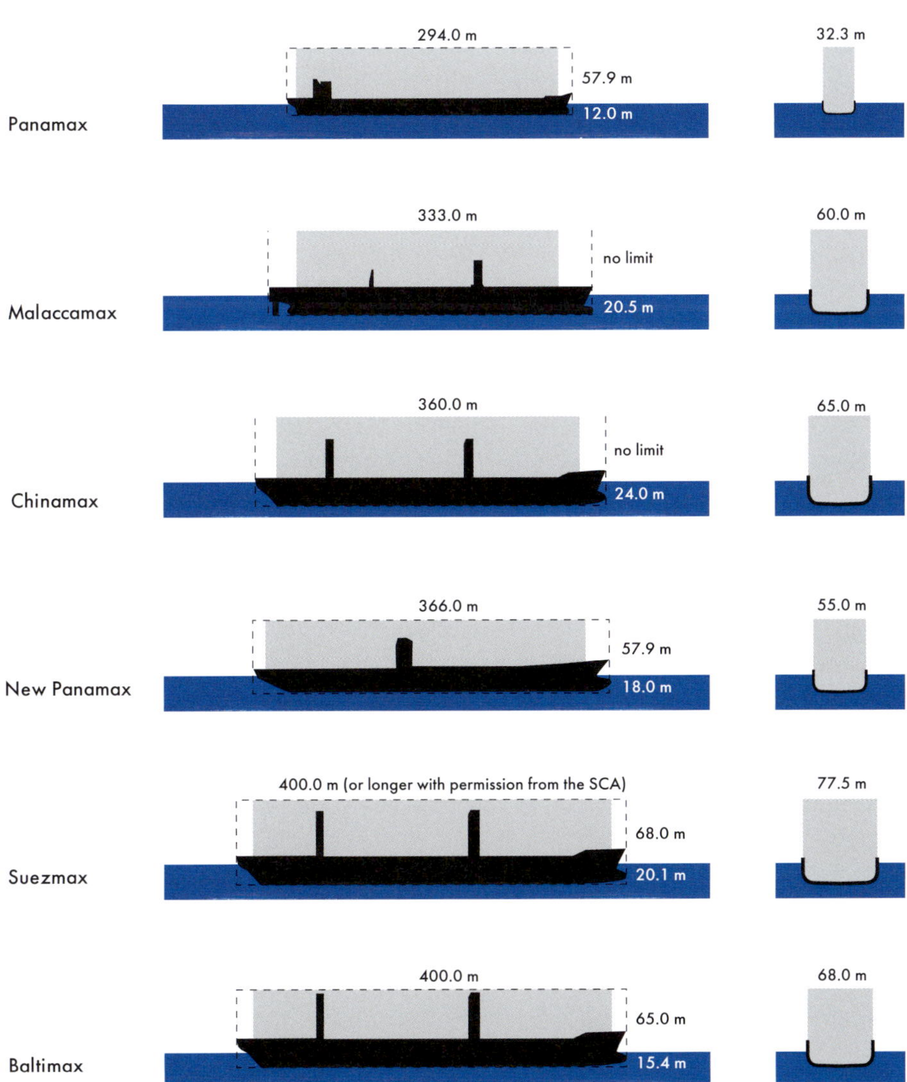

Panama Canal Expansion Project

since 1914: Panamax
max. 4,800 TEU

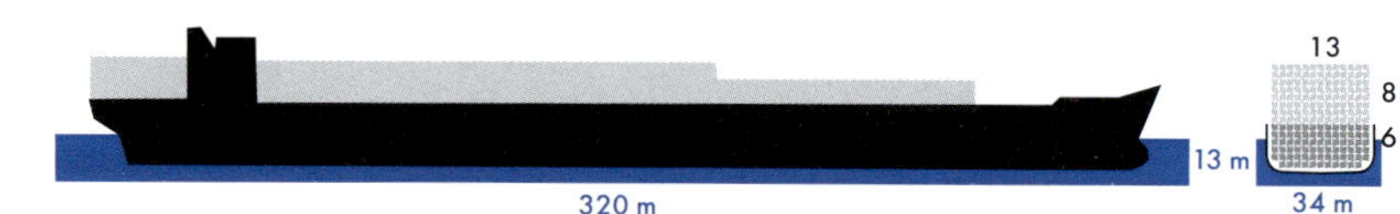

since 2016: New Panamax
max. 12,600 TEU

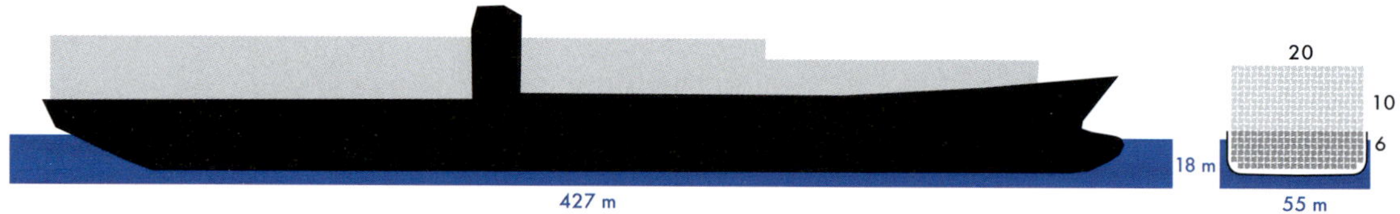

blue represents the lock size and lock dimensions

registered in Panama, and finally, its all-Indian crew of 25 people was employed by the German ship management company Bernhard Schulte Shipmanagement (BSM).[15]

The foreign registry of a ship, or "flag of convenience," started in the 1920s, when US passenger ships made the first cross-registry to Panama in order to be able to serve alcohol to their passengers during Prohibition. Since then, the ability to operate under Panamanian tax laws, or Liberian minimum wages, has picked up and become a lucrative business worldwide.[16] To fly the Stars and Stripes would mean operating the ship with US citizens, paying them US wages, and paying US taxes on their income – Panama, Liberia, and the Marshall Islands are all a much more appealing option as a result. By 2013, three-quarters of the global fleet was registered under flags different from the ownership flag.[17]

The COVID-19 pandemic caused an unprecedented disruption in international maritime trade, and containers were at the very heart of it. In fall 2020, almost a year into the pandemic, a sudden shortage of shipping containers seemed to appear, yet the problem wasn't a lack of containers, but rather that they were in the wrong spots. When China closed down because of the pandemic, cargo ships that were already en route to the Americas dropped off hundreds of thousands of containers full of goods, and so containers piled up in America's ports and inland rail depots. When its COVID-19 restrictions were loosened, China had no containers to fill, and the planet's economy went out of balance.[18]

To have a better picture of the whereabouts of the containers, the future of maritime logistics is smart containers.[19] Electronics are added to standard containers which enable tracking and monitoring during their journey. These also monitor the conditions under which the contents are transported: calculating the estimated time of arrival (ETA), optimizing the container flow as part of the fleet management, managing container utilization, monitoring the condition of the container, calculating CO_2 emissions for the journey, and performing predictive maintenance.[20]

All this technology sounds nice and fancy, but the vessel that carries these smart cubes remains rather stupid. Many vessels still burn heavy bunker fuel, a viscous, carbon-intensive petroleum product that's left over from the refining of crude oil. Consequently, the world's 15 largest ships emit as much sulfur and nitrogen as all the cars in the world.[21] Furthermore, these electronics do not monitor bilge dumping, a common but illegal practice in which container ships release their toxic waste into the ocean. Bilge water is a slurry of engine sludge, fuel oil, water, various chemicals, and heavy metals.[22] Over the course of one year in EU waters alone, an estimated equivalent of 5 times the amount of oil from the infamous 1989 *Exxon Valdez* spill was released into the oceans via bilge dumping.[23]

Melting polar caps seem to be no threat, but a blessing, to world trade. Rising temperatures promise the opening of new routes from Europe to Japan via the Northern Sea Route (or Northeast Passage), reducing the journey from Hamburg to Yokohama by 14 days, from 32 to 18 days.[24]

Yet the Norther n Sea Route is entirely part of Russia's Exclusive Economic Zone. All vessels taking that route are at the mercy of Russia making it ice-free and allowing them to refuel at one of the ports along the route.

The economic crisis around 2010, the COVID-19 pandemic, and the Russo-Ukrainian War present a trifecta of global uncertainties. In response to this, concerns about resilience and self-sufficiency have resurfaced. The international division of labor is a peacetime construct that depends on international cooperation and reliability. Institutions like the World Trade Organization (WTO), founded in 1995, are put in place to safeguard the smooth global exchange of goods.

New alliances will need to be formed and old ones strengthened. In the short term, countries are confronted with their own strengths and weaknesses.

Main Shipping Routes

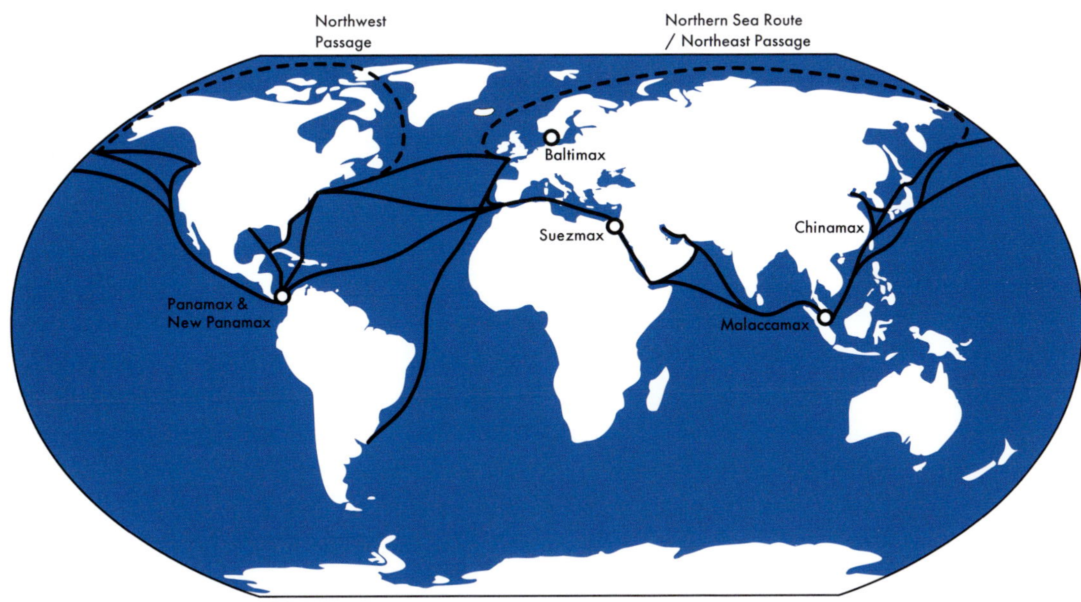

Wheat Trade

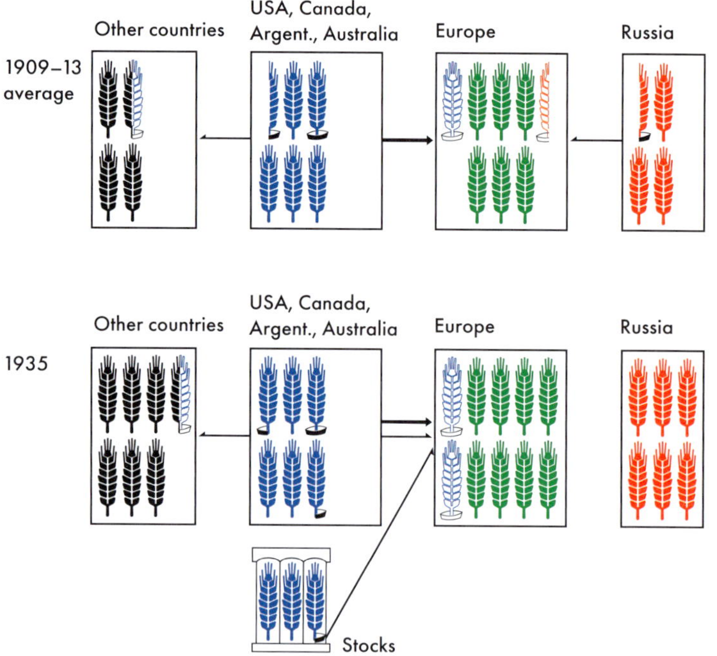

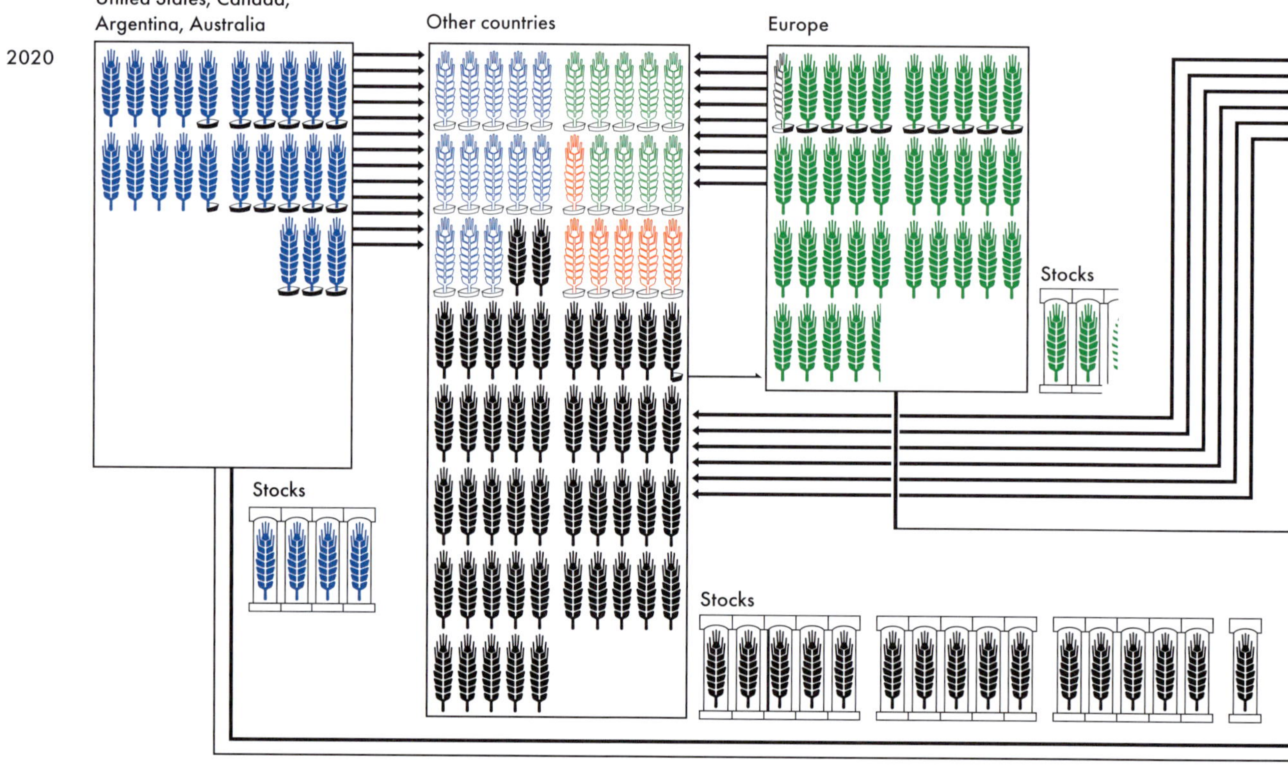

each symbol represents 200 million bushels

filled without ship: produced and consumed ad locum
filled on black ship: exported
outlined on white ship: imported
Stocks: total wheat in stock at the end of the year 2020

Supply Chain

The 1990s started a unique period of three decades of openness across the globe. The end of the Cold War brought the prospect of global peace but also the flourishing of global trade. The international division of labor was fully established during this period: storage grew out of favor and just-in-time production became the way to organize production. Abandoning stocks allowed companies to cut costs, since no warehouses needed to be rented or built, and just-in-time production allowed quicker adjustment to consumer desires. Supply chains with just-in-time deliveries connected subcontractors with assembly lines, resulting in a gigantic Earth-spanning web between countries of mutual trade and interest.

The event of 9/11 in 2001 was a first attack on this Earth-spanning system that had been propagated predominantly by the Western powers, mainly the US. It was a shot across the bow by a marginalized group of Muslim believers, by those who had been left out of this profitable system. Although shocked by the event, no correction, of course, has been made by the West. The aforementioned trifecta of economic slump, pandemic, and war in Europe finally closed this exceptional window of global cooperation and interdependence. The 30-year period of relatively smooth global trade, starting with the collapse of the Soviet Union and ending with the invasion of Ukraine by Russia, has now come to a halt.

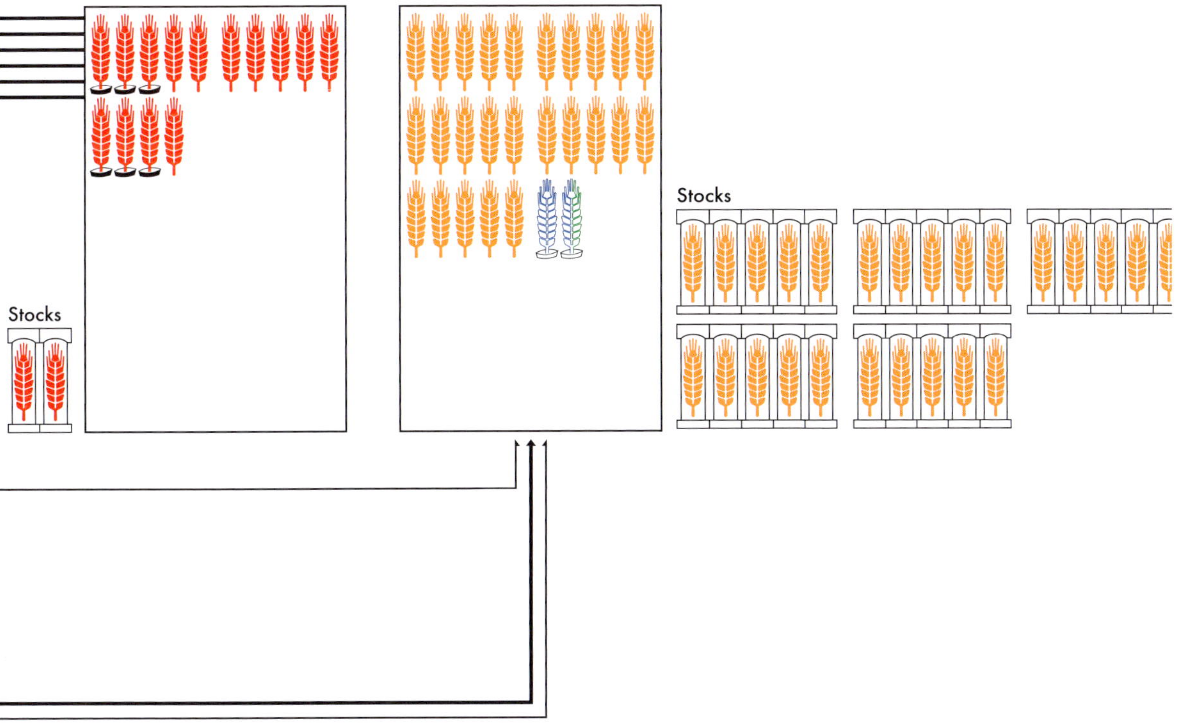

blue: US, Canada, Argentina, Australia
green: Europe; in 2020 European Union, UK, and Ukraine
red: Russia
orange: China
black: Other countries

Maximum Stocks in 1930
Compared with Annual Production

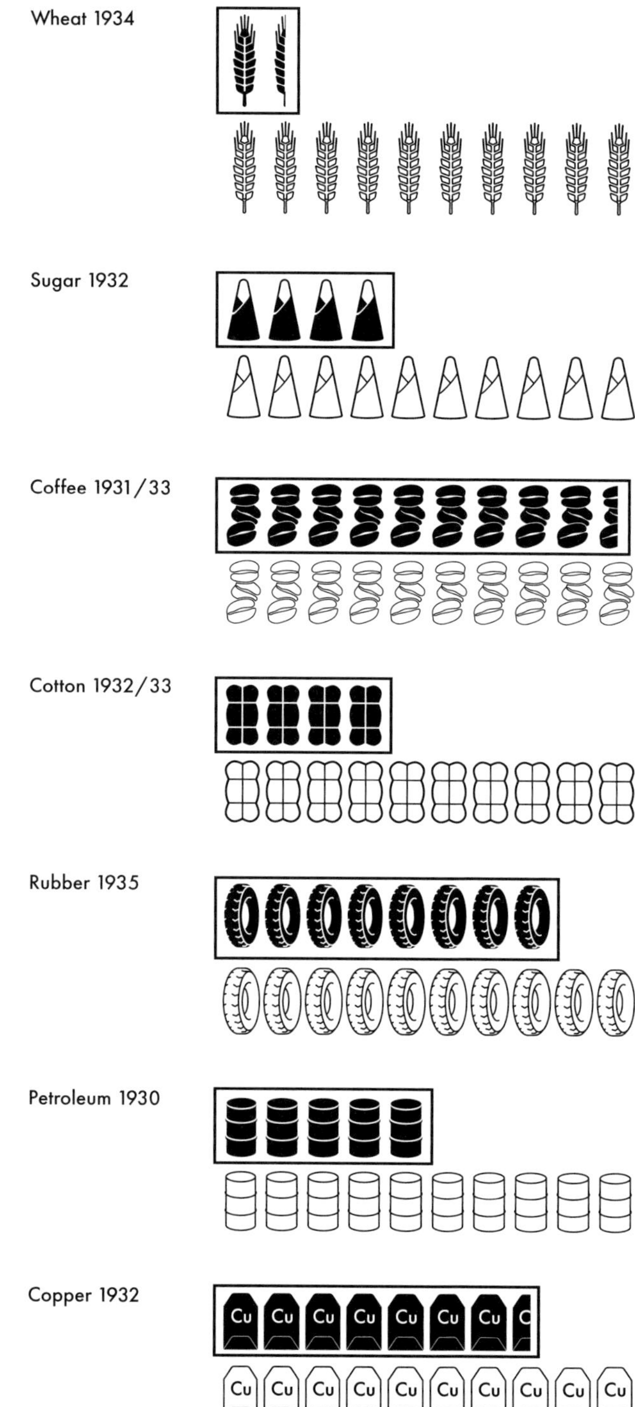

each symbol represents 10% of annual production
white symbols: produced annually
black symbols in rectangles: still in stock from previous years

Maximum Stocks in 2020
Compared with Annual Production

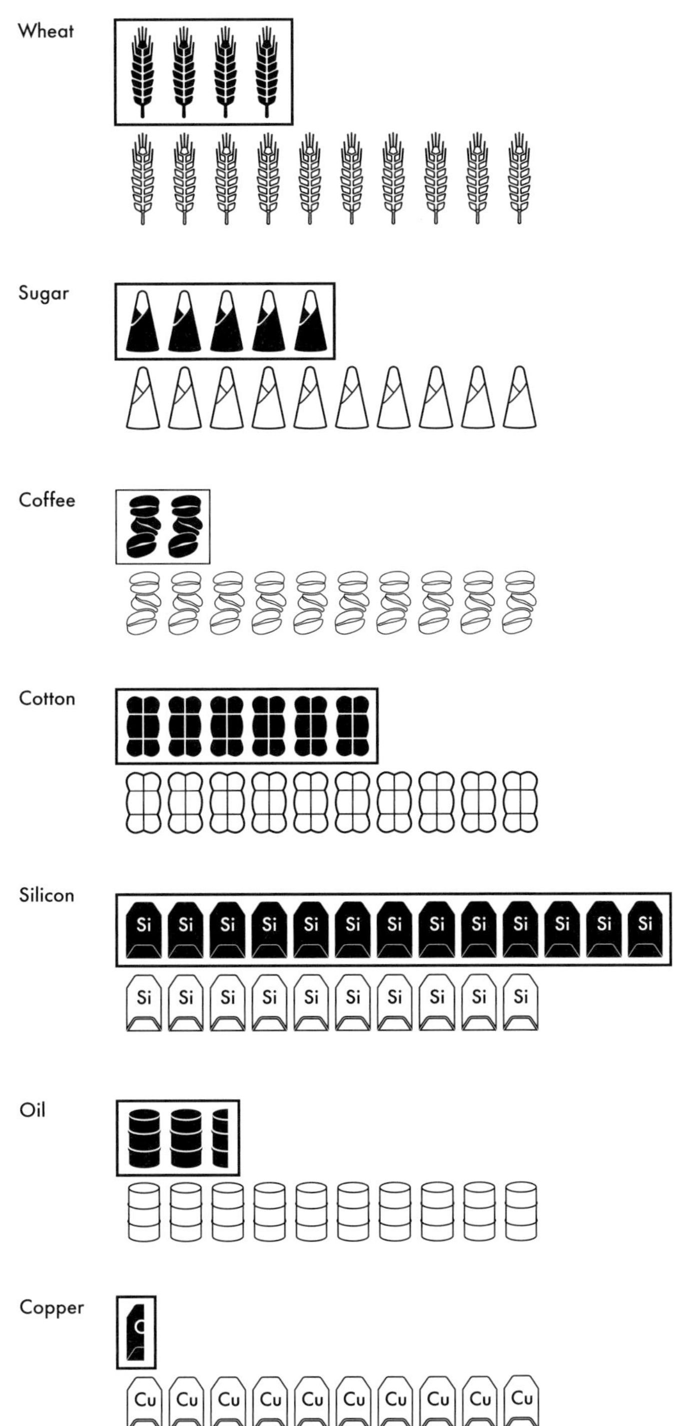

each symbol represents 10% of annual production
white symbols: produced annually
black symbols in rectangles: still in stock from previous years

Wheat Trade by the United States

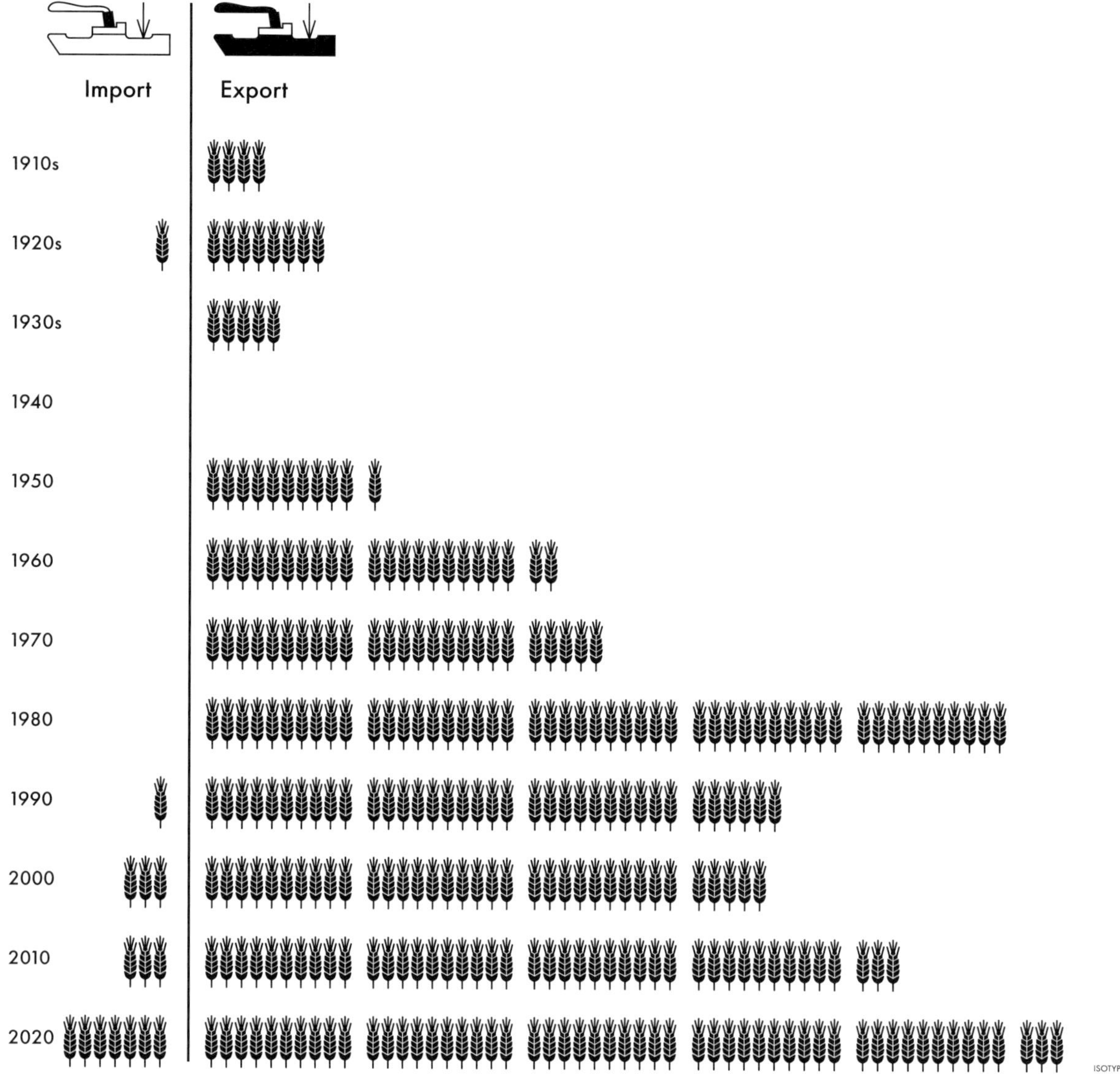

each icon represents 30 million bushels of wheat

As a consequence, the focus turned to self-sufficiency and even autarky. Neurath was not a fan, insisting that "autarky [...] lowers the quality of products and the standard of living."[25] It was 1938 when he wrote those words, and he had a gut feeling in what direction it would possibly lead as he continued on page 82, saying: "This [increasing self-sufficiency] is part of the international change in trade and production and is closely connected with preparations for war." It remains to be seen if Neurath's observation still holds true for today's war between Russia and Ukraine. It is a very ominous prediction, which turned out to be correct in the same year Neurath's book was published. Let's hope that this time it's different.

When a country aims for autarky, providing food for its population is the most important issue. Importing countries keep grain reserves to hedge against sudden price increases, while exporting countries hold grain reserves to hedge against over-supply and price-dumping in years of a good harvest. Kept in good condition, wheat can be stored in a silo for 4 years or more, thus leaving enough leeway to balance out peaks and troughs. China, home to 18% of the Earth's population, is currently stockpiling about 50% of the Earth's wheat reserves, 60% of its rice, and 70% of its maize reserves, which will enable the country to meet its domestic demand for one and a half years.[26] China has been keeping massive reserves since its agricultural production plateaued in 2015. The dispersion of farmland, soil contamination, and the migration of farmers to urban areas make it difficult to increase agricultural output, while the Chinese population is demanding more and more calories. To soften the future impasse and stress the importance of food security, China's national legislature, the National People's Congress, implemented a law in April 2021 that bans excessive leftovers.[27]

Wheat Production in Egypt

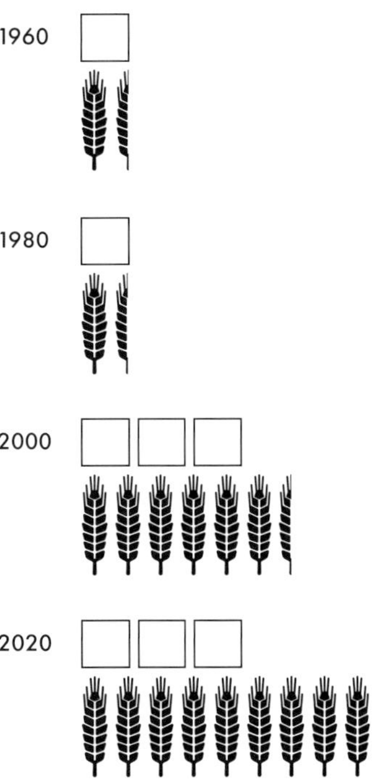

rectangle symbol represents 5,000 km² harvested land for wheat
grain symbol represents 1,000,000 tonnes wheat

Wheat Trade

Agriculture, though negligible in terms of workforce, remains essential to any country's stability by providing food close to consumers. The industrialization of agriculture in the US deeply affected its wheat production. Due to the "green revolution," output increased dramatically while the input of manpower decreased.

Today the USA is exporting 50% of its wheat, the third-largest field crop in the US, after corn and soybeans. The steady decline in wheat production in the US since the early 1980s is the result of changes in government programs and lower returns for wheat due to increasing competition on the global wheat market.[28] Russia, Ukraine, and the EU countries in particular produce large amounts of wheat today. The US share of global wheat exports went from 46% in the 1980s down to 10% in 2022.[29]

While the West is oversupplied with wheat, some countries in the Global South are heavily dependent on imports. For example, Egypt, the world's largest wheat importer, gets two-thirds of its wheat from outside the country, nota bene 82% of it from Russia and Ukraine.[30] Making matters worse, Egypt's population became dependent on their loaf of wheat bread due to extreme subsidies by the state. It's a tragedy, considering Egypt's push for domestic wheat production in the past 40 years. The country produces 6 times as much wheat as in the 1960s, but seems to end up much further away from self-sufficiency and thus food security.[31] That's because in the same period, Egypt had to deal with a fourfold increase in its population, eating up all its advances and even more, since its population also became more prosperous and so, too, gained in appetite.

Russia, on the contrary, is massively oversupplied. Having always been a wheat exporter, that country started an agricultural boom during the past 20 years. Within that time, the country doubled its wheat production.[32] 100% of these gains are produced for export, making it the world's largest wheat exporting nation today.
In the same time period, the proportion of Russia's workforce in agriculture declined from about 15% (2000) to 6% (2020).[33] With output figures like those, no silos for storage seem to be necessary.

But where food is concerned, the stakes are more than just pure economics. To withhold, excessively hoard, or even destroy crops for whatever reason endangers the very existence of millions of people.

War

Alliances

The political map of the world did not change much during the 1970s and 1980s. Yet following the dissolution of the Soviet Union and Yugoslavia, the map changed and continues to change tremendously, mostly following existing political and linguistic divisions. Since the late 2000s a different tone has been set, and large powers are ready to expand their turf. Russia has been expanding to the south and east by quasi-annexing parts of Georgia in 2008 (Abkhazia and South Ossetia) and parts of Ukraine in 2014 (the Crimean Peninsula and the Donbas region). As this is being written, war is raging across all of Ukraine as Russia tries to reimpose Soviet-era control over the country. China seems to have abandoned its promise of "one country, two systems,"[1] made before Hong Kong came under Chinese control in 1997, which was supposed to guarantee Hong Kong's independent democratic system of government until 2047. At the same time, China is flexing its military muscles against India in eastern Kashmir, claims large parts of the South China Sea, and is preparing to take hold of the country of Taiwan.

At the same time, the West and especially the EU is avoiding direct confrontation and is claiming to deescalate such situations. The above-mentioned acts by Russia and China were answered with heavy criticism and in the case of Russia with severe sanctions starting in 2014. They did no harm, but on the contrary made Russia's economy only more self-sufficient and robust in the years that followed. Little or no consequences for their actions seem to encourage Russia, China, and other powers to doubt the heretofore sacrosanct national boundaries. Turkey is secretly snapping up parts of northern Syria, Morocco has its eye on finally taking over Western Sahara, and Azerbaijan saw its chance to finally grab Nagorno-Karabakh from Armenia in 2020.

The USA as the former world-dominating power is showing signs of fatigue, which immediately results in the empowerment of its opponents. The second Iraq war ended

Current Armed Conflicts

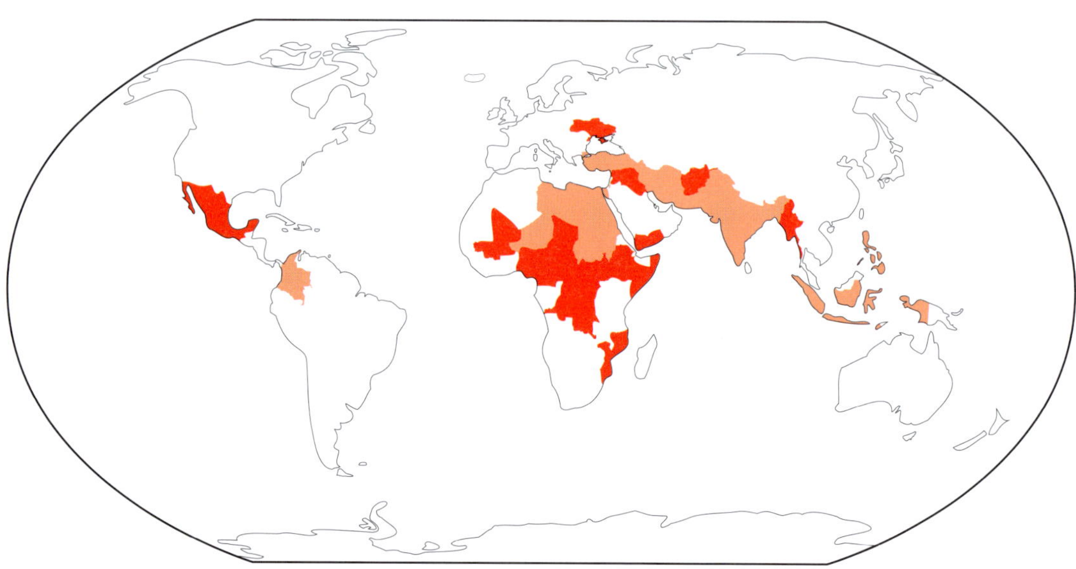

red: armed conflicts with more than 1,000 combat-related deaths
pink: armed conflicts with 100–1,000 combat-related deaths
(2020)

Global Arms Trade Versus War Deaths

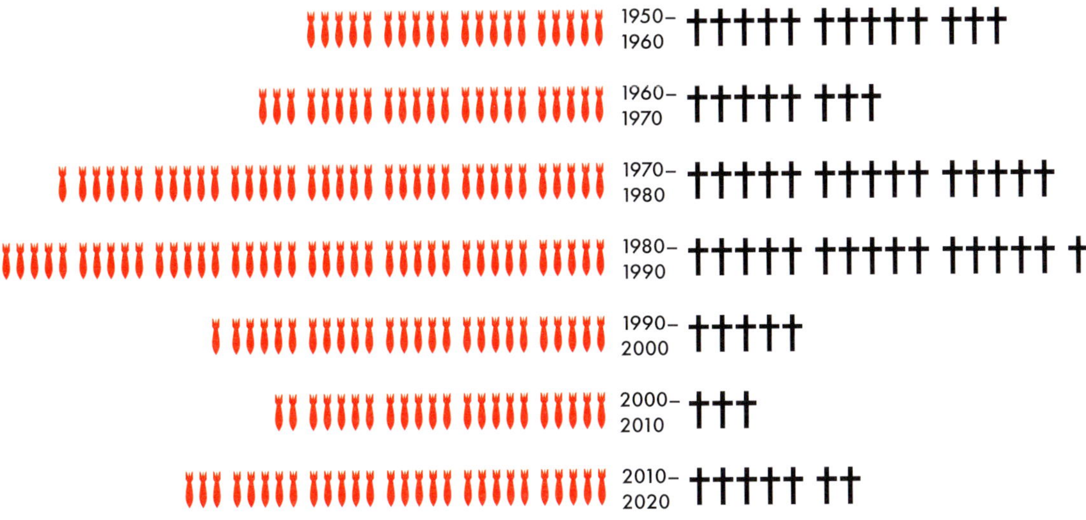

each red symbol represents 10 billion SIPRI trend indicator values for global arms export
each black symbol represents 100,000 deaths in armed conflict

unsuccessfully, leaving that country in ruins. Similarly, the 20-year war in Afghanistan ended with the victory of the Taliban, an Afghan group of religious radicals. At the same time, Russia has realized just how easy it is to sway US elections and destabilize its internal political discourse.

While the politics of the West might be exhausted, its war economy is a booming business. The countries of the Western world seem to be quite good at supplying the world with arms. 48 of the top 100 weapons-producing companies are US-based;[2] another 41 come from Europe (including 10 from Russia). Thus, most of the weaponry used in conflicts and wars, which do happen in the poorer South, are produced in the prosperous North of the planet. A rather cruel image appears: the West imports cheap plastic clothes, rare earths for mobile phones, and soybeans for the vegan diet, and in return gives weapons of mass destruction.

The world's top 100 weapons-producing companies sold US$ 531,000,000,000 worth of weapons in 2020.[3] That equals the economy (GDP) of Norway, the world's 30th richest economy. The hypocrisy of the war economy is highlighted by Western countries like the US, UK, and Germany, which are often involved in peace talks to solve conflicts and wars all around the world, while at the same time they produce and export weaponry to turn a profit from the wars they talk about stopping. Neurath explains that armament production belongs to the non-competitive activities of an economy, but today this is only partially true. The US government only provides contracts to US companies, yet on an international level, there is fierce competition between the arms-producing companies and countries.

The US is the major arms deliverer to NATO (the North Atlantic Treaty Organization), an intergovernmental military alliance of 30 member states founded in 1949 as a counterweight to its Soviet equivalent, the Warsaw Pact. As a security measure, NATO members are supposed to buy military gear from each other. But NATO member

Silhouettes of the War Economy

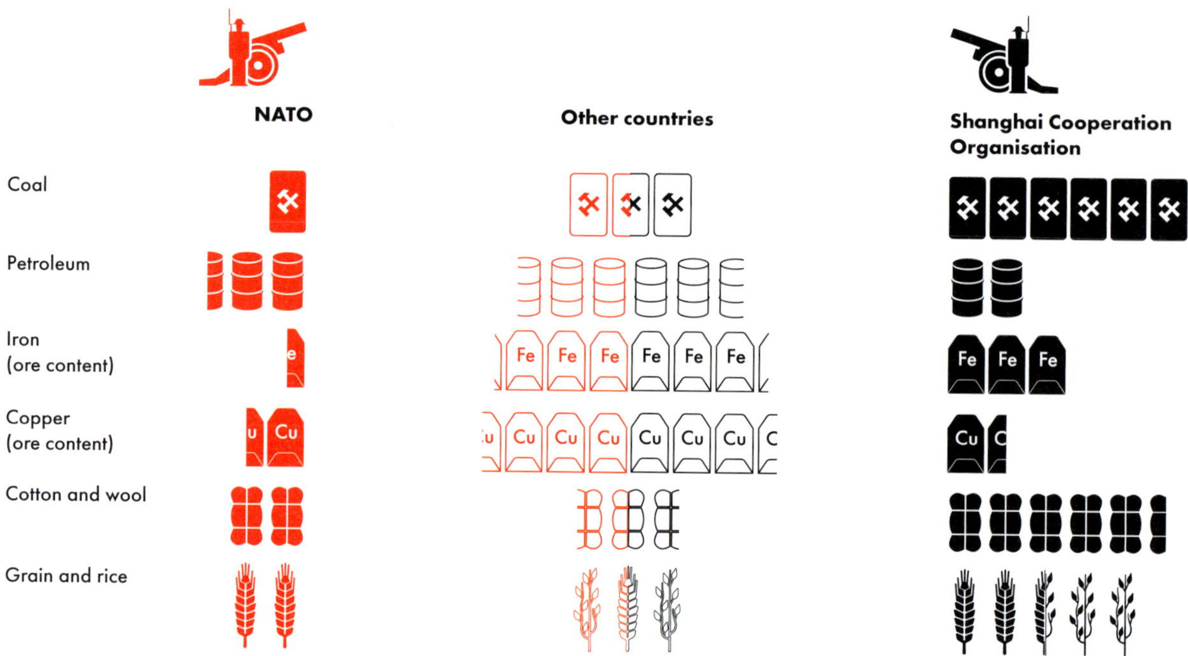

each symbol represents 10% of global production

NATO members

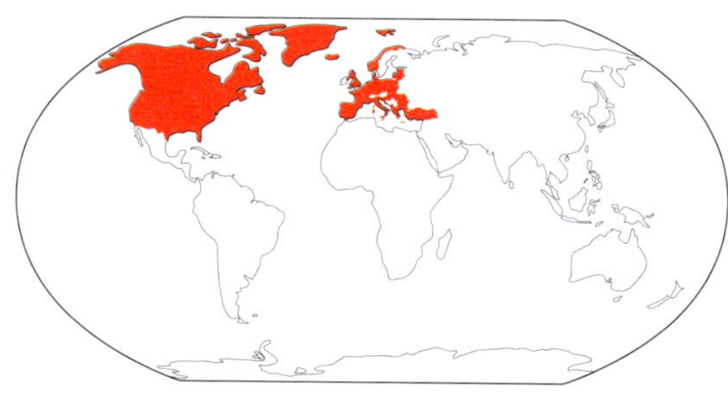

Shanghai Cooperation Organisation members

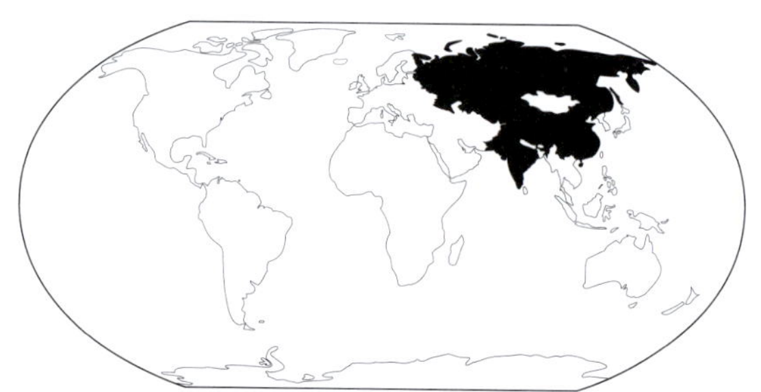

NATO soldiers

Shanghai Cooperation Organisation soldiers

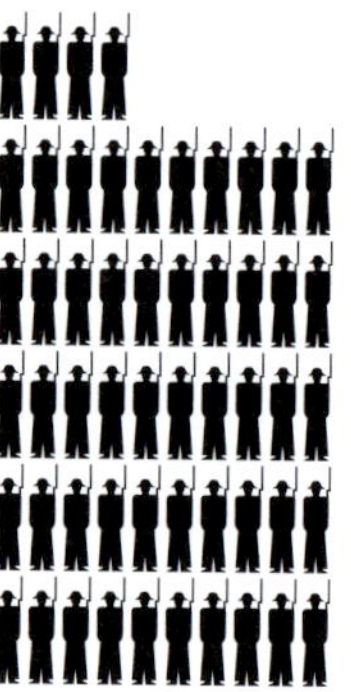

each symbol represents 100,000 soldiers

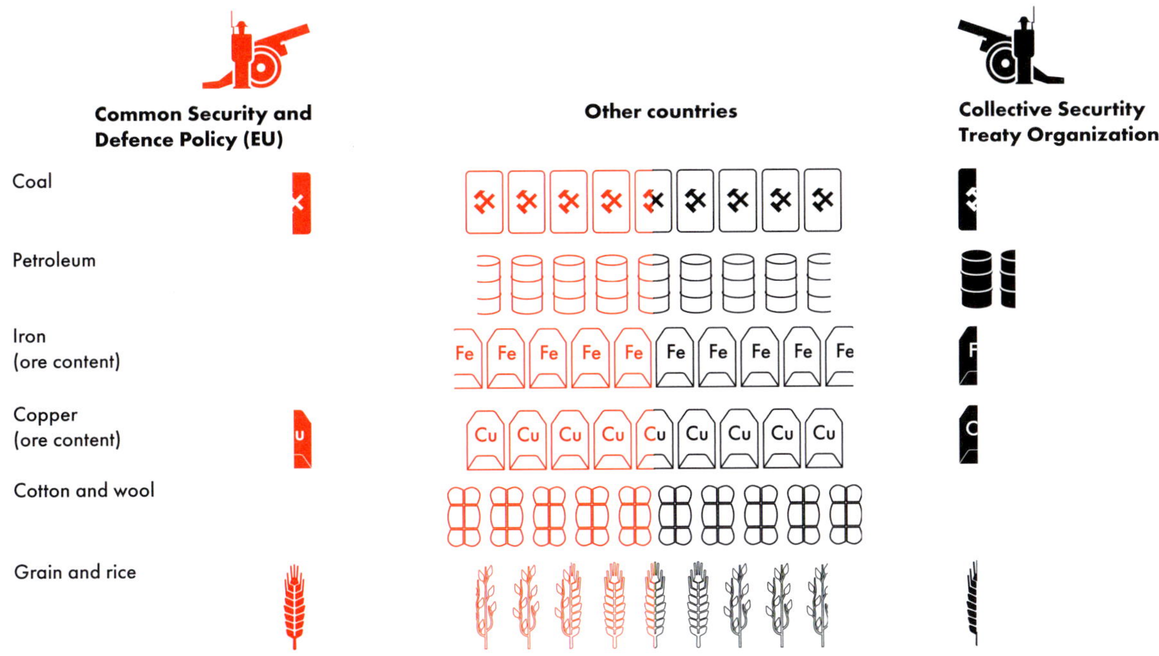

each symbol represents 10% of global production

Collective Security Treaty Organization members

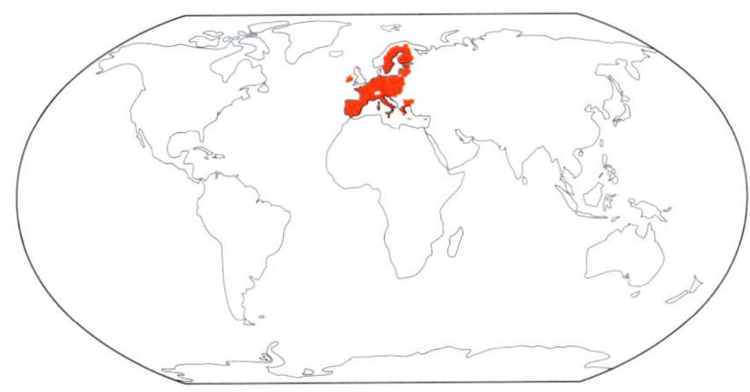

Common Security and Defence Policy (EU) soldiers

Collective Security Treaty Organization soldiers

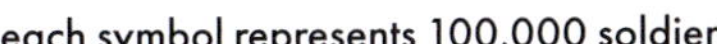

Silhouettes of the War Economy

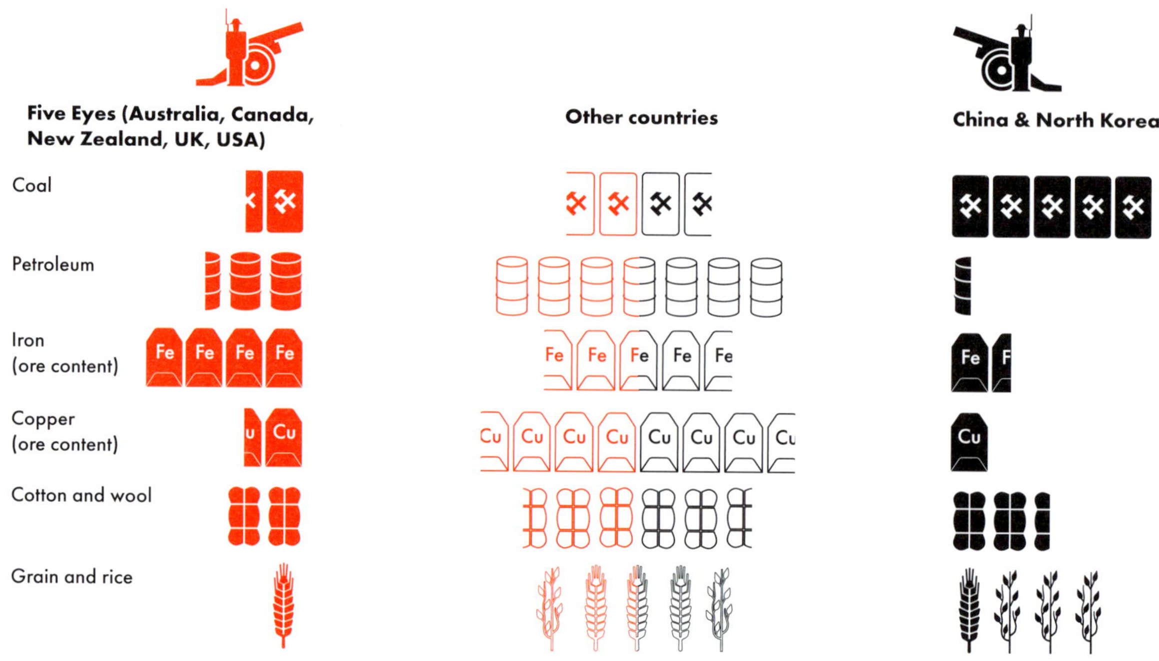

each symbol represents 10% of global production

Five Eyes members

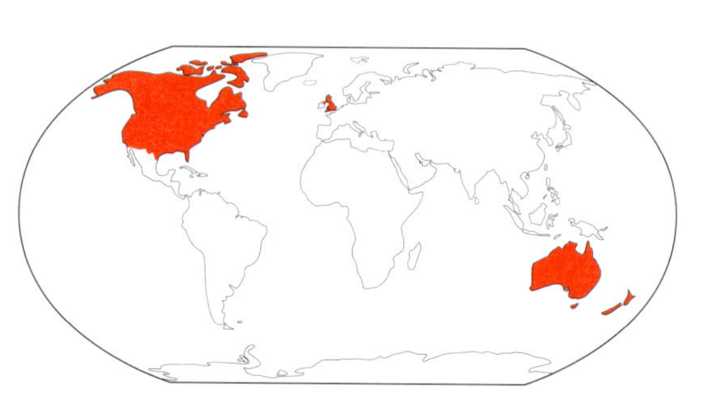

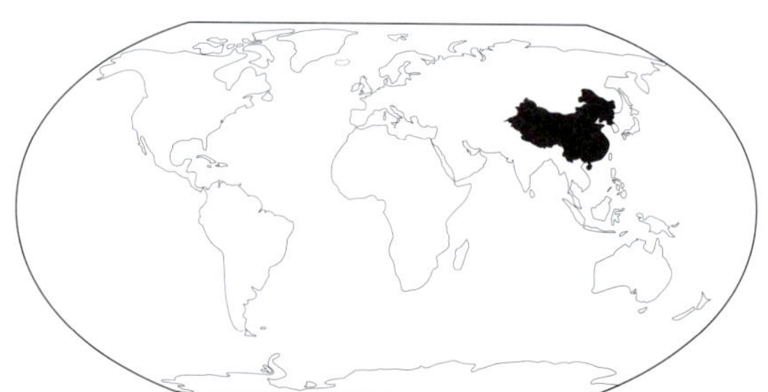

Five Eyes soldiers

Chinese and North Korean soldiers

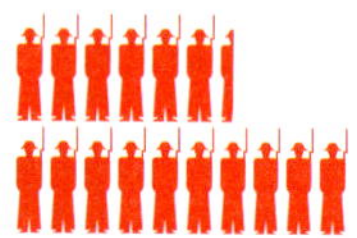

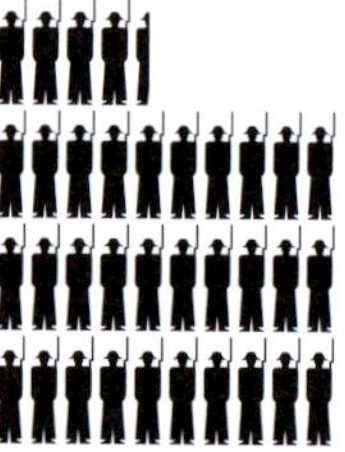

each symbol represents 100,000 soldiers

Turkey recently stepped out of line and bought air defense missile systems from Russia and is even eyeing to buy Russian airplanes instead of the US-produced F-16.[4] Paradoxically, Turkey and Russia were at the same time in a de facto war with each other in the short conflict over Nagorno-Karabakh. But Armenia's, and with it Russia's, quick defeat hints in the direction of a prearranged affair.

Thus, in a future war, as was the case in Neurath's day and age, military alliances will falter and be rearranged according to what's at stake. Even NATO, which appears to be the best-organized alliance, could falter under a deranged American president or a geopolitical conflict of interest. Turkey feels less and less connected to the West and could go either way. Israel, an underestimated military might, is forging regional alliances with Arab nations and former enemies like Bahrain, the Emirates, and Morocco.

China is a power in its own right. With more than 2 million soldiers, it has the world's largest army. Its secrecy about armament production makes it difficult to pin down, but without a doubt it has the fastest-growing military industry. China, and with it the entire globe, has one certain conflict ahead of it, which is invading Taiwan if the latter does not surrender. It has been reported that China has set a deadline of 2049 for the reunification of Taiwan with the mainland, which is the 100th anniversary of the founding of the People's Republic of China.[5] It's certain that a conflict lies ahead; it's only a question of when. Another question is how other countries will react. The West did not lift a finger for Hong Kong in 2020, and it is very likely that an invasion of Taiwan will be addressed with a mix of temporary sanctions and words of condemnation.

The reordering of the world seems to be occurring not so much because of the waning power of the West, but because the West cannot match the brutality of its opponents. The question the West is confronted with is how to react to genocide, mass rape, and nuclear bombs. Technology certainly does not provide the answer. Modernity is overstrained when confronted with pre-modern habits.

Contemporary Reasons for Going to War

As Neurath pointed out, modern wars don't start out of a scarcity of food, but "an entanglement of various interests."[6] Whatever the reason for war might be, the victor is often determined by the supply of resources and production. Should a war drag on, it ultimately comes down to a question of supply. In a hypothetical third world war, should today's alliances apply and the rest of world's resources otherwise be equally distributed, the Shanghai Cooperation Organization (SCO) would unequivocally dominate in a war of attrition. Including observer states in the SCO, the organization accounts for almost half of the world's population.[7]

The idea of disruption as an economic tool for profit-making has taken hold of the capitalist world since the 2010s. Web-based taxi services undercut the existing taxi industry by activating the public as potential drivers. A Web platform for letting private bedrooms to tourists bypasses official hotels. Disruptive economies loom with extra-ordinary profits through finding loopholes or undermining existing regulations. The final and big disruption concerns the war economy, which is the up-and-coming target for capitalists from the West. Investment in privatized military companies has keenly picked up since sharp cuts in traditional military spending were enacted at the end of the Cold War.[8] The privatization of war has the added benefit of a government's plausible deniability – since the military company is private, and contractors can be subsidiaries of larger companies, these companies act as an effective smoke screen, hiding spending and activities in spite of the fact that they essentially function as proxies of the state.[9] In addition to this, the legal definition of an employee of such an enterprise escapes the Geneva definitions of mercenary and remains a slippery slope as they are placed in a gray area between combatant and civilian.[10]

In the second Iraq war, which was not backed by the UN Charter and was thus illegal, the United States gave its largest contract of US$ 39.5 billion over 10 years to Kellogg Brown & Root (KBR), a then-subsidiary of Halliburton.[11] KBR provides the US with "military support services," and in its support in Iraq spent $ 400 million of its contracts hiring Blackwater, a US-based private military company, for its own protection, which was illegal, as the US should have provided military support.[12, 13] As a result of its subcontract, whatever Blackwater does is (legally speaking) not at the request of the US government.[14] Furthermore, knowing where all $ 39.5 billion has gone is almost impossible, as the private company is under no obligation to share that information publicly until audited. And even then, regarding a US$ 1.2 billion contract for Dyncorp, another private military contractor involved in Iraq, government auditors simply "could not determine exactly what was done for the money." In 2011, the US Department of Defense had more contractor personnel (52%) than uniformed personnel in Afghanistan and Iraq.[15]

For Russia, the Wagner Group serves as President Putin's private army, having carried out operations in Syria, the Central African Republic, Mali, Ukraine, Libya, Venezuela, Madagascar, Mozambique, and Sudan. The Wagner Group first emerged in 2014 in the Luhansk region of Ukraine.[16] The Wagner Group gets its name from the call sign of its founder, Dmitry Utkin, a Nazi-tattoo-adorned figure who named the group after Hitler's favorite composer, Richard Wagner. Today the group is owned by Yevgeny Prigozhin, a businessman nicknamed "Putin's chef" because his restaurants and catering businesses served the Russian military as well as hosted dinners for President Putin and his guests.[17] Legally speaking, the Wagner Group does not exist,

Russian Private Military Company Operations between 2016 and 2021

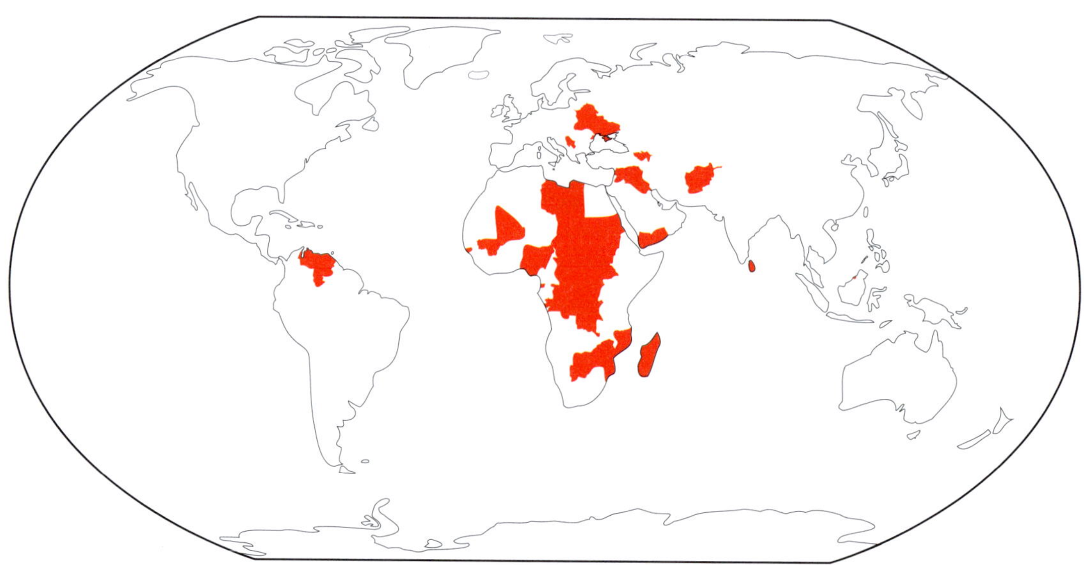

red: countries in which Russian PMCs have operated

since Russia bans private military companies. Thus Moscow denies knowledge of Wagner, which makes it almost immune to legal repercussion.[18]

What becomes clear from the increasing prevalence of privatized military activities is the removal of responsibility from nation-states in conflicts that are profitable. In addition to this, the authority of military operations is contested. The structure of military actions is changing and being commercialized. Without proper regulation and stricter legal definition, the state of warfare itself is becoming ever more opaque. Even after the withdrawal of the US from Iraq in 2011, a year later, some 36,000 men with arms were still operating under private military contracts.[19]

The USA and Russia are both working to undermine international agreements and organizations that were founded after World War II to prevent large-scale conflicts. Mercenaries don't count as soldiers, a detention camp at Guantánamo Bay in Cuba is not seen as US territory, and nuclear missiles are just below a threshold to be counted as such. The strategy of drafting an international law and then undermining it is not healthy in the long run and does not contribute to a peaceful future.

Like any society, international society is held together by mutual trust. It is the task of politics to build up trust within a country and between countries.

Private Military and Security Companies: The Montreux Document of 2008,[20] while not legally binding, reaffirms the obligations of states to ensure that private military and security companies (PMSCs) operating in armed conflicts comply with international humanitarian and human rights law.

Politics

Democracy

The cultural, political, and economic success of the United States and the European democracies after World War II gave reason to believe that the secret to a peaceful and happy society is individual freedom combined with a democratic political system. The collapse of the USSR in 1989 was largely seen as final proof that democracy is the only way to go.

Yet today only 30% of Earth's inhabitants live under fully democratic rule.[1] From today's perspective, the most successful political system seems to be electoral autocracy, which allows people to choose, but from a preselected and limited number of candidates who all belong to the same political party. The looming triumph of democracy in the 1990s did not pull through, and today democracy is in decline.

The quiet persistence of the Chinese Communist Party, backed up by the proof that it is able to lead Earth's second most populous country peacefully toward economic prosperity, poses very strong competition to the democratic cause. China's economic success is admired by a large part of the world and makes other world leaders excuse human rights violations in Tibet and China's imprisonment of its Muslim Uighur minority in reeducation camps in the Xinjiang province.[2]

China's success would seem to prove it right, even if that means that some people have to suffer. As the ancient Chinese philosopher Confucius once counselled, "Let the wind blow over the grass, and it is sure to bend."[3]

To the outside, China portrays itself as a more stable country than many Western democracies and proves that autocracy and modernity are not mutually exclusive. Countries like Russia and Turkey, which flirted with democracy at the turn of the 21st century because of the allure of the West, were ultimately convinced by China's uninterrupted rise to join its autocratic path. The Chinese way is so appealing that

Authoritarian Regimes Versus Full Democracies

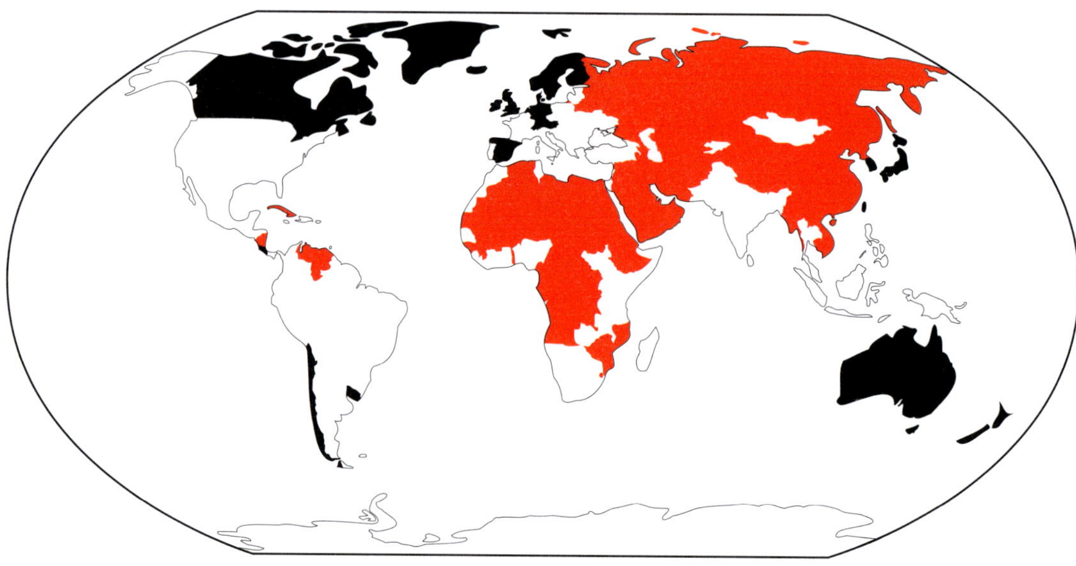

black: countries labeled as full democracies
red: countries labeled as authoritarian (2020)

Political Regimes

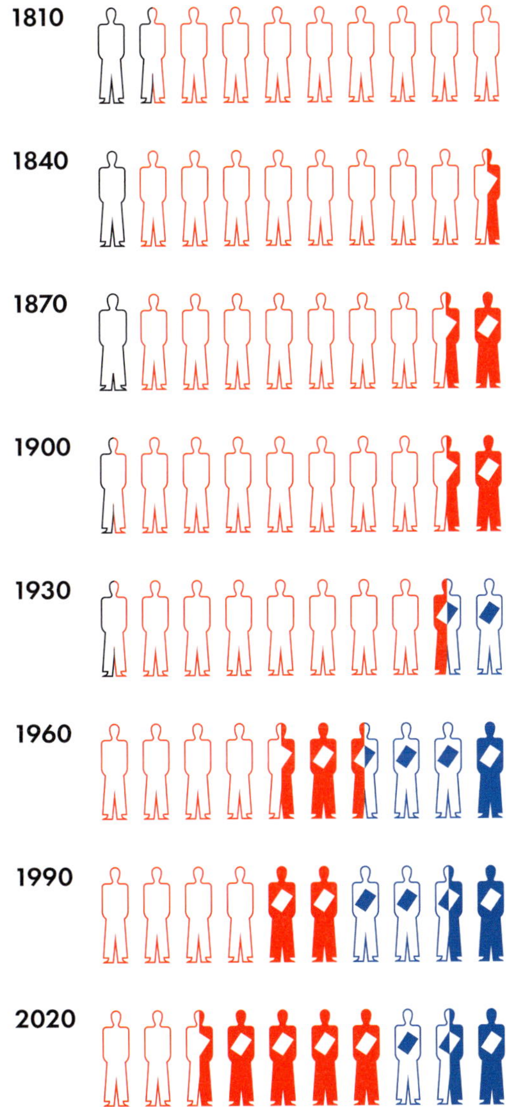

each symbol represents 10% of Earth's population

black outlined: people living in countries with missing regime data
red outlined: people living in closed autocracies
red filled with ballot paper: people living in electoral autocracies
blue outlined with ballot paper: people living in electoral democracies
blue filled with ballot paper: people living in liberal democracies

even the USA, Earth's oldest democracy, is falling for it. Donald Trump expressed admiration for the Communist Party's elimination of the two-term limit for President Xi Jinping and hinted that this might be a valid option for the US as well. Within the coming decades, China will overtake the US as the world's largest economy.[4] (According to some, this has already happened.) Losing its economic domination is another stress test that will show whether the US stands strong with democracy and holds on to its humanistic values or whether it falls for the appeal of a capitalist autocracy.

The liberal democracy is the world's most refined and fragile form of democracy, enjoyed by a meager 14% of the human population. According to Varieties of Democracy (V-Dem), an institute at the Department of Political Science at the University of Gothenburg in Sweden, a country is classified as a liberal democracy if its laws are transparent, men and women have equal access to the justice system, and the country features elements of a liberal democracy overall.[5]

The largest flaw of the democratic system, which is at the same time its biggest virtue, is its continual uncertainty. Elections every four to six years can result in radical changes, while people as well as markets love continuity and stability. That's why the most affluent countries have the most stable democracies, where changes of power barely result in radical changes of political direction.

As diverse as the world's political landscape might appear, the basis of all current political systems is a modern nation-state that relies on a pact between the people (citizens) and the territory (nation). This pact is closed at birth either through *jus soli*, a birthright to nationality or citizenship of the country of birth, or *jus sanguinis*, by which citizenship depends on the nationality of one or both parents. Regardless of the political system, a well-functioning bureaucracy is at the cradle of every successful modern nation-state. It begins almost with the conception of every citizen, whereafter they are indexed, taxed, educated, and accommodated for throughout their entire life.

Jus Soli

black: countries with unconditional birthright citizenship for persons born in the country
gray: countries with a modified or mixed system
white: countries where citizenship is determined by the nationality or ethnicity of one or both parents (jus sanguinis) (2022)

The Consolidation of the Nation-States

Despite their very different forms of government, the world's nation-states agree on a large set of tools that enable smooth communication (stamps, phone numbers, https), trade (containers, taxes, exchange rates), and travel (traffic signs, time zones, visas). At a conference in Paris hosted by the League of Nations in 1920, a set of standards was introduced for all passports issued by members of the League.[6] The passport and similar identification documents linked every single human being living on the planet directly to a territory and a political entity.

This is the theory, though effectively many do not own or not even account for a passport. With the standardization of the passport, the stateless citizen was introduced as well, due to the turmoil after World War I. The war unrooted masses all over Europe from countries that had ceased to exist, leaving thousands of stateless people behind. Predominantly Soviet Russia produced thousands of stateless people by revoking the citizenship of persons living abroad for more than five years, those who had left after 1917 without state permission, and those who were involved in anti-Soviet activities.

Gender Inequality in Nationality Laws

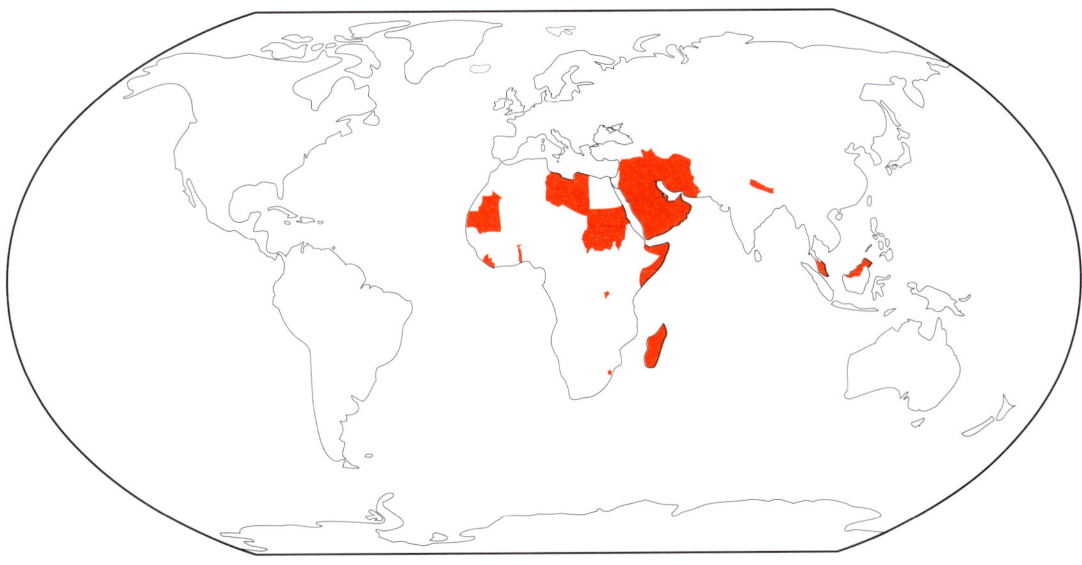

red: countries that do not grant women equality with men in conferring nationality to their children (2022)

To offer a way out from this impasse, Fridtjof Nansen, in his role as High Commissioner for Refugees for the League of Nations, introduced a "stateless person's passport" (aka Nansen Passport) in 1922. The issuing of Nansen Passports stopped by 1938, but was followed up by "refugee travel documents" that can be issued by the individual nation-states for registered refugees.[7]

Today no human being lives outside any of the 203 geopolitical containers called sovereign nation-states – physically, at least. In legal terms, no fewer than 10 million people are stateless[8] and thus do not legally belong to any nation-state although they live in one. At least 70,000 stateless children are born each year.[9] The causes are many; one of the worst is that mothers have no right to pass on their citizenship to their child. In the past 20 years, progress has been made and 14 countries have changed their laws, now granting equal rights to women and men to confer citizenship to their children; however, a group of 25 countries still differentiate between the father and the mother.[10] In these countries especially, the most burdened women are the most affected: widows or victims of violence and rape who end up alone with their kids. Without recognition as citizens, these children simply do not exist and struggle right from the start to acquire such essentials as proper healthcare, education, and food stamps.

In the past hundred years, the passport, once an unimpressive booklet, turned into the ticket to the world, and for some, the ticket to a better, or even longer, life. For example, by moving to Switzerland, a person from Chad could, statistically speaking, extend his or her life by 30 years, from 54 to 84. The sheer prospect of extending one's life by 30 years seems to be worth the risks.[11]

Very few win the lottery at birth and grow up in the affluent West with its social security and human rights. The introduction of the passport together with the solidification of the nation-state made migration from one country to the other ever more difficult. To ease the growing annoyance of border checks, a group of rich nations from Europe, mostly member states of the European Union, joined together in 1995 to create the Schengen Area. Within this zone, cross-border travel is possible without showing one's ID. Checks are done arbitrarily within that zone.

The Central America-4 Free Mobility Agreement (CA-4) between El Salvador, Guatemala, Honduras, and Nicaragua established a very similar agreement in 2006. Zones like the Schengen Area and CA-4 also share a visa regime for nationals traveling to their member countries.[12]

Failing States

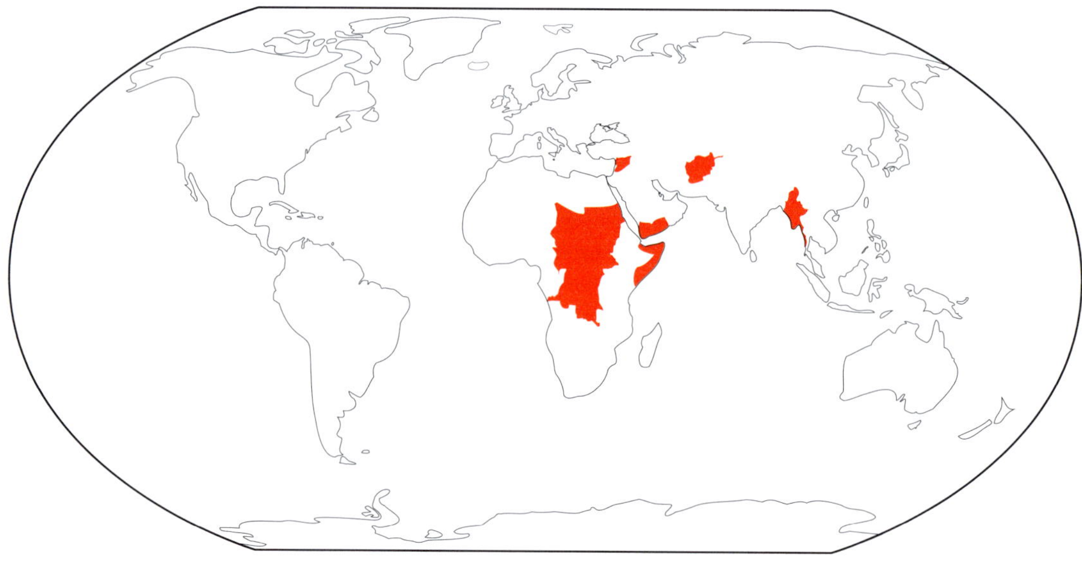

red: countries on high alert and very high alert to disintegrate; these are countries with a score of 100 and more on the Fragile State Index, based on economic, political, and social stability factors (2022)

Somalia

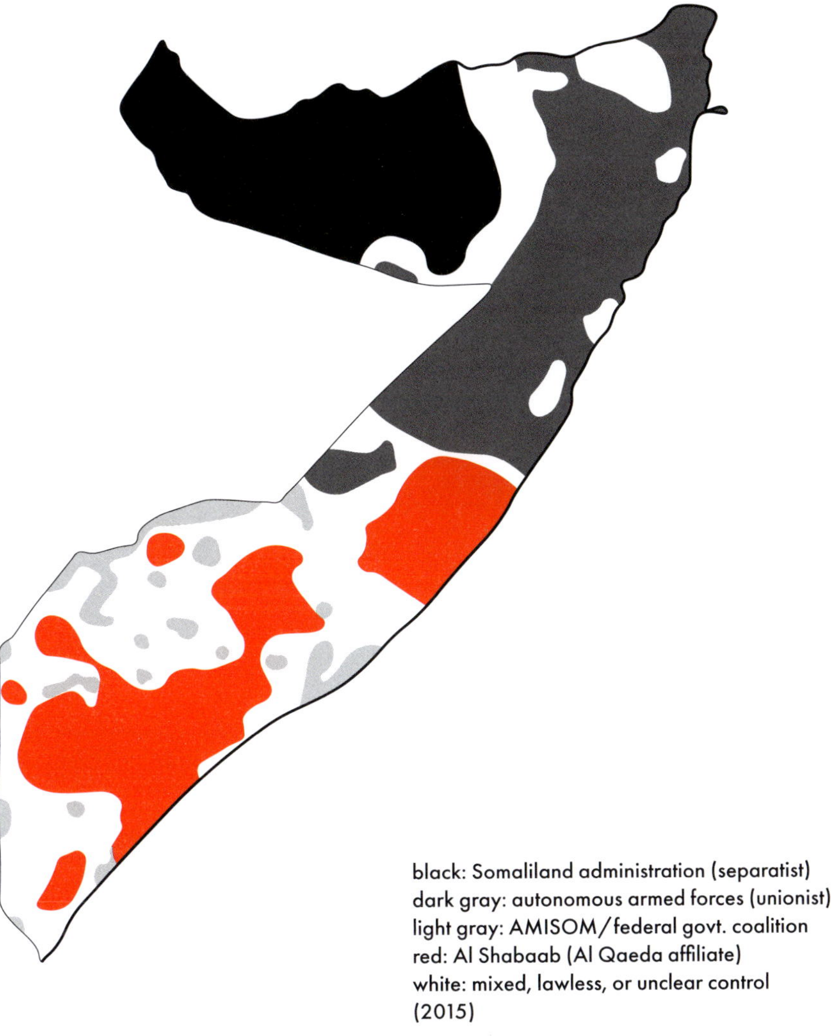

Somalia – the Dissolution of the Nation-State

The dissolution of the Soviet Union in 1991 resulted in many new countries in Europe and Asia. Some countries suddenly found themselves without a protective umbrella by one of the two superpowers because they had simply lost their strategic importance. A good example of this is the fall of Somalia in 1991, when an autocratic president tried desperately to hold onto power. Instead of uniting the nation behind him, he made use of tribal animosities and the systematic genocide of the Isaaq people, creating 500,000 refugees in neighboring Ethiopia.[13] Foreign aid was cut in response to the humanitarian abuses of the regime – causing the eventual collapse of the state when pressured by factional guerrilla groups. For 30 years, since the outbreak of the civil war, Somalia has been considered a failed state (the first of its kind), thus a country without a common functioning government.[14] Libya has experienced the same fate since 2011, and Yemen is following in their footsteps. The disintegration of nation-states can present a political aspect of de-modernization, as the states tend to fall apart into tribal zones governed by warlords. Secular laws are often replaced by religious codes without a clear separation of powers. When states dissolve, international agreements vanish and ties to the rest of the globe are cut. For example, the passport from Somaliland, a breakaway region of Somalia which is not officially recognized by any country or international organization, allows its citizens to travel to only 16 countries.[15]

Wars, lawlessness, and political prosecution by autocratic rulers force people out of their home country and turn citizens into refugees and asylum-seekers.

Refugees, Asylum-Seekers and Internally Displaced People Versus Walls and Fences

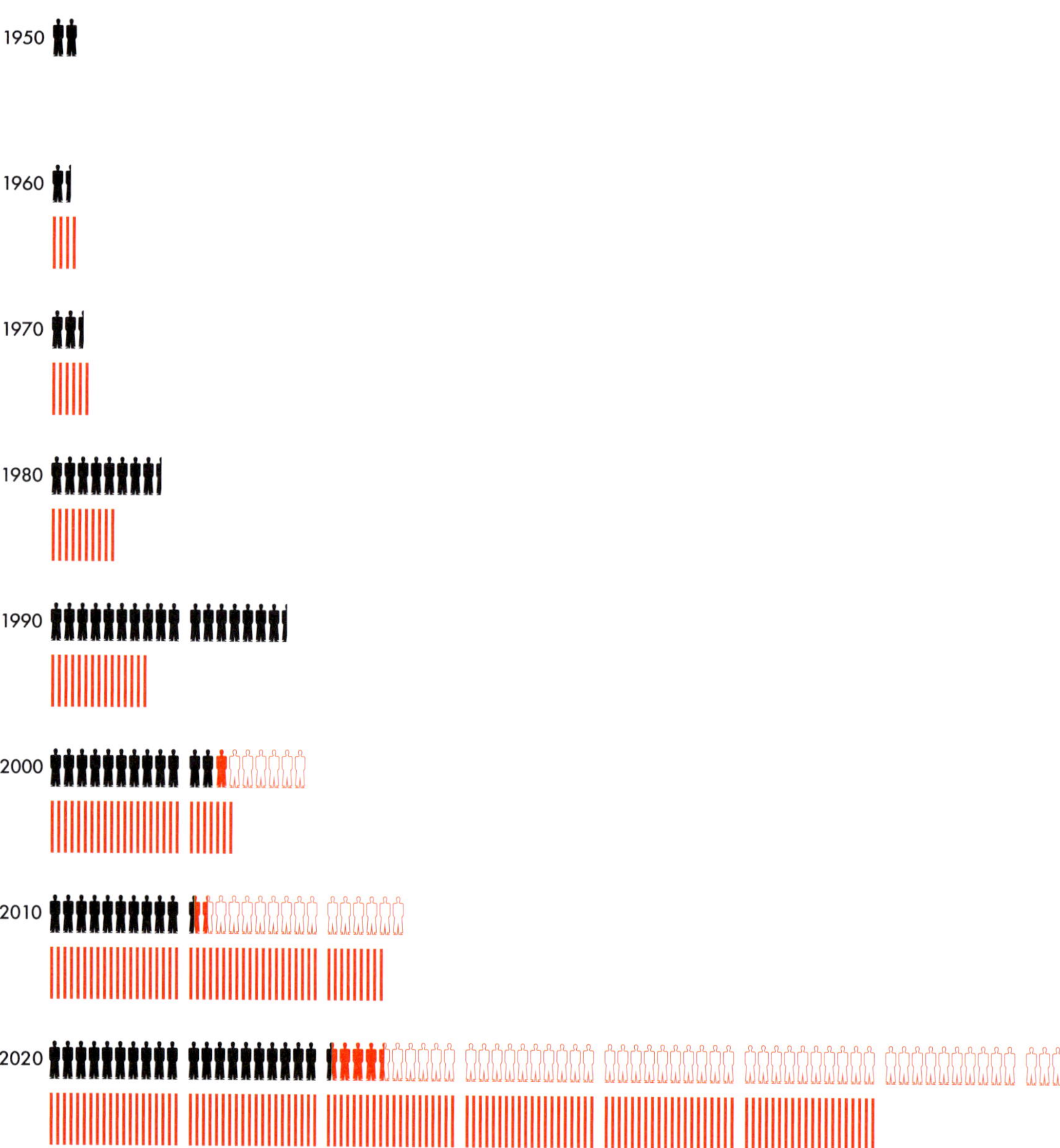

each black symbol represents 1 million refugees under UNHCR mandate
each red symbol represents 1 million asylum-seekers
each outlined symbol represents 1 million internally displaced people of concern to the UNHCR
each vertical bar represents an existing wall or fence structure between two nation-states

On the Move – Refugees

The 1951 Refugee Convention[16] and its 1967 Protocol outline the rights of refugees as well as the legal obligations of states to protect them. The core principle is non-refoulement, which asserts that a refugee asking for asylum cannot be returned to a country where they face serious threats to their life or freedom.

Once feet are set on the soil of a country, asylum can be requested, and must be granted by the 1951 Refugee Convention until a ruling has been made in court.

Internally Displaced People

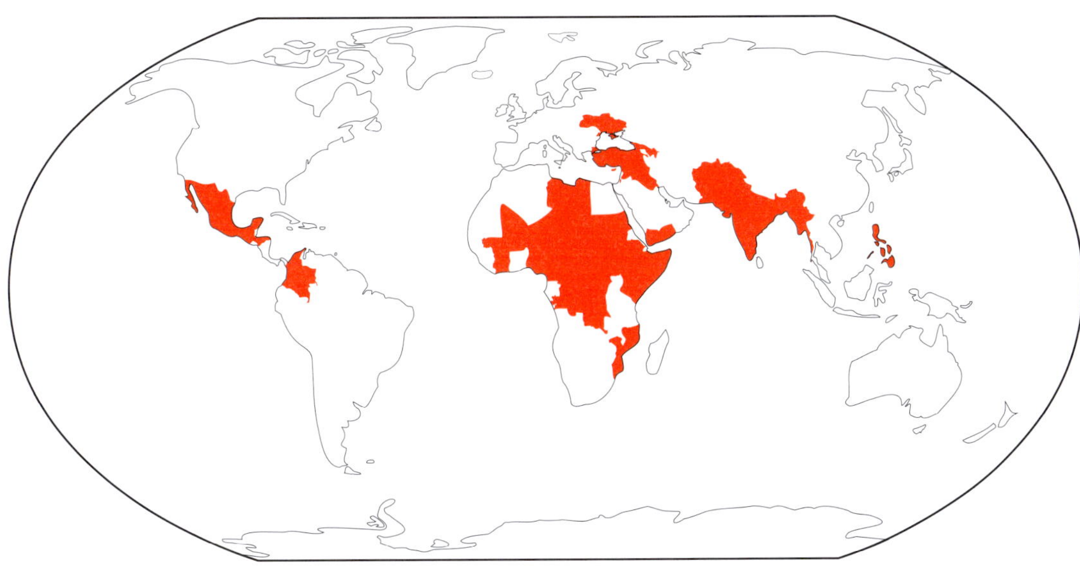

red: countries with more than 100,000 internally displaced people (IDP) as a result of conflicts (2021)

As a consequence, the USA and the European Union reinforce their borders with walls, fences, and security forces, to prevent people crossing into their territory. In violation of the Refugee Convention, this policy targets all people who wish to enter these areas, including refugees from war and terror.

Since the lifting of the Iron Curtain in 1991, over 30,000 kilometers of border barriers have been erected all around the world.[17] Some countries, like Israel and Turkey, have shut themselves off from the outside completely. Within three years, between 2015 and 2018, TOKI, Turkey's state-owned housing developer, working with local contractors, completed a 764 km structure that seals off most of the 911 km border between Turkey and its southern neighbor, Syria.[18] The 3-meter-high prefab concrete wall it built, topped with 1 meter of razor wire, is equipped with sensors, radar, detectors, cameras, and military patrols. The Turkish government is about to expand the structure along the entire 295 km border with Iran, which is expected to be finished in 2023.[19]

The extreme increase in the number of internally displaced people (IDP, people who have fled but have remained within the same country)[20] since the 1990s goes hand in hand with the wall-building hype. The more barriers there are, and the more heavily

Refugees and Asylum-Seekers – Destination and Origin

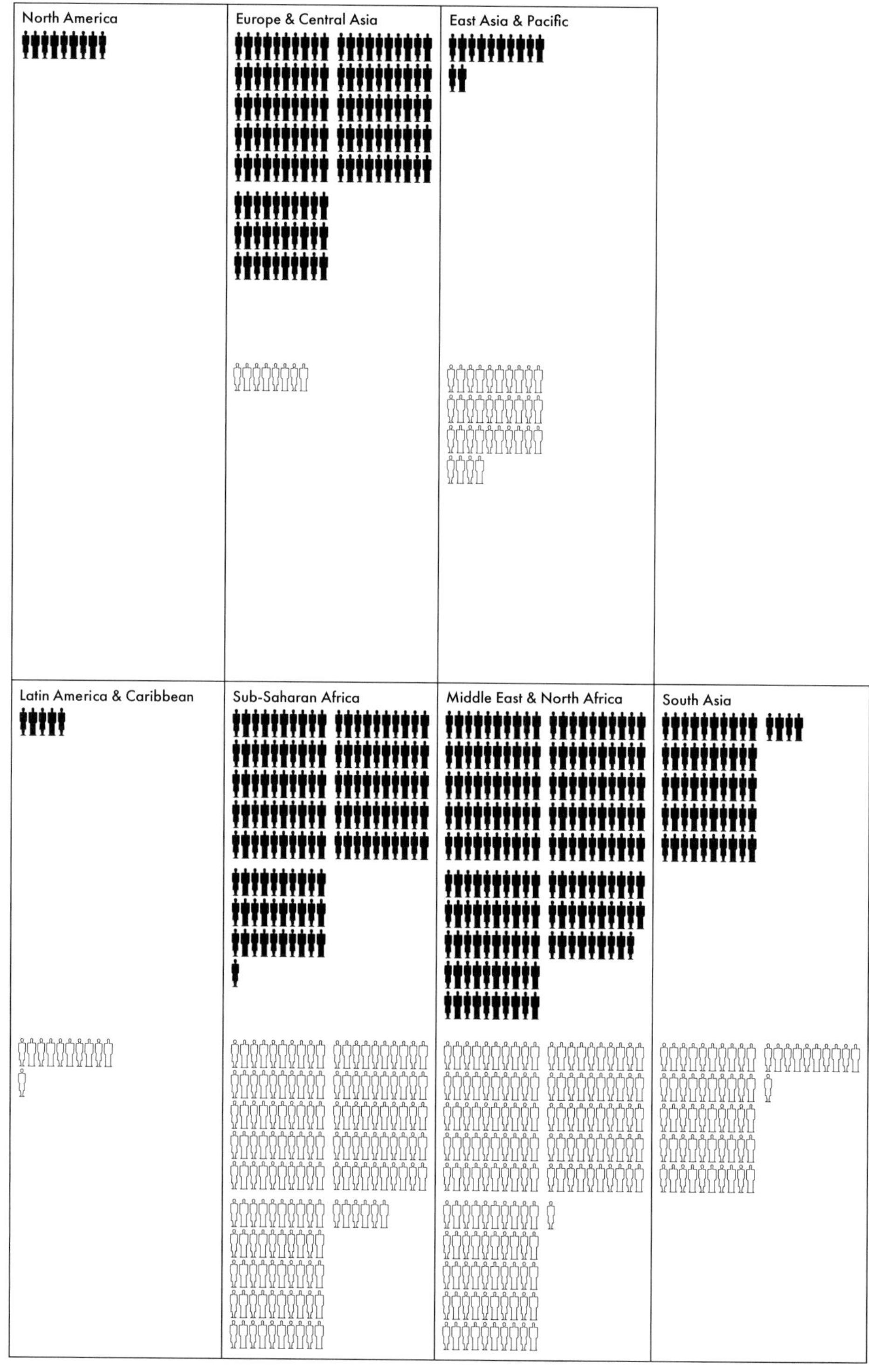

each filled symbol represents 50,000 refugees taken in as asylum-seekers by the specific region
each outlined symbol represents 50,000 refugees originating from the specific region
(2021)

borders are guarded, the more difficult it becomes for people to cross over to a neighboring country for refuge.[21] The bureaucratic truth is that people who flee but do not cross national borders do not count as refugees, according to the mandate of the UN. It is the responsibility of every state to protect and care for its own citizens. It would mean an infringement on the sovereignty of a state if the UN were to help internally displaced people of its own accord. Help is only possible if a state agrees to intervention by the UN, as happened in 2012, when an agreement was made between the Syrian government and the United Nations to help the 6.7 million internally displaced people produced by the Syrian civil war (since 2011). An equal number of refugees left the country, resulting in over 50% of the total population being on the move.[22]

Recent wars reveal a terrifying pattern. As in medieval times, cities are being turned into major battlefields, with citizens as targets. Wars of attrition try to "break" citizens in order to force a surrender. Cruelty against citizens has become a tool of contemporary warfare. The Russian army in particular, with the help of its mercenaries (Wagner Group), has turned itself into a master of brutality and a major aggressor against the weakest in a war, the civilians.

Gastarbeiter – Foreign Workforce

The affluent West is continually short of cheap labor, something which is plentiful in the Global South. Thus, both areas, the USA and the EU, have created loopholes in their system which give them access to people who keep their economic engine running. The USA has chosen to turn a blind eye to illegal immigration from Central and South America if cheap labor is needed. In 2020 there were about 11 million undocumented immigrants in the US – people who officially do not exist.

The EU has chosen a more formal way: expansion. Poorer countries, like Romania and Bulgaria, to the east of the club provide a cheap workforce as they are absorbed into the EU. While a worker from Luxembourg comes home with about € 6,000 every month on average, their EU colleague in Bulgaria is fobbed off with a meager € 860 per month.[23] In addition to internal work migration, EU countries, like the US, take on migrants by handing out work permits. The parameters for getting a work permit are written such that only highly educated workers have a chance of becoming an expatriate.

The wealthy Middle Eastern oil-rich countries might have the most radical approach by flying in cheap labor from India, Nepal, Sri Lanka, Bangladesh, and Pakistan. In some countries like the United Arab Emirates, migrant workers account for 88% of the population and 95% of the workforce.[24] People from India, Pakistan, and Bangladesh account for more than 50% of the foreign workforce, while people from the West contribute only about 2% to it.[25]

While 50% of the workforce (mainly construction workers and cleaners) earn less than € 500 per month, only 8% of the workforce receive more than € 1,300; the cost of living is comparable to the UK.[26]

In the UAE, migrant workers are allowed to enter the country via a sponsor (employer), who must be a UAE resident or citizen.[27] Until 2021, it has been impossible for any foreigner to naturalize into the UAE, customary within the Gulf Cooperation Council states. Today, however, investors who spend at least 10 million UAE dirhams (equivalent to nearly € 2.5 million) in the country, or people with a "special talent," can apply for citizenship – although whether they benefit from the public welfare system remains ambiguous.[28]

Migration as a Weapon

When Neurath points out back in 1939 that "migration is not yet the subject of international planning,"[29] then one must realize that things have only gotten worse. Today migration is a subject of restrictive national planning and is used as a political tool especially by the growing number of populist right-wing politicians. In the best case, host countries look at migrants as a potential rejuvenation factor for an aging population, to keep the pension funds afloat. At the same time, ill-minded neighboring countries use migrants as a human weapon. In 2020 Turkey sent thousands of refugees toward the border of Greece to demand support from its NATO allies for its military operation in Syria.[30] Turkey's prime minister, Erdoğan, threatened the EU that if it did not comply, it would be overrun by millions of refugees.[31]

A similar event was staged in late 2021, when Belarus' self-proclaimed president Lukashenko organized flights from the Middle East to Belarus to send thousands of refugees toward the border of Poland.[32] Mister Lukashenko's demand was to be recognized as the lawful president by the EU, since the countries of the club refused to do so after a rigged election in 2020.

The influx of people is increasingly seen as a threat. As the economies of the rich nations have turned from manufacturing to service, immigration has turned from an economic to a social issue. In times of low unemployment, the loss of a job by a migrant seems to be less of a threat than the loss of culture.

The Rise of the Welfare State in Europe

each symbol represents a 1% share of the annual tax revenue
the evolution depicted here is the average of Germany, France, Britain, and Sweden

Standard of Living

The biggest lure of the West is its high standard of living. Otto Neurath tried to measure it in terms of per capita sugar consumption, which seems a rather odd parameter today.[33] High sugar consumption is not really a good measure. In a globalized economy, sugar has become cheap and easily available. For example, Iran and Germany consume more or less the same amount per capita.

Today the standard of living is not so much about food, living, and clothing, but about medical care, education, security, and personal freedom. Europe, with its well-functioning bureaucracy and well-organized welfare state, is a particularly attractive role model for many.

The Welfare State

The welfare state is a magnificent invention. Its development goes hand in hand with a radical shift in the fiscal policy as well as an ideological turn of the nation-state. While the 19th-century version of nation-states mainly focused on law and order, the modern welfare state takes on full responsibility for the education of its citizens, for their health, care of the elderly, maternity care, public infrastructure and the administration of land, finance and labor laws. The welfare state took over large parts of the tasks that had been handled by the family in pre-modern societies.

The basis for the economic clout of the welfare state is redistribution through a series of tax schemes on income, trade, goods, and services. What sounds like a Robin Hood scheme is, when done well and with the help of good bureaucracy, a key to an equitable society. The trick is to know exactly how much tax one can ask for and to make sure that it is spent wisely so that society as a whole can profit. In France, the total tax

black: army, police, justice, administration
blue: education
green: retirement and disability pensions
red: health
orange: social transfers like family and unemployment
gray: other social spending

Tax Revenue

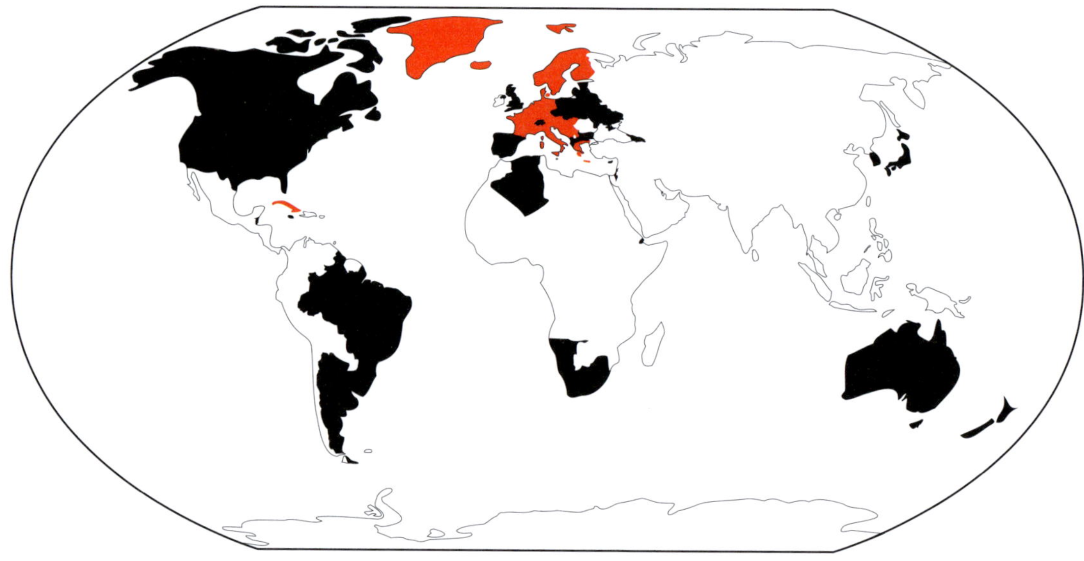

countries' tax revenue from social contributions, direct and indirect taxes, as a percentage of GDP (2020)

red: more than 35%
black: 25%–35%
white: less than 25%

revenue as a percentage of national income increased from 9% in 1900 to 49% in 2010.[34] This financial boost allows the nation-state not only to pamper its citizens and seduce them with smaller and larger gifts before general elections, but also to plan, operate, and regulate the national economy. For example, in times of an economic downturn, a country can decide to build or renovate national infrastructure like highways, hospitals, or schools in order to boost the construction industry.

Distribution of Global Wealth

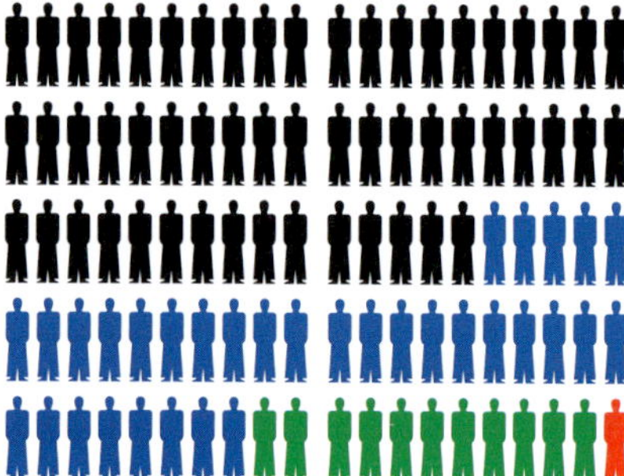

100% of Global Wealth

one symbol of a person represents 1% of the global adult population (2020)
one symbol of a stack of coins represents 1% of global wealth (2020)

black: adult having less than $ 10,000
(55% of global population = 1.5% of global wealth)
blue: adult having $ 10,000 to $ 100,000
green: adult having $ 100,000 to $ 1 million
red: adult having more than $ 1 million
(1% of global population = 41% of global wealth)

Life Expectancy Versus Infant Mortality

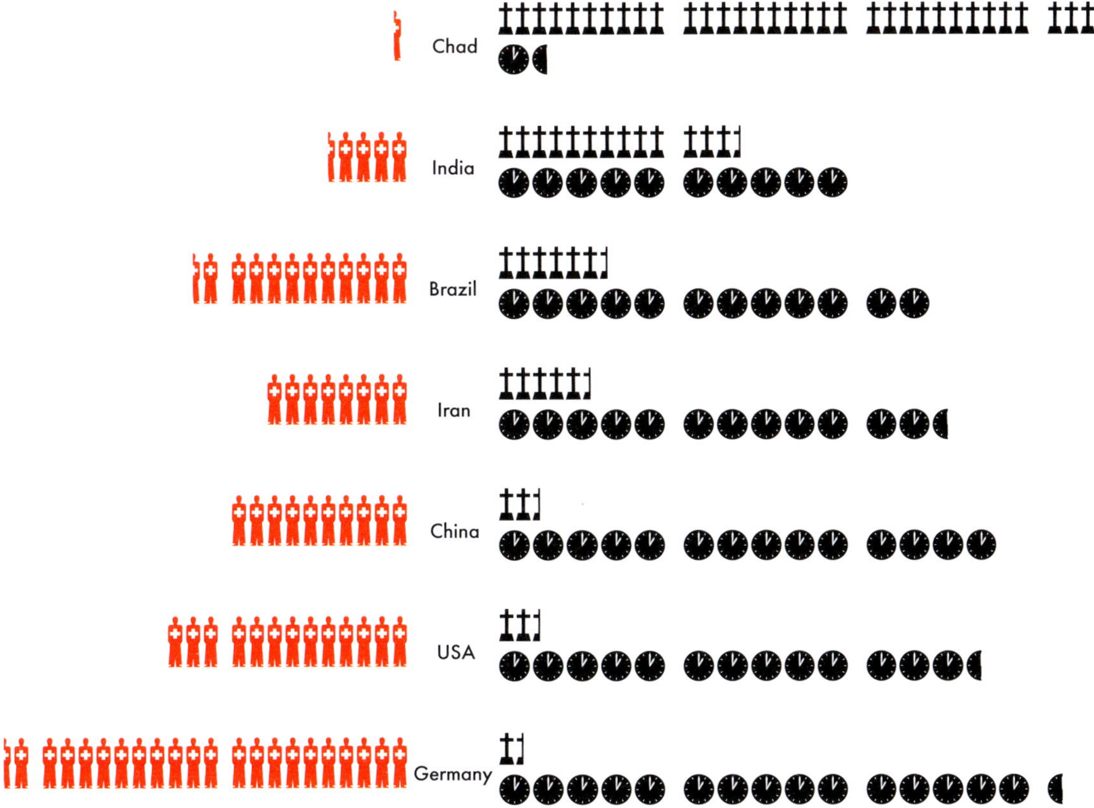

each human symbol represents 2 doctors per 10 people
each cross represents 2 deaths per 1,000 births
each clock represents 2 years of life expectancy beyond 50 years

This ability makes the modern nation-state much more resilient than its harbinger in the 19th century, which relied predominantly on expenditures for the army and bureaucracy. This provided much less leverage to maneuver a country in difficult times.

Next to the model of the modern, democratic welfare state prevalent in Europe, a large variety of systems that protect citizens from hardship exist across the globe. Egypt, for example, spends $ 5.5 billion a year on a food subsidy, mainly for bread. This program serves more than 60 million Egyptians, or nearly two-thirds of the population, who get 5 loaves of bread every day for 50 cents a month.[35] The price of a subsidized loaf has remained constant at 0.05 pounds ($ 0.002) since the 1980s. Attempts to remove the subsidy have failed. In 1977 the World Bank advised Anwar Sadat, Egypt's president at the time, to end the subsidies for flour, rice, and cooking oil. This proclamation led to the notorious "bread riots" of 1977, which resulted in 79 casualties and 1,000 injured persons.[36] Egypt's food subsidy, a legacy of World War II, comprised as much as 20% of total governmental expenditure. Today this is down to 5.5%, but it still accounts for a large part of the budget.[37] The fact that Egypt is one of the Earth's largest importers of wheat makes this system more interesting and of global importance.

What is made evident in the example of Egypt is that social welfare programs can be looked at from two sides. The social aspect of welfare programs highlights helping the poor and underprivileged. Yet there is also the governmental side of these programs which makes certain to keep the masses calm. Historian Walter Scheidel argues that the very idea of the European welfare state is more honestly based on a fear of the masses uprising than on the good intentions of social welfare.[38] The close proximity to the communist system with its radical view on equality and targeting the rich pushed western European leaders, predominantly people from the conservative-leaning upper class, toward the welfare state.

The Inheritance Flow in Europe

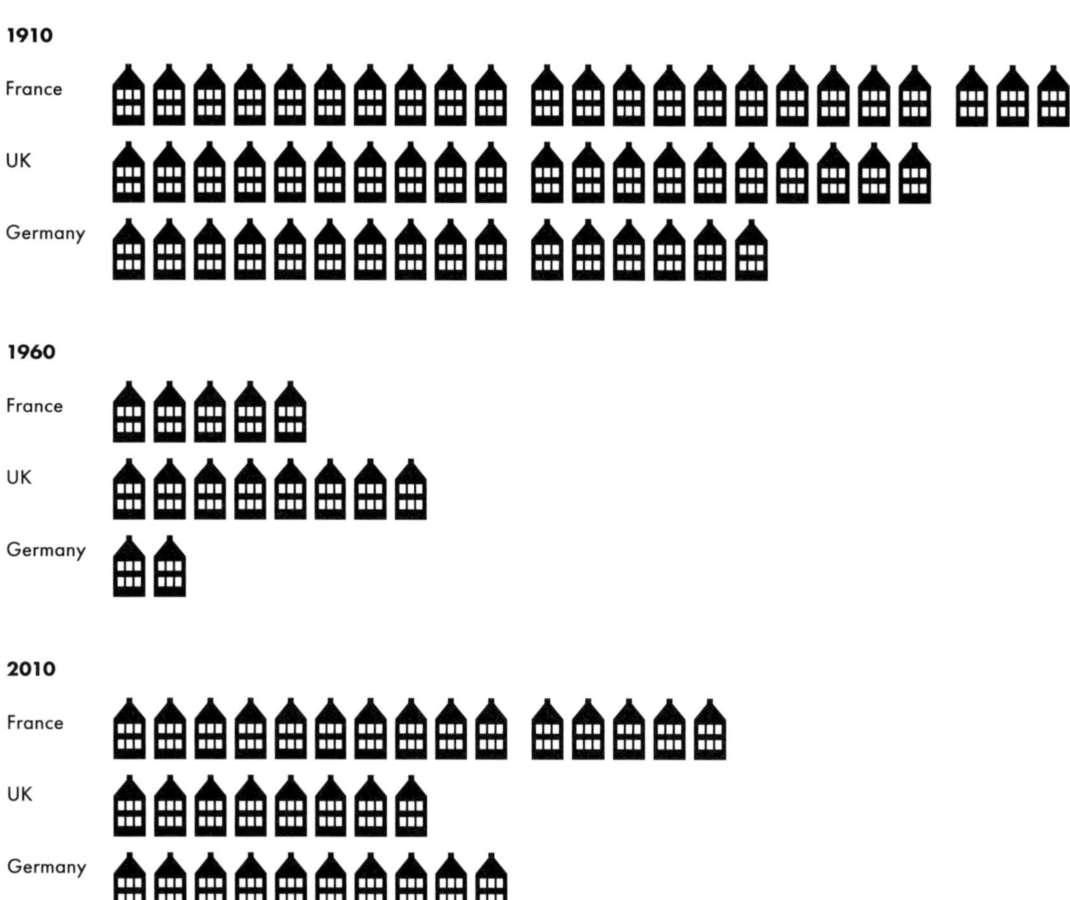

each house symbol represents 1% of national income from bequests and gifts inherited

In contrast with communism, the democratic welfare state has never targeted the rich, but takes care of just enough reallocation to keep the masses well-fed, healthy, and quiet, and at the same time not annoying the rich. With the end of communism to its east, ultra-high-income holders' fears of the angry masses waned and consequently inequality rose throughout the West.

Another, more brutal reason for more equality in Europe after the two world wars was the physical destruction of real estate. The removal of real estate as inheritable wealth functioned as an economic equalizer throughout society. In Germany and France, 25–30% of capital was eliminated due to physical destruction.[39] As a result, the volume of inheritance in Germany shrank from 16% of the national income in 1910 to 2% in 1960.[40] Large landowners lost their properties and financial and business assets were slashed in value, resulting in smaller dividends and bonuses.

In 2010 the volume of inheritance in Germany was up again to 10%, and throughout western Europe the mature middle class has turned into a generation of homeowners. No country in the EU has a home ownership rate below 50%.[41] People invest and hold on to real estate as capital that is supposed to work for them and that can be passed on to their heirs.

A global society needs to address inequality and care for the welfare of all humans. While the European Union is combating an average annual income gap between € 72,200 in Luxembourg and € 10,300 in Bulgaria,[42] the task on a global is scale is much more extreme. The highest average income – € 76,700 in Bermuda – is 150 times the € 500 per year in Somalia.[43]

To counter this, the West developed the system of foreign aid or development aid, which often is used as a tool of foreign policy. Here again, there is surely a genuine desire to help, but (especially) the rich European countries openly talk about and admit that foreign aid, particularly to Africa and the Middle East, helps to keep the people where they are. Foreign aid is seen as one of the most appropriate tools for preventing people from moving, especially from moving north or northwest toward Europe. For example, Austria doubled its foreign aid "to address the root causes of migration," while there is little evidence that this might result in the desired effect.[44]

Essentially, it all comes down to reducing inequality, within a country and across the globe, not only based on self-interest and goodwill but also based on genuine concern about our society. The redistribution of wealth from the rich to the poor, equal health-care, education, and political participation (all genders and all classes) is at the heart of a well-governed state and part of the magic formula for a healthy society.

Inequality in the USA Versus Europe

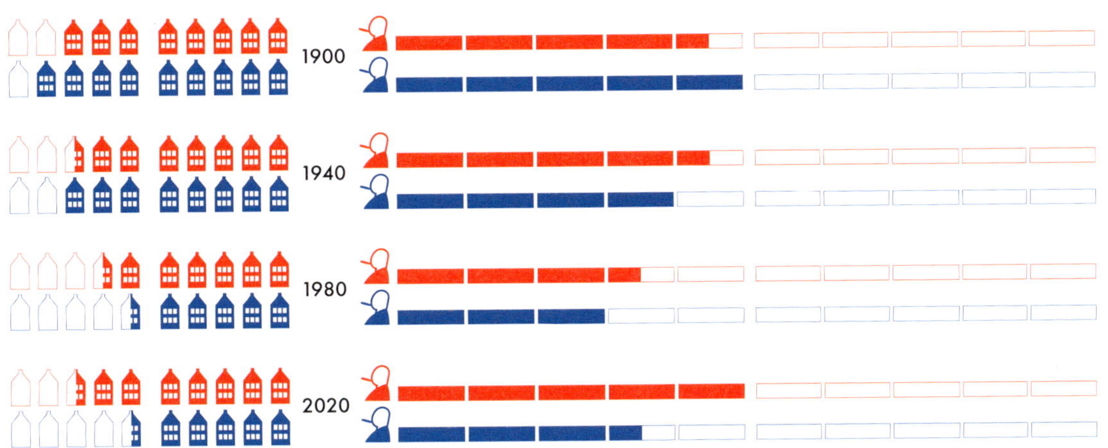

each house symbol represents 10% of private property
filled symbols: share owned by the top 10% wealth-holders
red: United States
blue: Europe

each bar represents 10% of the total income
filled symbols: share held by the top 10% income-earners
red: United States
blue: Europe

Consumerism

The Start of Consumerism

Democracy was empowering the people, offering them a choice of whom to be ruled by. Election campaigns and election battles are short and fierce struggles to elect a ruler. The young proto-democratic nation-states of the 19th century were struggling to keep their citizens calm and united during these times of elections which easily could lead to civil war-like situations. Political interest was needed for a high voter turnout, but not too much interest, which easily could translate into extremism. Many European nation-states struggled to find this balance after World War I.[1]

After World War II, the European democracies learned from the United States to entertain the masses with the help of consumerism. The USA, which had no war damage and thus no delay, extended its prewar experiences from the New Deal, a series of public spending programs enacted to counteract the Great Depression in the 1930s.[2] The New Deal proved that public spending could stimulate private spending.

In Europe, the Marshall Plan was enacted as an extension or offshore variant of the New Deal.[3] The huge influx of money, which fueled production and subsequently everyone's salaries, resulted in an ever more affluent society. Simultaneously, affordable products like the dishwasher, washing machine, and vacuum cleaner were offered to the masses, allowing people to have more spare time, meaning more time to spend money.

Global Textile Consumption

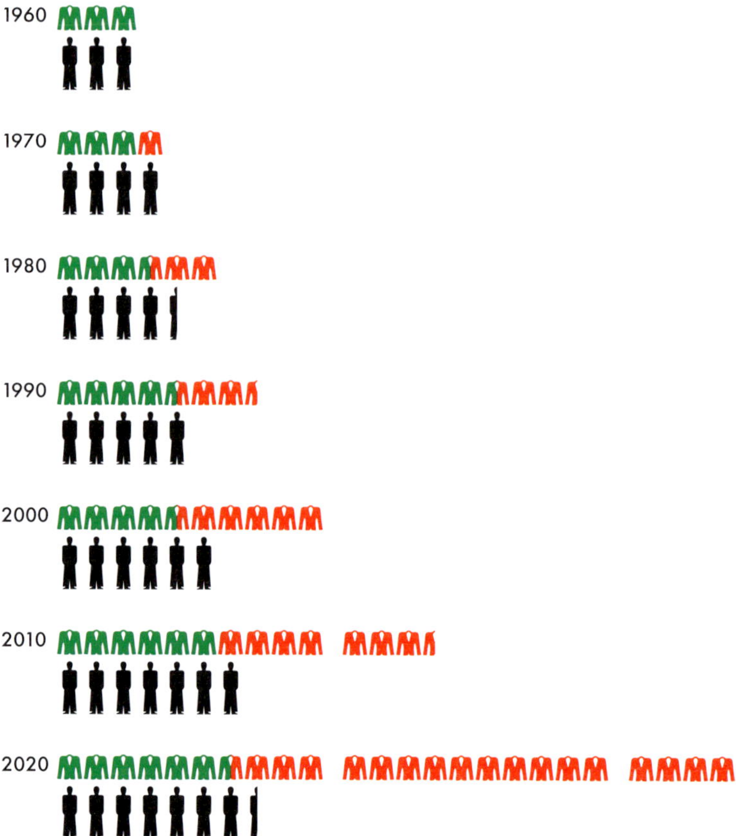

one shirt symbol represents 5 million tonnes of garments
one person symbol represents 1 billion people

green: fiber from a natural base
red: synthetic chemical fiber (fossil-based)

Telephones and Automobiles per 100 People

Germany	South Korea	China	India
1920	1920	1920	1920
1940	1940	1940	1940
1960	1960	1960	1960
1980	1980	1980	1980
2000	2000	2000	2000
2020	2020	2020	2020

"As a mass consumption-driven economy made possible a more adequate standard of living for more people than ever before in the decades after World War II, the consumer in the economic realm became increasingly identified with the citizen in the political realm."[4] The "citizen consumer" is the result of a new alliance between politics and the economy, triggered in response to the major shocks of the 1970s: the oil crisis, stagflation, and the collapse of the Bretton Woods monetary order. Politics became more cooperative, outward-oriented, and market-friendly, and global institutions such as the International Monetary Fund (IMF) were given a major role in order to fuel what was later perceived as the high time of "globalization." In order to sustain profits, with the new means of mass production came the need for mass consumption. And so, a demand for goods and services was elaborately contrived with advertisements that "kept the consumer dissatisfied"[5] and encouraged them to board the "escalator of desires" to an ever more affluent life. The notion that humans have everything they need is the biggest enemy to the capitalist consumer culture of today – the manufacturing of demand has ensured that the modern human is insatiable.

Major architectural typologies of modern life were already invented and fully developed in the early 20th century. Examples include the modern office tower and the supermarket in the 1930s, and the shopping mall in the 1950s. The invention of the supermarket empowered customers and enabled them to literally take what they want. At the same time, it led to a display of exuberance – shelves always had to be full of a large variety of similar products. The shopping mall, developed by Victor Gruen, an Austrian-born architect and American immigrant, delivered the need for experience and transformed shopping from a nuisance to an amusement.

The power of this time was the abundance and the overwhelming, almost unlimited, freedom of choice. Biblical or mythical images of the "land of plenty" or "shopper's paradise" appeared. At the same time, communist countries, sickened by the vulgarity of consumerism, served their people with what was needed, but not one inch more.

With the collapse of the Soviet Union in the early 1990s, consumerism eventually did win. The increasingly televised comparison between empty shelves in Moscow and full supermarkets in New York during the 1980s had contributed to cracking the regime. On January 31, 1990, the McDonald's fast-food chain, the grail of American consumerism, opened its first branch in Moscow, marking the beginning of a new world for the Russian people. More than 5,000 of them came to its opening to be the first customers. That day, the Moscow McDonald's set a world record by serving more than 30,000 visitors.[6] People stood in line for over 6 hours. On May 16, 2022, 32 years after its opening, McDonald's announced it would cease all operations in Russia due to the Russian army's invasion of Ukraine. A month later, some restaurants opened under the new name "Tasty," offering a Russian version of fast food.[7]

Consumerism has proven to be extremely resilient and adaptable. Today there is not one country in the world without a supermarket, and almost all have shopping malls. Consumerism has become a worldwide phenomenon. No matter the regime, whether it's Chinese communism, Arabic Islamism, or European welfare state, exuberance, affluence, and plenty to go around seems to be the way for politicians to satisfy the masses. All economies seem to agree that the combination of "good worker" and "good shopper" creates fantastic results for the national economy.

Waste, McDonald's, and Credit

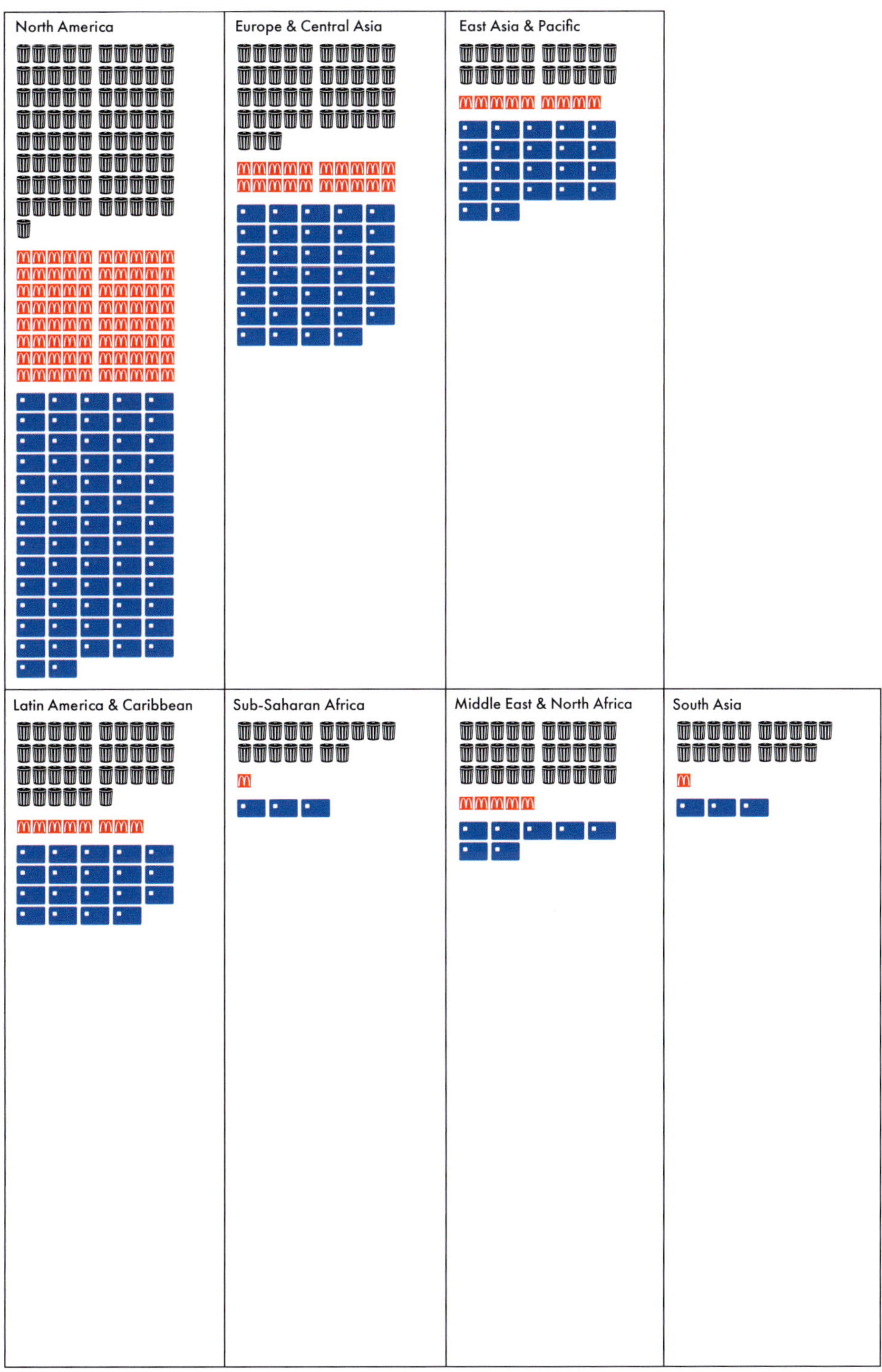

each waste symbol represents 10 kg of waste per capita per year
each M symbol represents one McDonald's restaurant per 2,000 people
each card symbol represents 1% of the adult population owning a credit card
(2020s; various years)

The Plastic Age

In 1989, plastic production surpassed steel production by volume.[8] That was the year when the Iron Curtain was lifted as well as the year when humankind entered the plastic age. Regardless of the efforts to end the world's dependency on oil, the rapid transition from mineral-based to fossil-based material is still going on and is expected to do so in the future.

Plastic is much cheaper and lighter than its competitors. In the past 50 years, many household goods, toys, and packaging changed from natural materials like wood, cardboard, metal, and glass to fossil-based plastics. 60% of all plastic produced globally between 1950 and 2015 ended up in landfills and another 10% in incinerators, which release toxic gases into the atmosphere.[9]

Steel Production Versus Plastic Production

1950

1960

1970

1980

1990

2000

2010

2020

each symbol represents 10,000,000 m³ of steel/plastic produced globally in the specific year
black: not recycled
green: recycled

Plastic and Its Fate

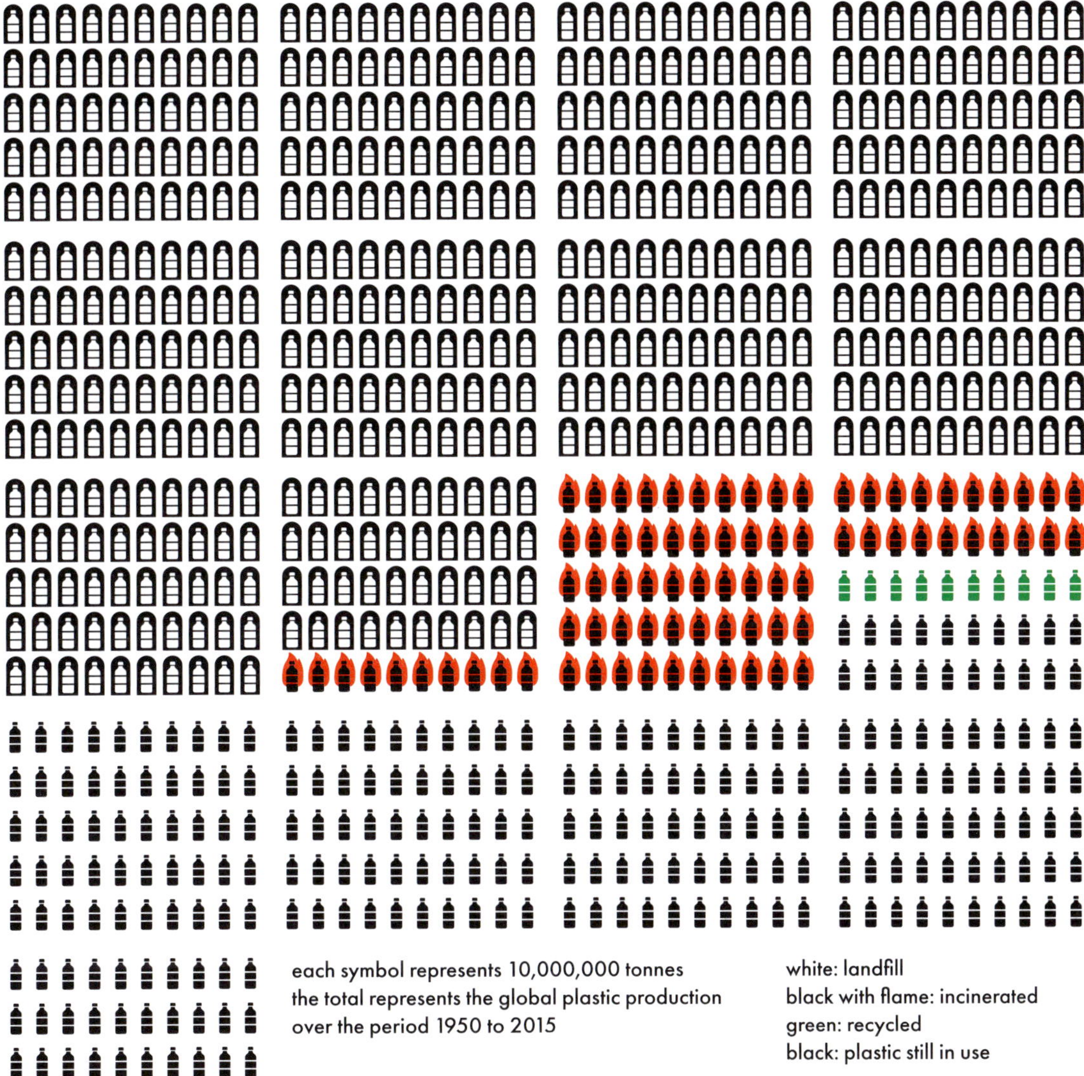

Only 1% of this plastic is still in use as a recycled product, which can only be done a maximum of three times.[10] Then plastic loses all of its virtues and it, too, is ripe for the incinerator or the landfill. Unlike plastic, glass and metal can be recycled infinitely without losing quality or purity in the product.

Since the 1960s, the "material world" has been heading in the wrong direction at high speed. Biodegradable and perfectly recyclable materials are replaced with harmful, toxic, and non-degradable synthetics. Research on ocean floor sediments has found that the number of microscopic plastic particles has doubled about every 15 years since the 1940s.[11]

After car tires, through their abrasion, synthetic clothing is the largest contributor to microplastics in our waters. For an average wash load of 6 kg, over 700,000 fibers can be released per wash.[12] Plastics and especially microplastics are so embedded in a person's life cycle that it is believed that one consumes at least 50,000 microplastic particles a year through food and water.[13] The health impact is unknown, but microplastics can lead to metabolic disturbances, neurotoxicity, and an increased risk of cancer. In 2022, microplastics were found in human blood for the first time; 80% of a study's blood samples contained microplastics from plastic bottles, polystyrene packaging, and plastic bags. Research must still be conducted on the interaction of micro- and nanoplastics with human cells.[14]

Plastic is so persistent and ubiquitous that even nature is adapting to it as a source of energy. In 2016 Japanese scientists discovered *Ideonella sakaiensis*, a bacterium that consumes polyethylene terephthalate (PET), a type of plastic.[15] This discovery was made while collecting samples of PET-contaminated sediment near a plastic bottle recycling facility.

Apparel to Waste in the USA

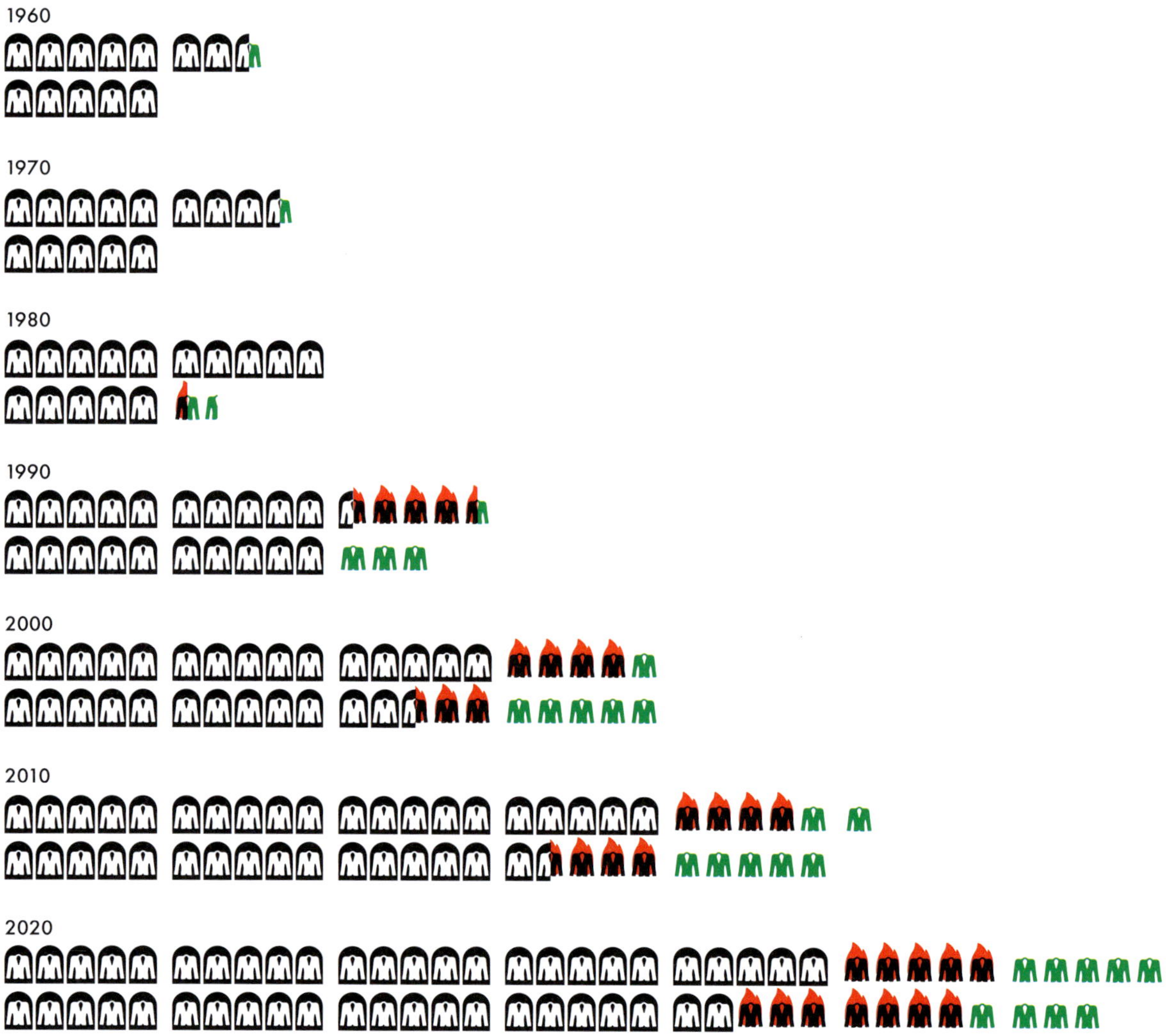

1960

1970

1980

1990

2000

2010

2020

one shirt symbol represents 1 piece of apparel per person for the specific year ending up as municipal solid waste
white: disposed of in landfill
black with flame: disposed of by incineration
green: recycled

Wrapped in Plastic

Of all solid materials, plastic packaging is the world's most devastating environmental catastrophe, adding up to almost 50%, or 140 million tons (2015), of global waste.[16] An insane waste of resources, considering that the average duration of use is a mere six months, but very often the package spends only a few minutes in the hands of consumers.

The invention of plastic packaging and the supermarket are closely interlinked. The fact that people help themselves to their groceries makes it necessary to protect the goods from possible germs and dirt. Humans of today are absolutely used to the idea that every product comes with packaging. They are used to material whose sole destiny is to be thrown away.

This so-called throwaway society discards not only the wrapping, but also the products themselves. Clothing, for example, contributes 14%, or 42 million tons (2015),[17] to the global garbage pile, making it the second-largest polluter after packaging. As mentioned above, 65% of the world's textiles are made from fossil-based synthetic fibers – thus are plastic. In the UK, the total amount of clothing in active use has an estimated volume of 3.6 million tons (2016), while 1.1 million tons of clothing were purchased in the same year. This means that the entire British clothing stock is replaced every three years, twice as fast as it would need to be, since most of the apparel can be worn for 6–7 years.[18]

It is estimated that about 107 billion units of apparel and 14.5 billion pairs of shoes were purchased around the globe in 2016.[19] On average, every person in the US buys 68 units of apparel per year[20] and simultaneously throws away almost the same number of garments. Only 9 of the 68 pieces per person get recycled, while the rest end up in landfills (47 pieces) or are incinerated (12 pieces).[21]

The end of functioning is seldom the reason for a product's disposal. In the case of apparel, seasonal fashions, not the durability of the material, are what determine the span of usage. Seasonal colors and cuts make consumers long for new garments, thus on average items are worn seven times. "Fast fashion" was the latest and greatest hit of the '90s, with the arrival of brands like Zara, which had a mission to move its products from design to purchase in the space of 15 days. That's no small feat when the design is created in Spain and the clothes are manufactured in Turkey, then sold in New York City.

One of the major successes of modernity is eliminating scarcity in large parts of the world. The lure of modernity was its promise of abundance. One will not just have enough, but much more than enough. Wardrobes are full of clothes that are barely worn, cars can go 180 km/h while the maximum speed limit is 130 km/h, and supermarkets are filled with fresh food that goes to waste just to assure the customers that there is no shortage.

Convenience and Lifestyle

Convenience

Modernity holds the promise of convenience. To release humans from physical drudgery, machines have been designed, providing spare time. Machines are the modern servants that turn every human into a queen or king who spends their spare time musing on the joys of life.

These servants are nowhere better visible than in the form of household appliances. The washing machine inside the apartment replaces a long walk to the communal washing house or even the river. While a washing machine is a standard household item in the West, only 20% of the households in India have one of their own, and considering that a third of India's washing machine owners live in India's six major urban areas, one can posit that the majority of India's rural population still wash their clothes by hand.[1]

Striving for convenience in the battle for modernity is best explained by the "Kitchen Debate" between US President Nixon and his Russian colleague Khrushchev at the 1959 American National Exhibition in Moscow. Standing in front of a built-in washing machine, Nixon pointed out the device and explained, "What we want to do is to make life more easy for our housewives." Khrushchev assured him that Russian houses are equipped with these devices as well and went on to explain that Russia's economy would soon overtake that of the US and would wave bye-bye as it did so.[2]

Devices and Connections per Person

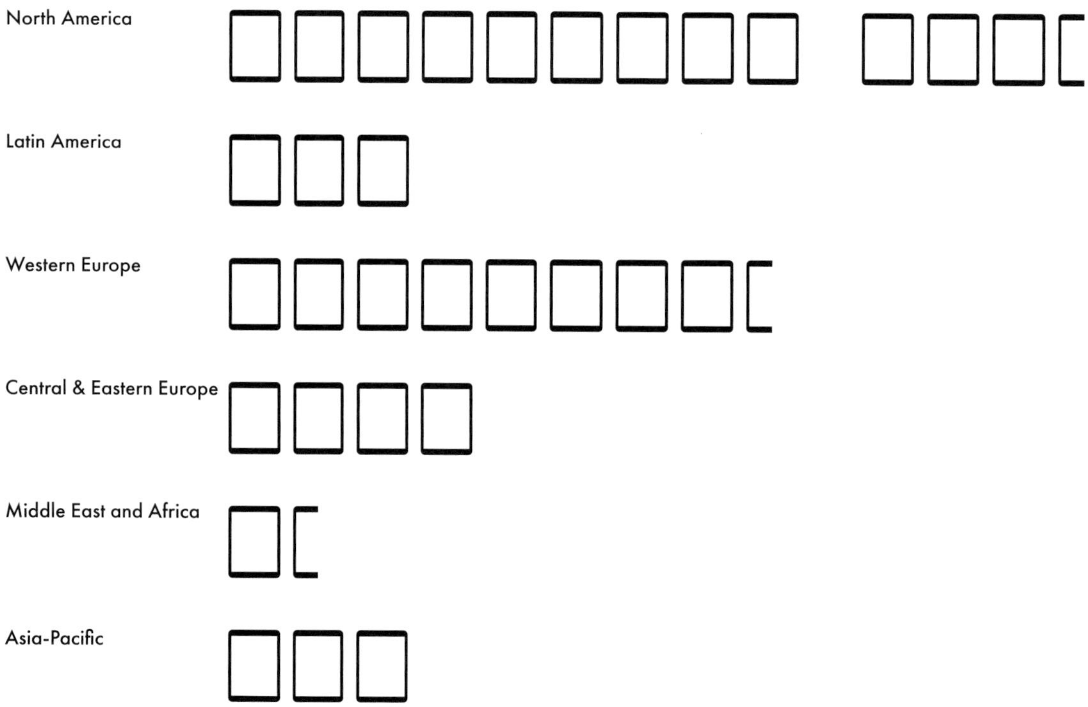

North America

Latin America

Western Europe

Central & Eastern Europe

Middle East and Africa

Asia-Pacific

each symbol represents one device per person (2023)
(devices = tablets, PCs, TVs, non-smartphones, smartphones, machine-to-machine devices, and others)

Otto Neurath[3] was right in the assumption that the number of robots is growing faster than Earth's population. Today humans are surrounded by such a number of appliances and machines that their existence is barely noticed anymore. Alongside old-school mechanical devices, electronic tools equipped with artificial intelligence have recently been introduced. Computers, smartphones, sensors, and detectors are just the very beginning of a new wave of robotization, an era in which robots replace not only human muscle power but also human brain power.

Once again, the already established and wealthy nations are those which are populated by an already pampered society which is, regardless of income levels, well-served with (for them) relatively inexpensive household appliances.

To someone with a net monthly salary of € 1,750 (the minimum wage in Germany), a refrigerator for € 250 seems affordable. In the case of Chad, where the price of a washing machine equals the *annual* minimum wage, this looks very different.[4] Yet it's not only the price that hinders Chadians in buying a washing machine; it is also the missing plumbing and the nonexistent or unstable electricity supply.

The large differences in the distribution of "modern devices" that Neurath observed within the income groups of the US city of Columbia, South Carolina does not present itself today as much within the Western societies as it does instead on a global level. It is again the Global South that is heavily underserved. This often concerns not just a group within a society, but an entire country and with it an entire region, which is caught in a very different definition of modern living. Without the "push-button conveniences,"[5] there is no spare time, no leisure, and much less convenience, and thus a very different way of living.

Silhouettes of Amenities

United States

Germany

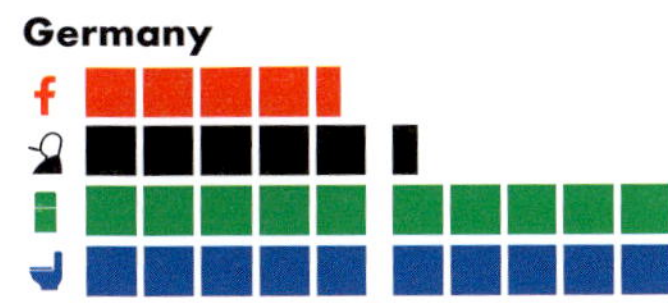

China

Iran

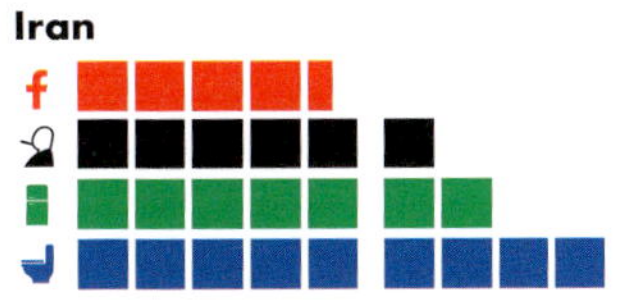

Brazil

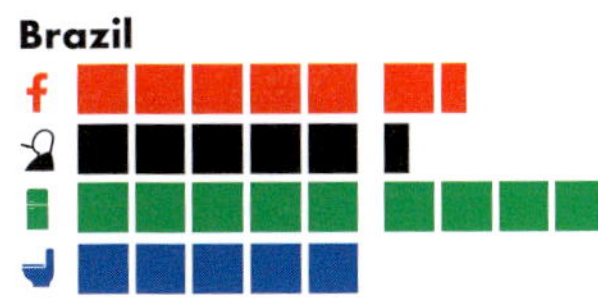

India

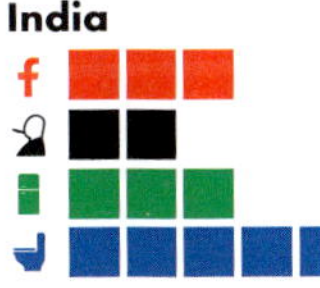

Chad

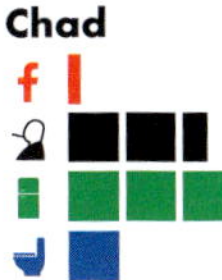

each square represents 10% of the population

- Facebook (China = WeChat) users (2023)
- adults who are overweight or obese (2016)
- refrigerator ownership (various years)
- people using safely managed sanitation services (various years)

Amenities in the USA

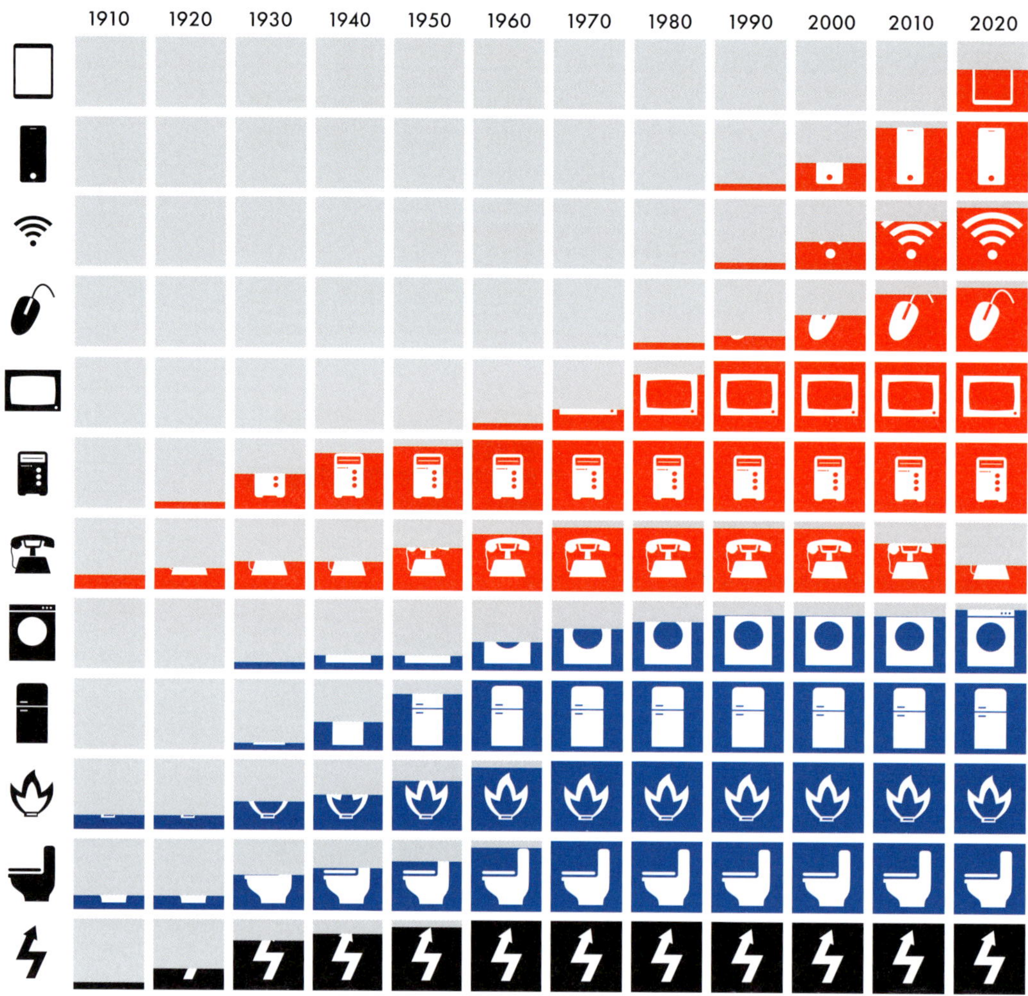

empty box = 0% ownership of item per household
entirely filled box = 100% ownership of item per household

While the people of Chad have been caught in a standstill for decades, the countries of the West are heading toward an ever more convenient way of living. Robots already take care of lawnmowing, window cleaning, and vacuum cleaning, and soon driving might be obsolete as well, due to self-driving cars and drone delivery. This is interesting only for countries like the USA with 800 cars per 1,000 people, much less so for the people of Chad, where only 6 out of 1,000 people own a car.[6]

It is safe to say that countries like Chad have not modernized (developed) much in the past 80 years. The West – the avant-garde – did not wait for the rest of the world to catch up, but started to revel in its front-runner position. This might eventually prove to be very short-sighted thinking. Humankind as a whole started to walk the road toward modernity. In order to not get lost, humanity ought to stick together during this walk; staying with the group and helping each other will offer the best chance of survival. It's simply wrong to make a race out of it; there is no finish line.

Maybe the West's version of modernity has taken a wrong turn while running ahead. Today the people of Chad appear much more contemporary in certain respects.

Radios, Telephones, and Automobiles in the 1930s

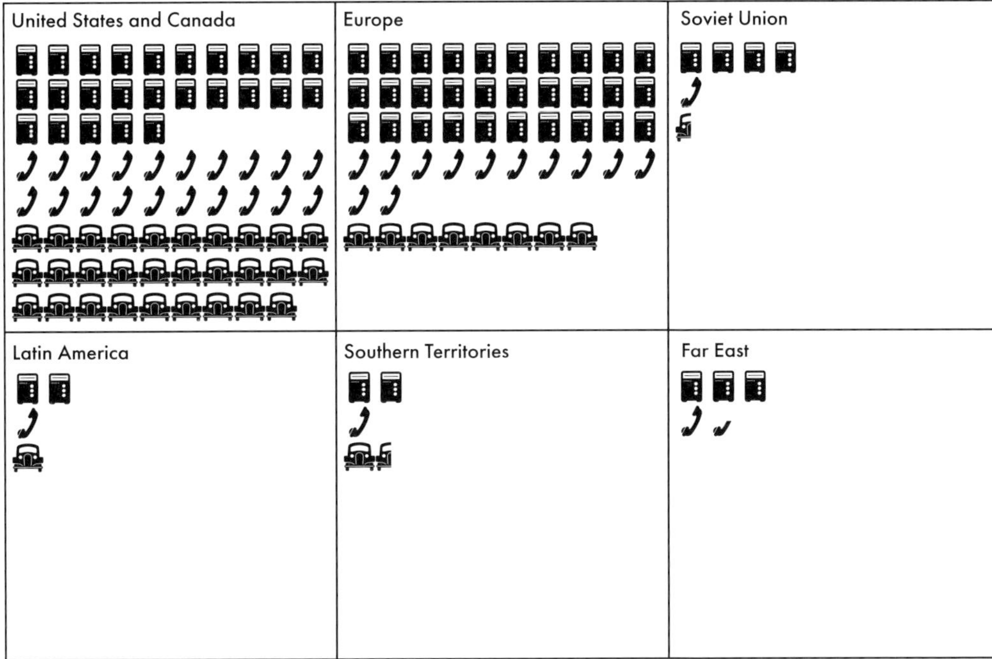

each symbol represents 1 million radios, telephones, or automobiles

Radios, Telephones, and Automobiles in the 2020s

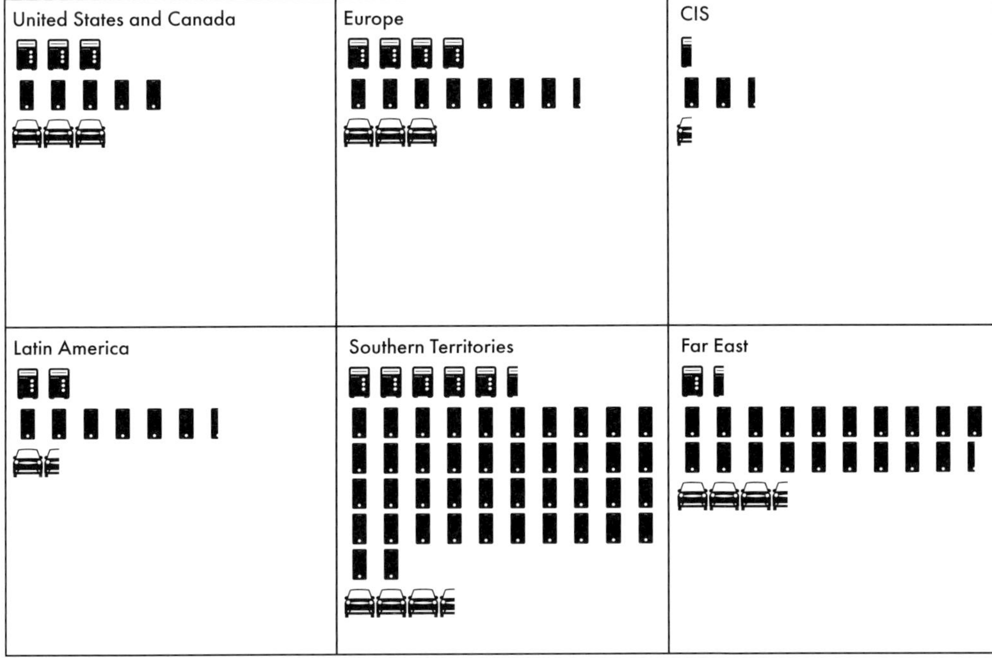

each symbol represents 100 million radios, telephones, or automobiles

Screens in Germany

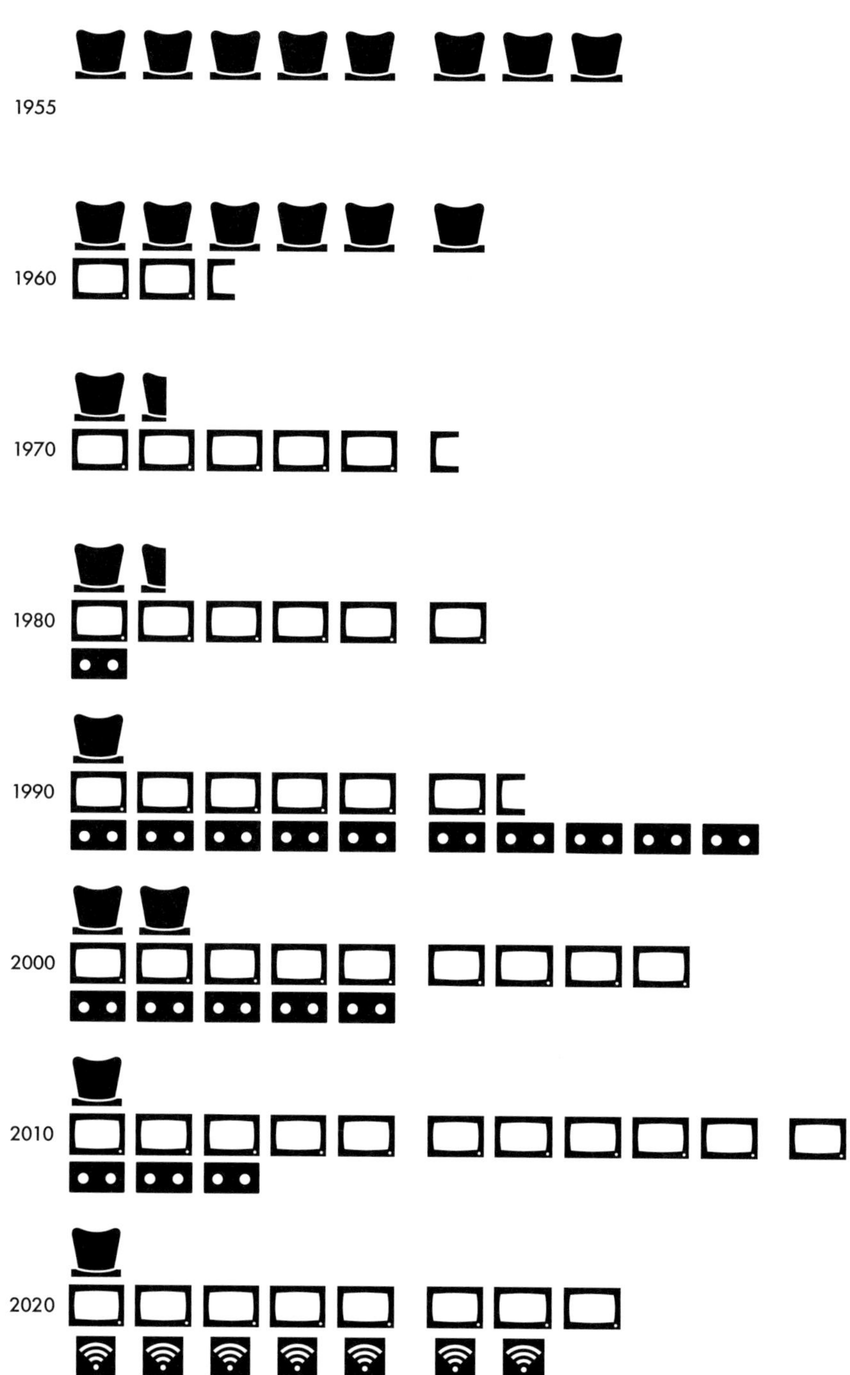

each chair symbol represents 100 million moviegoers
each TV symbol represents 20 minutes of TV per day
each tape symbol represents 1,000 video rental stores
each Wi-Fi symbol represents 1,000,000 Netflix subscriptions
(Data prior to 1990 only for West Germany)

The West should want to get the recipe for an entire society surviving on 6 cars per 1,000 people rather than 800 like the US. One might even state that if all people on Earth were to live like the Chadians, there would be no global warming, nor air pollution, and there would be enough food for everyone.

Unfortunately, this lifestyle "in sync with planet Earth" comes at a high price to the people themselves. The average life expectancy in Chad is one of the world's lowest, at 53 years. Similarly, only 22% of its population can read.[7] Only 2% of the rural households in Chad have running water, and only 8% have electricity.[8] Chad's electricity grid, which suffers from frequent outages, is limited to N'Djamena, the capital, home to about 1 million people.[9] This renders the purchase of household appliances beyond the capital a waste.

What little infrastructure, and thus convenience, there is in Chad is concentrated in the cities.

Urban Lifestyle I

Modern life is urban life. The cities are the places where architectures of modern amusement and culture such as concert halls, theaters, opera houses, and cinemas are concentrated. Throughout the past 80 years, these architectures have faced strong competition from radio and TV, and have lost some seats, but are now standing stronger than ever. The radio and TV, in turn, have been receiving competition from the services provided by the Internet since the 1990s. Streaming platforms bring live and prerecorded events from all over the world into the living rooms of the well-connected. Concerts, theater plays, movies, lectures, political assemblies, and real-time natural events all can be delivered by a single device. Smartphones make it possible to enjoy all of this while being on the move. And again, cities seem not to suffer, but continue to gain inhabitants and interest.

The introduction of the TV almost killed the cinema. Admissions to German cinemas dropped from 800 million in 1955 to a mere 100 million in the 1980s, but have been stable ever since.[10] In music a similar trend is happening. Income from record sales is close to nothing for many musicians, but the concert business is thriving. The more entertainment the Internet swallows, the higher the value of live events seems to become. Disruptions like the COVID-19 pandemic give an extra push to the development of holograms, worlds of virtual reality, and metaverses that create scenes of virtual entertainment.

Yet it remains to be seen if these can compete with the real experiences of the senses. The longing for surprises and the annoyances of waiting or getting a bad seat, which people can then complain about afterward, is underestimated. In a virtual world there is little to complain about, since everyone gets a front seat, but in the real world, the laws of physics still hold, and it makes people happy to perceive them once in a while.

Urban Lifestyle II

Modern city planning formalized the segregation of space to protect citizens from noise and the toxic exhaust of factories and mines. Dividing the city into quarters for living, working, and leisure produced a society on the move. The everyday functions are frequented during a daily journey which resembles the very conveyor belt one was working on at the factory: leaving home in the morning, dropping the kids off at day care, working at the factory, shopping at the supermarket on the way home, and picking up the kids to finally arrive home – only to repeat the round trip on the days that follow.

Beans in Vienna

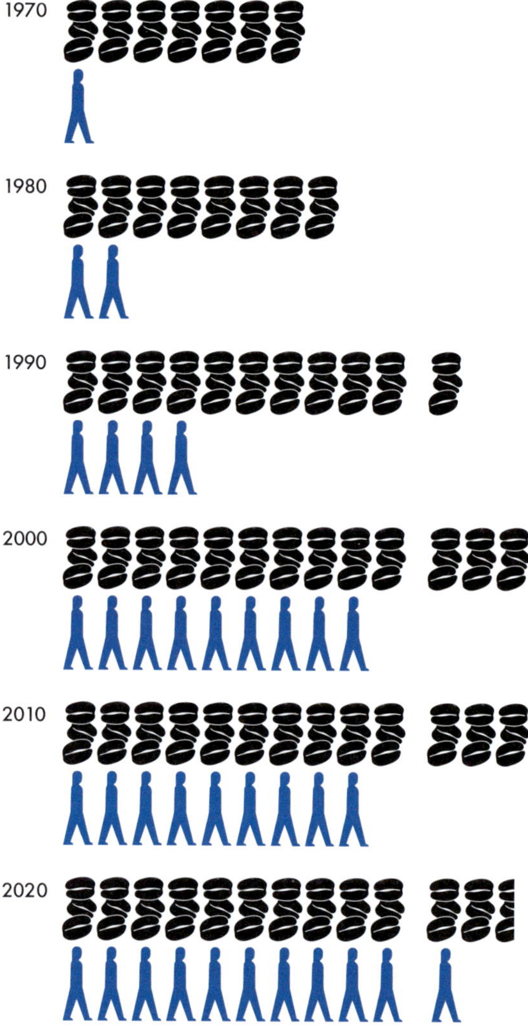

each bean symbol represents
200 coffeehouses

each human symbol represents
a 2,000-meter pedestrian zone

High car ownership increased individual mobility and the size of suburbs. A home with a garden was the middle-class equivalent of the aristocrat's palace. In the suburbs everyone could be a queen and king, with the car as their carriage (with ever more horsepower). Today, however, the suburbs are out of fashion. Long commutes in endless traffic jams are ruining the glamorous image of individual freedom.

Throughout the 1990s, cities were rediscovered as places to meet, places to shop, and especially places for having coffee. Sipping on a cappuccino, a coffee with milk foam on top, has become synonymous with the good life. Contrary to the mass mobilization by the automobile, which resulted in an urban sprawl of shopping malls outside historic city centers, the current verve in urban living is based not on a new mode of transport, but on "image." It seems to be the result of city marketing campaigns, which have

Coffee Imports to Europe

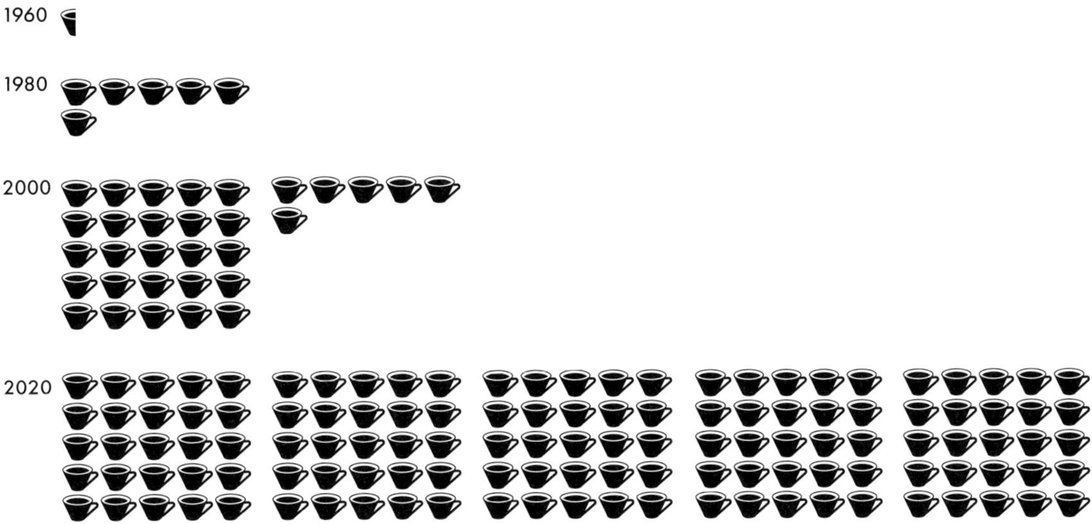

each symbol represents 1 cup of coffee imported to Europe per person

resulted in a cultural shift. To attract more tourists and investment, Western cities started to introduce city marketing by inventing catchy slogans, hosting movies (such as those featuring James Bond), and investing in placative architecture. The strategy worked, and more people than ever want to move to the cities in the West. Some cites have even been too successful. London, for example, has been struggling with ever-soaring rents throughout the past 20 years, which is driving less affluent renters ever further away from the city center.

Distribution of the Urban Population in London

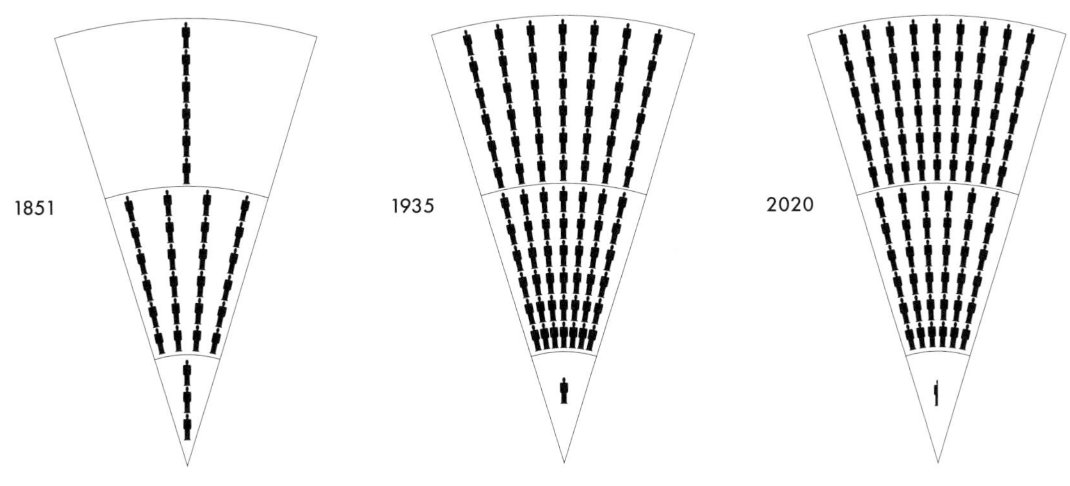

innermost circle: City, Finsbury, Holborn
second circle: County of London
outer circle: Greater London

each symbol represents 100,000 people

Family

Modern Family

Neurath described the only child as an urgent modern social problem. He shared the thought of his time that a child needs "not only playmates but also close relatives" for its social development.[1] To compensate for the missing siblings, he highlights the importance of the kindergarten in children's social and mental health. Aside from the social benefits for the kids, kindergartens allow parents to pursue a profession while the kids are taken care of. With the advance of the welfare state after World War II in many countries around the world, the kindergarten and school system allowed women to work and contribute to the wealth of a nation. The last point might deliver the reason that even in the USA, a country that is averse to any socialist ideas, the network of kindergartens and schools is dense and attendance rates are high. Today in the EU, 93% of all kids between age 3 and the age of compulsory education attend formal early childhood education programs (kindergarten).[2]

Another step toward the equality of women and men came with the introduction and proliferation of household appliances. Vacuum cleaners, dishwashers, and washing machines diminished the time needed for household tasks, so that women could pursue a regular job. In addition, these devices do not require special skills, so they can be used equally by both sexes. Step by step, appliances, workspaces, and social lives have been designed to become ever more "gender-neutral" (a term that has gained significant attention in academic and social discourse only in the past 50 years) –

Gender Pay Gap in Europe

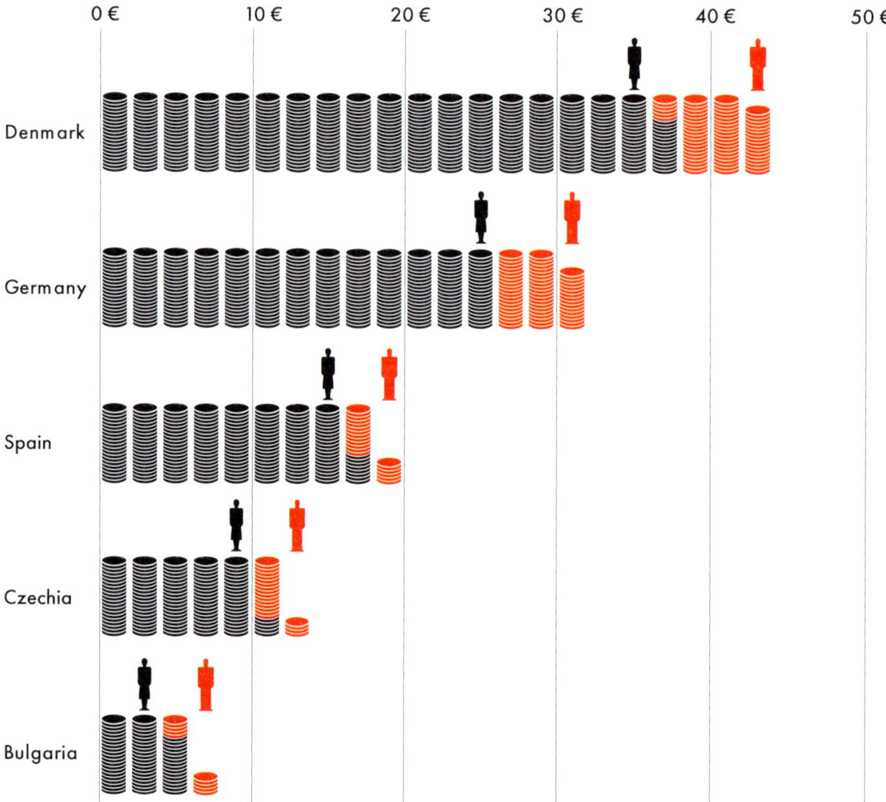

each stack of coins represents € 2 of wages and salaries per hour (2021)
black: female salary
red: male salary exceeding female salary = gender pay gap

on the one hand, because the sexes' way of spending their spare time and the nature of work have become more similar, and on the other hand, because women have demanded and fought for equality. Men might not be able to bear children, but this does not make them unfit to change diapers. And just as men can be better at changing diapers, women can be better at running companies. Yet the sheer numbers disagree. Of the Fortune 500 companies, a list of the world's 500 largest companies published by *Fortune* magazine, only 38 are run by a woman.[3] Just as leading positions are difficult to achieve, so is equal payment. The gross hourly earnings of women in the EU are still 14% below those of men – for doing exactly the same job![4]

While they still have a lot of work to do themselves, the countries of the West are promoting women's rights and democracy in other parts of the globe. It is true that progress has been made. Today universal suffrage for women has been introduced all around the globe except in Saudi Arabia, Brunei, and the United Arab Emirates. But large discrepancies still exist. Polygyny, the marriage of a man to several women, is legal in many countries, while female rights in education, inheritance, and property ownership are limited. Add to this a routinely disrespectful attitude toward women, and the image of a very asymmetric global society appears that is still dominated by men.

The joyful "veils are vanishing" trend in the Muslim world of which Otto Neurath spoke in the 1930s continued up to the 1970s, but came to a halt soon after that.[5] Sometime in the 1980s, the promise of modernity for Muslim and Arab society disappeared. Today, radical patriarchal systems based on religious justifications are back in force. The expanding gap between Western "modernity" and other societies is volitional and is used as a political tool. Radical patriarchal movements like the Taliban of Afghanistan refer to the West as degenerate and immoral. The Taliban enforce their strict interpretation of Sharia law, which limits women's access to education, labor, and travel drastically. According to Taliban law, women and girls are banned from secondary and higher education, and female labor is limited to education and healthcare.

Marital Rape

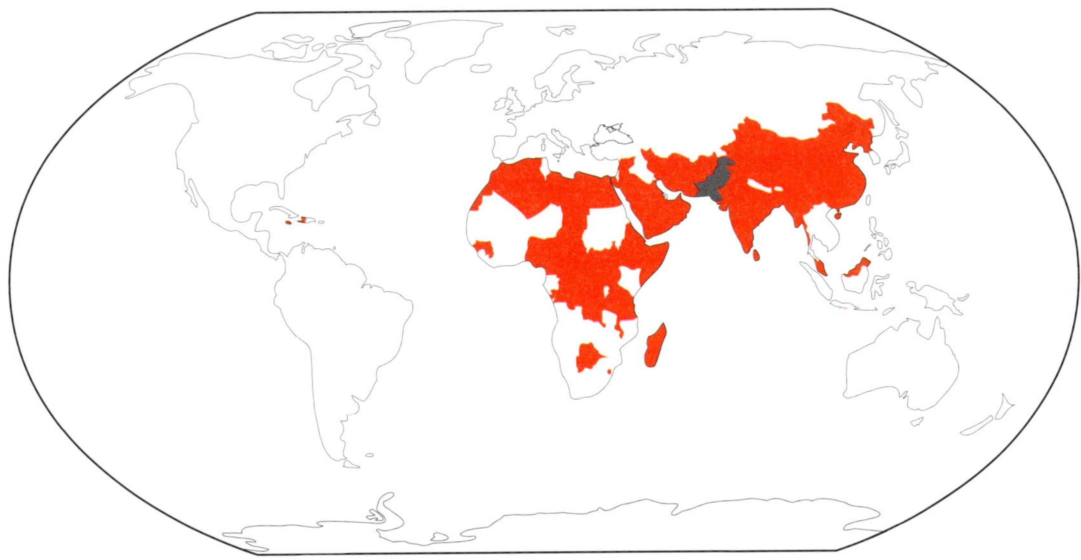

red: countries in which marital rape is not criminalized
gray: status unclear (2021)

Legal inequality against women is widespread. Among the 193 member states of the United Nations, 54 do not consider the rape of a woman by her husband as a crime.[6] Some countries like India, Syria, and Tanzania even explicitly exclude marital rape as, for example, in the case of Tanzania on the grounds that "husbands, by virtue of paying a bride price, have the legal right to have unlimited sexual access to their wives."[7]

Modernity is often misunderstood as a technological and economic project, while it is primarily a social project that depends heavily on the re-engineering of existing social structures. Family ties need to be weakened in order to increase the ties with the nation-state and its institutions. Kindergarten, school, work, and senior care centers are the contemporary markers of modern human beings. The more modern a society, the more present these institutions are.

The most severe opposition to modern life comes from religious fundamentalists. Embedded in a modernized society like the Quakers or the Amish in the USA, these groups remain local minorities which thrive on the modern waves around them. The Taliban in Afghanistan, on the other hand, dominate an entire country and therefore dictate how the entire society must perform.

Since female emancipation from the home and family is the very basis of social modernization, it is exactly female emancipation which is targeted by religious fundamentalists like the Taliban. Getting a grip on women means getting a grip on modernity. Modernity's opposition groups want women to fulfill tasks that the modern nation-state and modern appliances would otherwise take care of: childcare, senior care, cooking, cleaning, and socializing (entertaining). These groups call modernized societies cold and antisocial. Kids and old people disappear into institutions, women have to work dull jobs instead of being with their family, and men are vacuuming and diaper-changing wimps. In short, this view states that Western countries (= modern societies) are inhabited by a rotten society. Euthanasia, LGBTQ+ people and abortion

Abortion

black: countries in which abortion is allowed and allowed with restrictions (2021)

Euthanasia

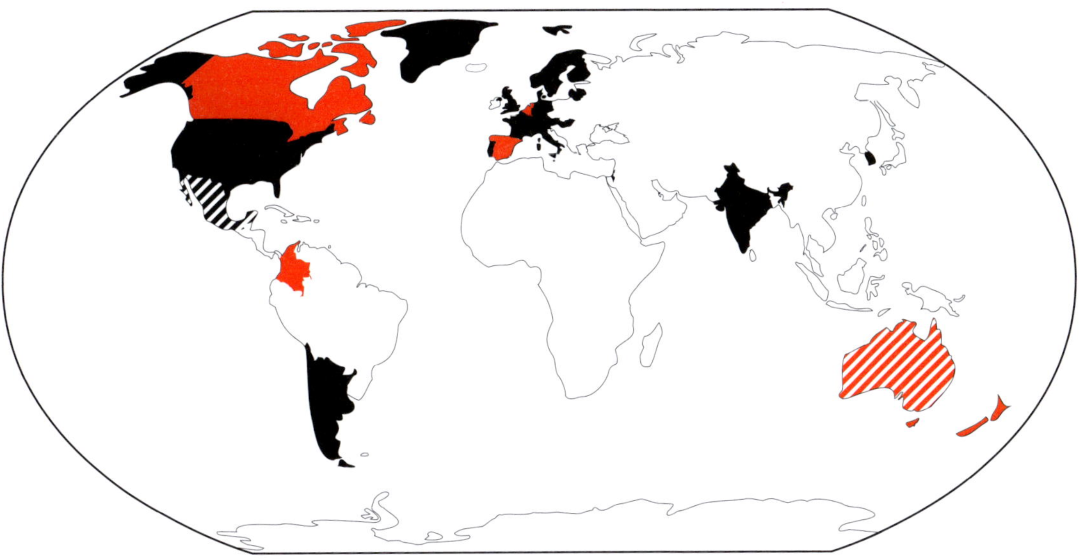

black: countries in which physician-assisted suicide or passive euthanasia is legal
red: countries in which active euthanasia is legal
hatch: not applicable to the whole country (2022)

laws add further proof to this postulation. To oppose groups like the Taliban, answers need to be given to the following questions: How can societies that see human rights as their cornerstone kill unborn children and allow the killing of their seniors? What definition of humanity is that?

Let's try to answer this. Euthanasia, LGBTQ+ people, and abortion exist all over the world. In free and democratic countries, it is possible to talk about them and protect the vulnerable. Abortions also happen in countries where they are forbidden by law, with the difference that there they cause more maternal fatalities due to unprofessional treatment. It is estimated that in Pakistan, where abortion is forbidden, 10 times as many abortions are performed each year as in Switzerland; 50 in 1,000 women in Pakistan compared to 5 in 1,000 in the case of Switzerland.[8] The big difference can be explained partially by the lack of contraception methods and by the non-criminalization of marital rape as mentioned above.

The answer regarding euthanasia is trickier. Modern healthcare allows people to extend their lives beyond their will to live – beyond their consciousness even. Hospital treatment has reached such a level that humans can be kept alive with the help of pumps, respirators, and automatic feeding for an indefinite amount of time. Euthanasia is to a certain extent about determining the legal right or framework to switch off this machine. Alongside several other rules, depending on the country, patients need to be seriously or terminally ill and a death certificate must be issued and filed personally by a notary.

It was the USSR that legalized abortion in 1920 as the first modern state to do so.[9] In 1994, it was the Netherlands that became the first country to legalize euthanasia.[10] A moral dilemma will always remain. The question about the direction and the value of modernity reaches its climax when I must deal with death.

Maternal Mortality

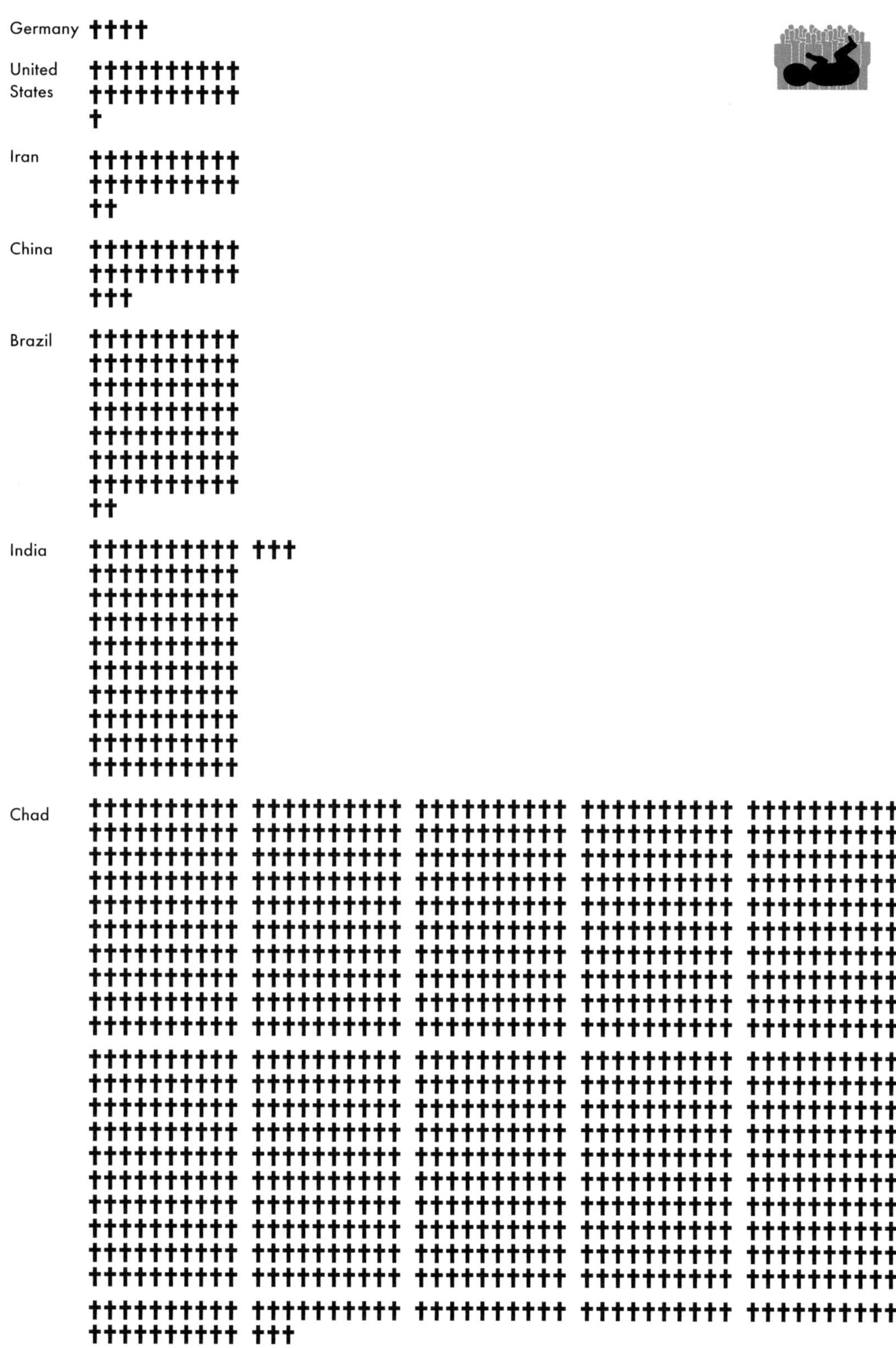

Each symbol represents one death of a mother per 100,000 live births during pregnancy or within 42 days of pregnancy (2020)

Children

Earth has become a much safer and healthier place for children over the past 100 years. Child labor is restricted, alcohol and cigarette consumption are forbidden until a certain age, and primary-school education is mandatory in many countries around the globe. While in 1900 on a global scale about 40% of all kids died before their fifth birthday, today this number has dropped to 4%. In the same period, the number of kids per woman has dropped from 5.5 to 2.5.[11, 12]

Modern parents don't need children to support them in their old age; for this they have a pension scheme. Yet looking at countries like Chad, the number of births per woman is still 6.3, and kids as well as mothers are at risk of premature death. On average one-fifth of all women in Chad die during childbirth. This should come to no surprise, considering that only 17% of births[13] are attended by skilled health personnel.

As difficult it might be to survive birth in Chad, when reaching the age of six, Chadian kids enjoy compulsory public education till the age of 12, as is practiced by most countries.[14] But following class in Chad is a challenge when 57 kids face one teacher on average. Thus it is no wonder that only 20% of children who finish their primary-school studies have a good foundation in reading and math in the two classroom languages, French and Arabic.[15]

The people of the Global North enjoy decent social equality, no matter their level of income. Birth control is largely accepted; thus having children is often a rational choice after evaluating a series of parameters.[16] Higher income is associated with a decrease in childbirths. Young couples make a rational decision at what point they "can afford" to have children – financially and psychologically – and settle around 2 kids per family. On the contrary, people in Chad usually choose to have children precisely so that they can survive financially as a family. Consequently, in 2004, about 50% of children between the ages of 4 and 15 are working full-time and contributing a large share to the family income.[17]

Pupils per Teacher

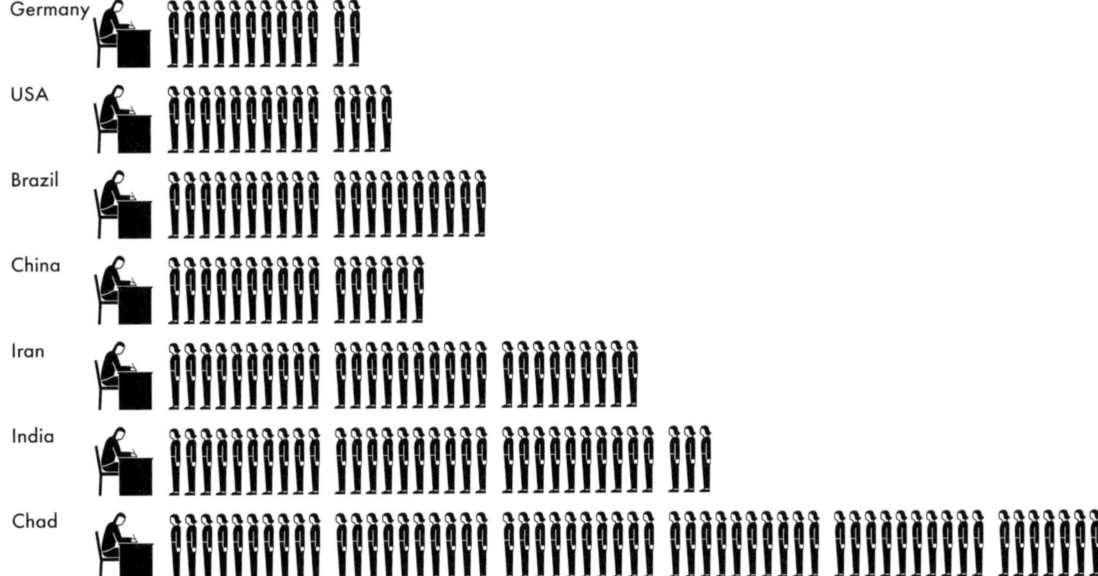

Age Groups in England and Wales

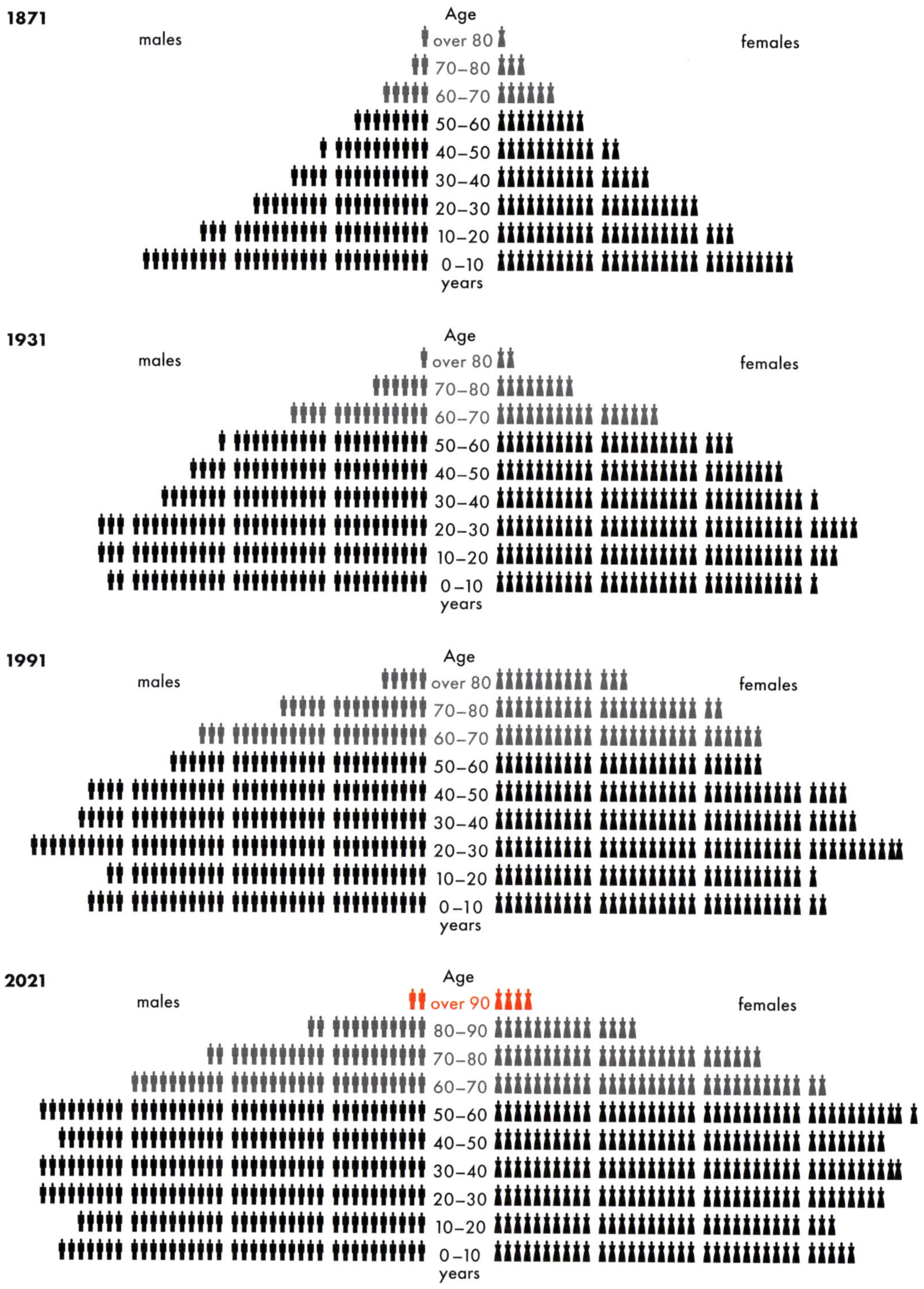

1871

males | Age | females
over 80
70–80
60–70
50–60
40–50
30–40
20–30
10–20
0–10
years

1931

males | Age | females
over 80
70–80
60–70
50–60
40–50
30–40
20–30
10–20
0–10
years

1991

males | Age | females
over 80
70–80
60–70
50–60
40–50
30–40
20–30
10–20
0–10
years

2021

males | Age | females
over 90
80–90
70–80
60–70
50–60
40–50
30–40
20–30
10–20
0–10
years

each symbol represents 100,000 people

Growing Old

The lower death and birth rates that Neurath mentioned[18] persisted and reshaped the population pyramid. In his time, the pyramid had already developed into what he described as a crown, which has further morphed into the beehive shape of today. These structural changes are caused by a continuing decline in the birth rate as well as increasing life expectancy.

The increasing life expectancy coinciding with a stagnating number of people of working age makes countries worry about the viability of the pension system. Today, there are twice as many people in England and Wales who are over 90 years old as there were 80+ in the 1930s.[19] People in the West are living longer and staying healthy for a longer time, and as a reaction, the retirement age for women and men is rising all over the Western world. To compensate for stagnating population growth, economists and the governments welcome migration.

This seems to be the worst incentive to stimulate migration or help refugees to a new home. Exemplary is a 2022 speech by US president Joe Biden in which he suggests making it easier to acquire migrant workers for businesses and reuniting families, saying, "It's not only the right thing to do; it's the economically smart thing to do."[20] This reduces people to a factor in a socioeconomic calculation, a multiplier in a spreadsheet, which might be a very efficient way to acquire a cheap workforce but has nothing to do with respect for humanity and/or with long-term thinking.

Years of Retirement

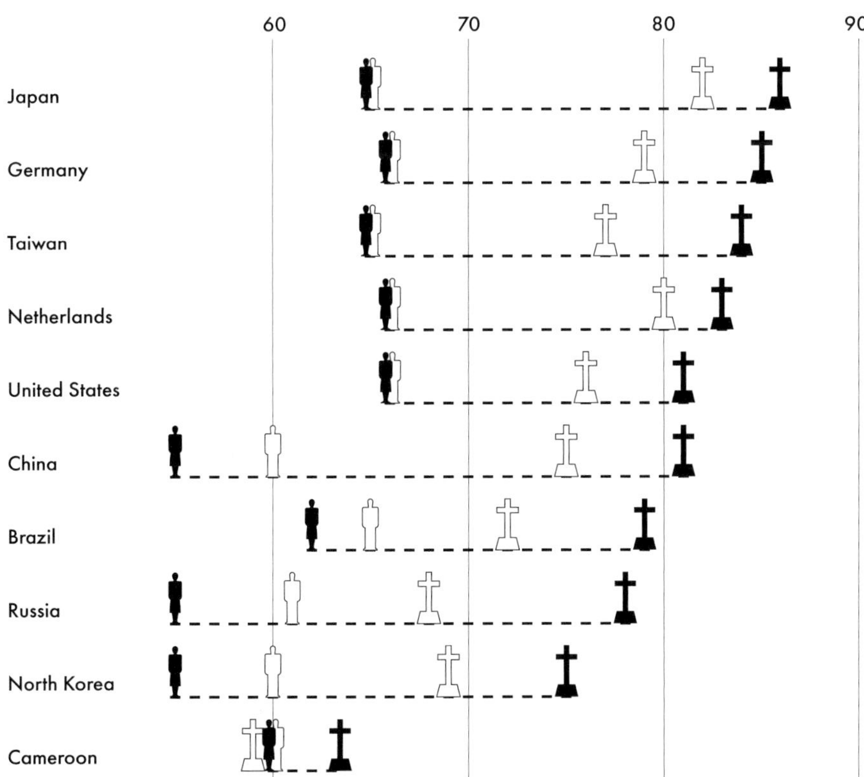

person symbol: female (black filled) and male (black outlined) retirement age
gravestone: average life expectancy
(various years throughout the 2010s)

Silhouettes of Social Progress

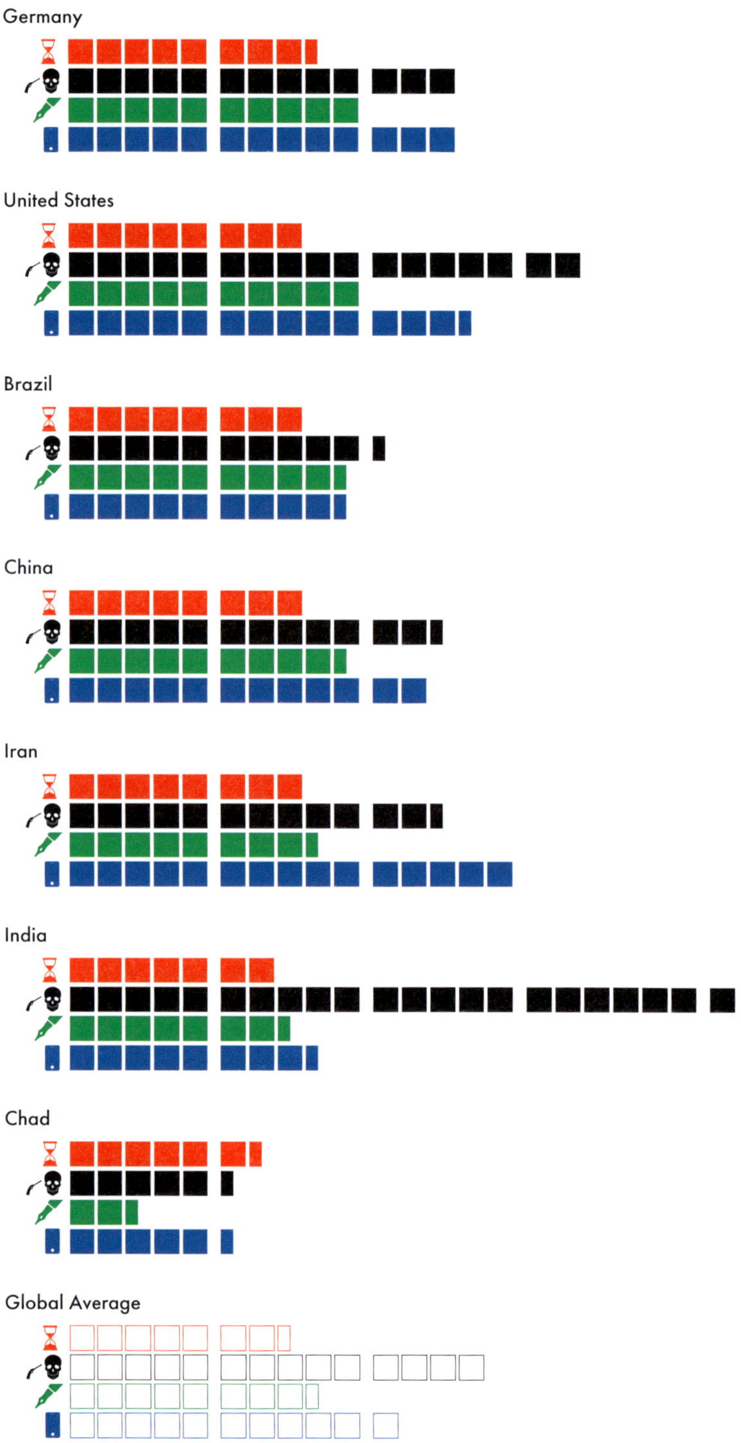

Germany

United States

Brazil

China

Iran

India

Chad

Global Average

average length of life of female population: each unit equals 10 years (2020)
suicides: each unit represents 1 per 1,000 population (various years)
literacy: each unit represents 10% (various years)
mobile phone subscription: each unit represents 1 per 10 population (2017)

Overall, a lot of progress has been made. Today the average life expectancy of the global female population is 75 years, and the overall literacy rate is 83%.[21] The rich countries' life expectancy is plateauing at a very high level, and literacy rates have been at 100% for decades. Looking at the scale of individual regions and countries, it becomes clear that humankind still has a long way to go toward achieving social equality. Especially in Africa, the numbers are much different, although incremental progress is being made there as well. The life expectancy of women in Cameroon has risen from 42 years in the 1960s to 63 years in 2020.[22]

But growing old in Cameroon is no fun. Earning the minimum wage of € 55 per month in Cameroon entitles a person to a minimum pension of € 25 per month.[23] The thought that "maybe this isn't so bad, since it's cheap to live in Africa" is unfortunately not true. Shopping for a kilo of rice (€ 1), a liter of milk (€ 2), a kilo of bread (€ 1), a kilo of chicken filet (€ 5) and a kilo of tomatoes (€ 1) costs € 10[24] in total for the most essential food. Without extra income and the support of one's family, there is no way to get by while relying solely on a pension. Yet the fact that 90% of the working population is part of the informal economy[25] and the retirement is set to the age of 60, while the average life expectancy is 59 for men and 63 for women,[26] lets us assume that very few people in Cameroon can enjoy a pension at all.

If the countries of the globe could learn to act together, it would be possible to create more equal living conditions and pursue overall social progress around the globe – what is sorely needed is a "social globalization." The affluent West especially could do more for the Global South than selling cheap food and goods like mobile phones. Mobile communication technology creates the illusion of a modern lifestyle, but without decent education, healthcare, and infrastructure, it will remain just a digital window into a seemingly better world.

Good and free education for both sexes, reliable healthcare in close proximity, and safe public infrastructure are the key components to save millions of lives and lengthen life spans around the globe. At the moment, there is no technology other than academic medicine, a healthy diet, and a healthy physical condition, to prolong human life.

Leisure

Free Time

Modernity introduced a new concept of time: the regime of the clock. The clock allowed time to be measured accurately, which resulted in management and consequently enabled the workforce to be synchronized.

The mechanical weaving loom – the harbinger of industrialization – enabled mainly women to work from home, while watching the kids and caring for the household. At this time, workers were paid for the piece they produced, no matter how long it took. And payment was made frequently in form of material, food, or accommodation. The term "working hours" was unheard of.

This changed radically during the 18th century. The planet's first factory was the silk-throwing mill by Thomas Lombe in Derby, England, built in the 1720s.[1] At the same time, in Barrow upon Humber some 100 km to the north, John Harrison[2] was working on his maritime clock – a clock so robust and precise that it could be taken on board ships to eventually sail the oceans and help to colonize the world for the British crown. In the long run, Harrison's invention allowed workers to take the clock with them in their pockets or on their wrists. The modern workplace – the factory – and the modern working hours – the clock – were developed hand in hand, and together they created the rhythm of modern life.

Throughout the 19th century, hourly wages were introduced in all sectors of work, and by the mid-20th century they had been introduced in almost all countries around the world. New Zealand introduced a legal minimum hourly wage in 1894; Australia and the rest of the world followed in the 20th century.[3]

Free time, or leisure, was a luxury no longer reserved for the upper class! With the advent of hourly pay, it was in the interest of the employee, and the employer, to reduce the hours of production, and to give people the ability to spend their hours on consumption instead. Today it is hard to imagine that for thousands of years a daily rate or sometimes even a yearly salary had been issued. "Time is money" became the modern workers' battle cry.

By defining a specific number of hours as "working time," the remaining time was consequently "leisure." After-work hours, the weekend, and holidays were formalized,

Industrial Robots

each symbol represents 200,000 operational industrial robots
red: industrial robots in Asia and Australia
black: industrial robots in Europe and the Americas

and with this, days, weeks, years, and the lives of the working population were systematically divided up. Today, humans are used to planning their lives along these lines – the modern rhythm of the masses.

Every working day, the phenomenon of the rush hour takes place as everyone goes to work and then travels back home in time for their favorite TV shows and live streaming platforms, with peak viewing between 7 and 10 pm. Shopping centers are packed on Saturday afternoons and beaches are full on sunny summer days. Free time turned into a large chunk of the Western world's economy.

Henry Ford's economic maxim that every worker should earn enough to buy a car that his workers built in one of his factories can be applied to today's time management. Every saleswoman or man should have enough free time to spend the money on the goods and services as was earned by selling goods and services. Without free time for consumption and an incentive to buy things, the contemporary economy would collapse. Thus, people need to be provided with time and desire. Since time is finite, the economy can only grow by constantly creating new desires. The World Wide Web opened a totally new (shopping) window, generating unknown desires for spending free time. Applications do everything at the tip of the finger. Spending time on the Web has become a major free-time activity around the globe. For example, in Nigeria and the Philippines, people spend an average of 4 hours per day on social media platforms – leading the worldwide ranking of screen-time.[4]

The initial promise at the very beginning of industrialization that the machine would do all the work so that humans could sit back and relax has not been fulfilled – although there does seem to be a clear link between working hours and the level of automation. Highly industrialized Germany slashed the average annual working hours almost in half, from 2,427 h in 1870 to 1,354 h in 2017.[5] Excluding Saturdays and Sundays,

Work, Leisure, and Sleep

19th Century

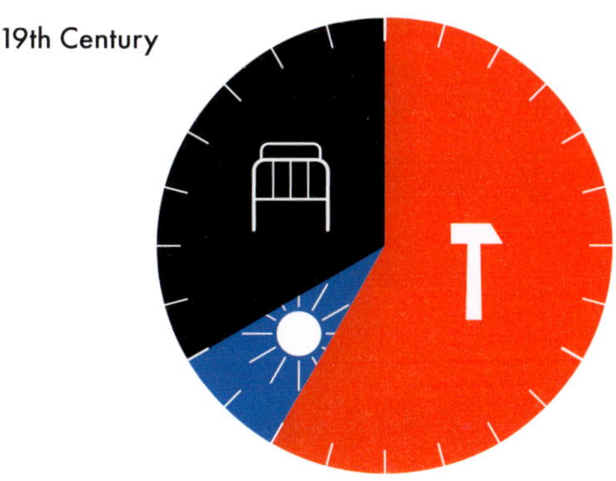

20th Century

Now

Subdivision of the 24 hours of a day

red: work
blue: leisure
black: sleep
with monitor: average screen time

Working Hours Versus Productivity

Germany

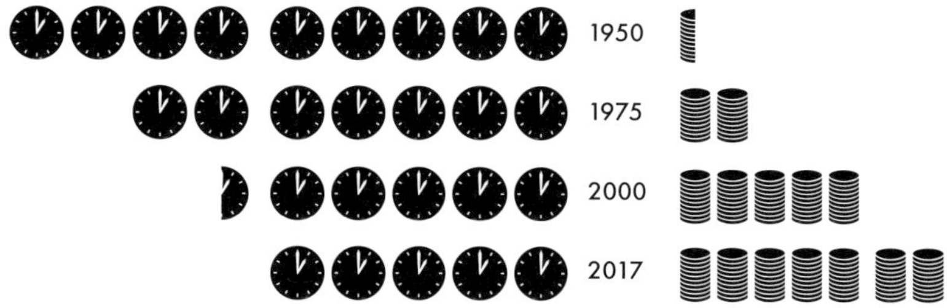

Brazil

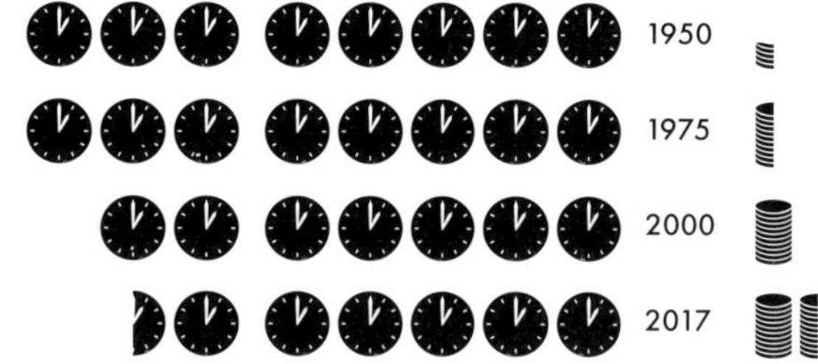

each clock symbol represents one hour worked per day
each stack of coins represents 10 €/h generated – measured as gross domestic product (GDP) per hour of work

this means a reduction from 9.0 to 5.0 working hours per day. Brazil, which started from a very similar level of productivity as Germany in the 19th century, developed differently. Productivity increased only slightly, while working hours are still as high as they were in Germany in the 1980s.[6]

One striking difference between the two countries, which is directly linked to the above-mentioned promise that the machine will replace humans in the long run, is their difference in automation. While Brazil provides only 10 robots per 10,000 workers,[7] Germany has 346 and Singapore even has almost 1,000.[8] Although several factors influence automation, labor costs are the most important parameter. Brazil's minimum monthly wage (€ 200/month) is a fraction of Germany's (€ 1,750/month), thus replacing a German worker with an expensive, energy-consuming robot makes much more sense.[9] Once acquired, installed, and running, a robot gives a boost to productivity since it is rarely sick, does not want to fly to the Bahamas, or change its employer. Thus, despite fewer working hours, the value added per working hour in Germany has increased tremendously. The formula is not that simple, but is applicable if an economy is growing and energy is cheap: higher wages force automation and lead to more value being added per hour.

A highly efficient workforce generates the highest value in the shortest amount of time. Consequently, this workforce can leave earlier and has more time to spend money. This achievement is rewarded with more spare time; for German workers, the amount of vacation and holidays grew from 29 to 43 days per year between 1950 and 2000.[10] Brazilian workers are granted less spare time and once on vacation have less money to spend. Regardless of what people earn in their home country, the ice cream on St. Mark's Square in Venice costs € 3 for everyone.

Robots per Human

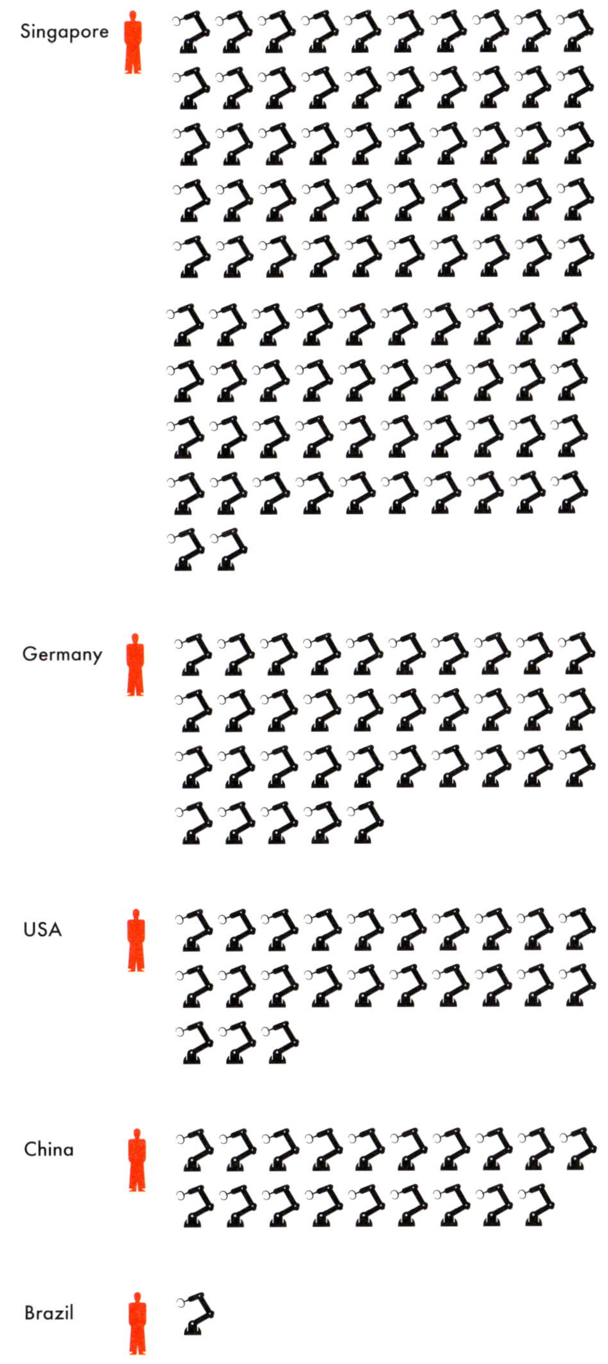

each symbol represents 10 operational industrial robots per 10,000 employees (2019)

International Tourism

In Western countries, birth, the very beginning of a modern human being's life, is already covered by health insurance. This is followed by kindergarten, school, maybe higher education, work, and retirement – with the clear focus on work as the modern human's main purpose in life. Most people in the modernized world live with this rhythm, the classic rhythm of modernity.

The climax of leisure time is vacation, usually some weeks filled with travel and relaxation. Around these cravings grew the tourism industry, the world's largest service

International Tourism

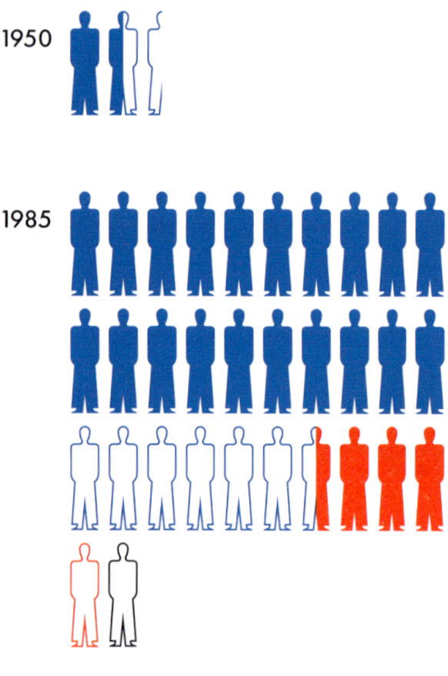

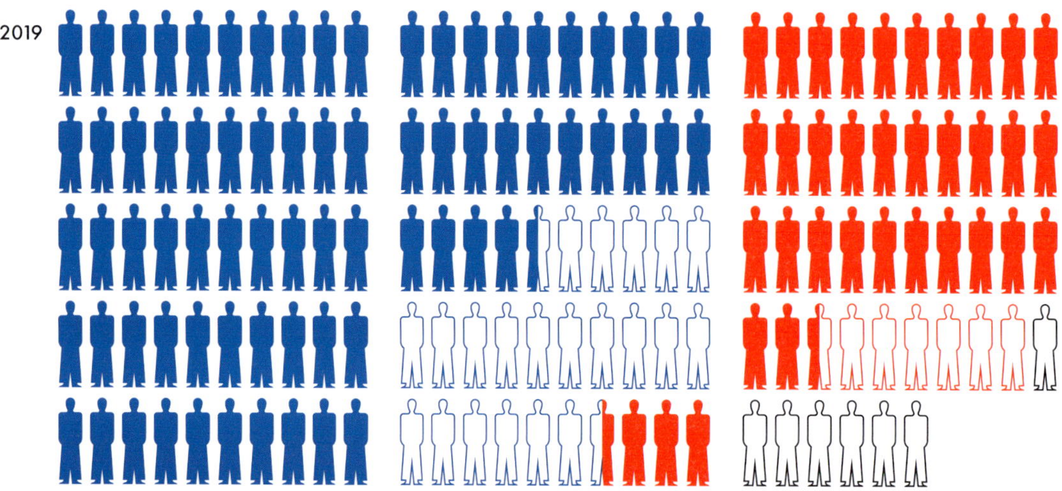

each symbol represents 10,000,000 tourists arriving in a given region (international tourist arrivals)
in 2022, international tourist arrivals were still 40% lower than in 2019 due to the impact of COVID-19 restrictions

blue filled: Europe
blue outlined: Americas
red filled: Asia & Pacific
red outlined: Middle East
black outlined: Africa

Global Aircraft Fleet

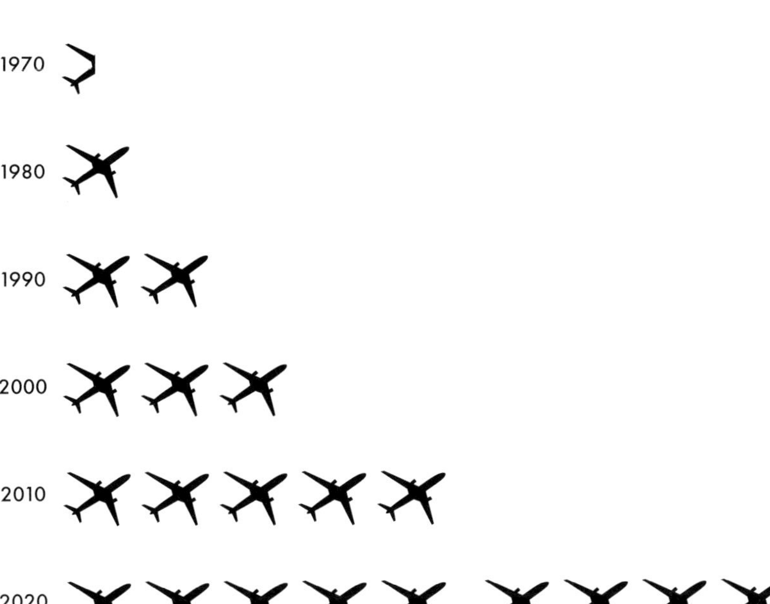

each symbol represents 500,000 aircraft

sector with 334 million people involved around the globe in 2019.[11] Humans show an enormous desire to spend time somewhere else; from day trips to a neighboring city to a vacation overseas. To be an international tourist, one needs time, money, and the right passport. Reluctance to allow visa-free travel to certain countries is directly linked to the fear of illegal immigration. The countries with the weakest passports are precisely the countries that score highest in international asylum-seeking. The 2.6 million Afghan refugees are equipped with Earth's least valuable passport, which allows them to enter only 35 countries without applying for a visa. None of these countries border Afghanistan. The situation is very similar for the 6.2 million Syrian refugees. Their passport opens the door to only 36 countries – again, none of which are neighbors. The most welcoming countries without any visa restrictions are either faraway islands in Oceania or are war-ridden themselves, like Somalia, Yemen, and South Sudan.[12] The tourist destinations in the West use their visa policy largely to filter the wealthy and desired tourists and businesswomen and -men from the poor migrant countries.

While work time is highly regulated, leisure time is left open for any activity. People are free to fill it in; most fill it with travel. In 2019, 1.46 billion people arrived at international vacation destinations.[13] About 50% of them arrived in Europe, which is no wonder, since a day trip from the Netherlands to Belgium already counts as an international arrival. The many nations of Europe skew this image a bit, yet the general trend is set. Tourism made up 10% of global GDP in 2019 and was worth € 9.6 trillion.[14] These jobs in hospitality are also difficult to automate and replace by machines. Being greeted, served, and recognized by other humans is the essence of tourism; this is especially true for trips to faraway destinations.

Not only nature and sights, but also the people and their culture, want to be experienced and consumed. Tourism turns culture into a commodity, into a good that can be advertised, sold, and consumed. The most successful destinations offer something unique and iconic, like the pyramids of Egypt. Attached to that, other bigger and smaller authentic products and services like food, clothes, and folkloric dances are sold. Consequently, mass tourism sometimes results in extreme simplifications and stereotyping as, for example, the round, thatched huts that can be found all over Sub-Saharan Africa as tourist accommodations.[15] The originally one-room house with a mud floor is now recreated for tourism, fully equipped with a sauna, jacuzzi, and a wooden floor that extends to a spacious veranda. Naively, tourists want to have the real African experience, just with more comfort and safety.

In Europe, the liberalization of the aviation industry in the mid-1990s, which moved aviation from a monopolistic, state-owned and -administered economy into a competitive market economy,[16] was a game-changer for the tourism industry. The resulting arrival of budget airlines turned a once luxurious mode of transport into a cumbersome affair with the allure of a bus ride. As an effect of liberalization, the prices went down to the level of a bus ride and city tourism in particular picked up rapidly.

Visitors Versus Inhabitants in Venice

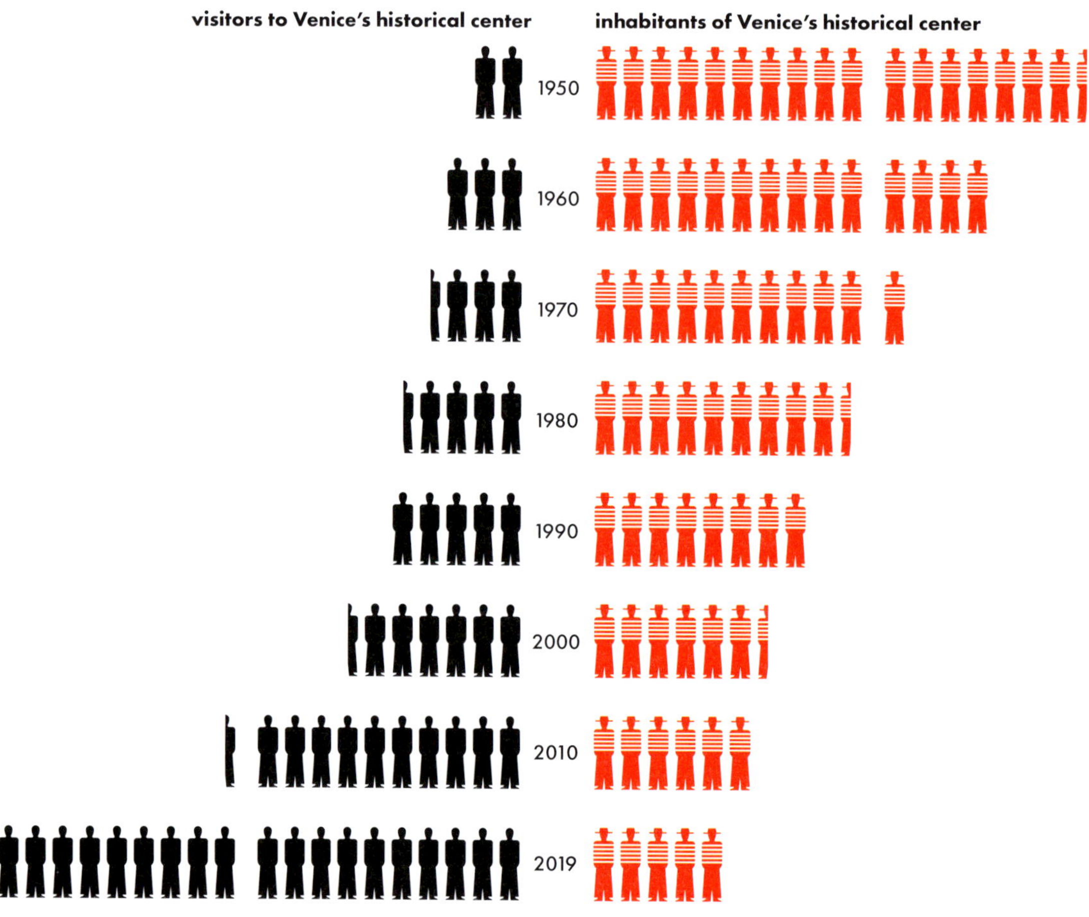

each black symbol represents 2,000,000 visitors (overnighters and day-trippers)
each red symbol represents 10,000 inhabitants

Visitors Versus Inhabitants in Venice – 2019

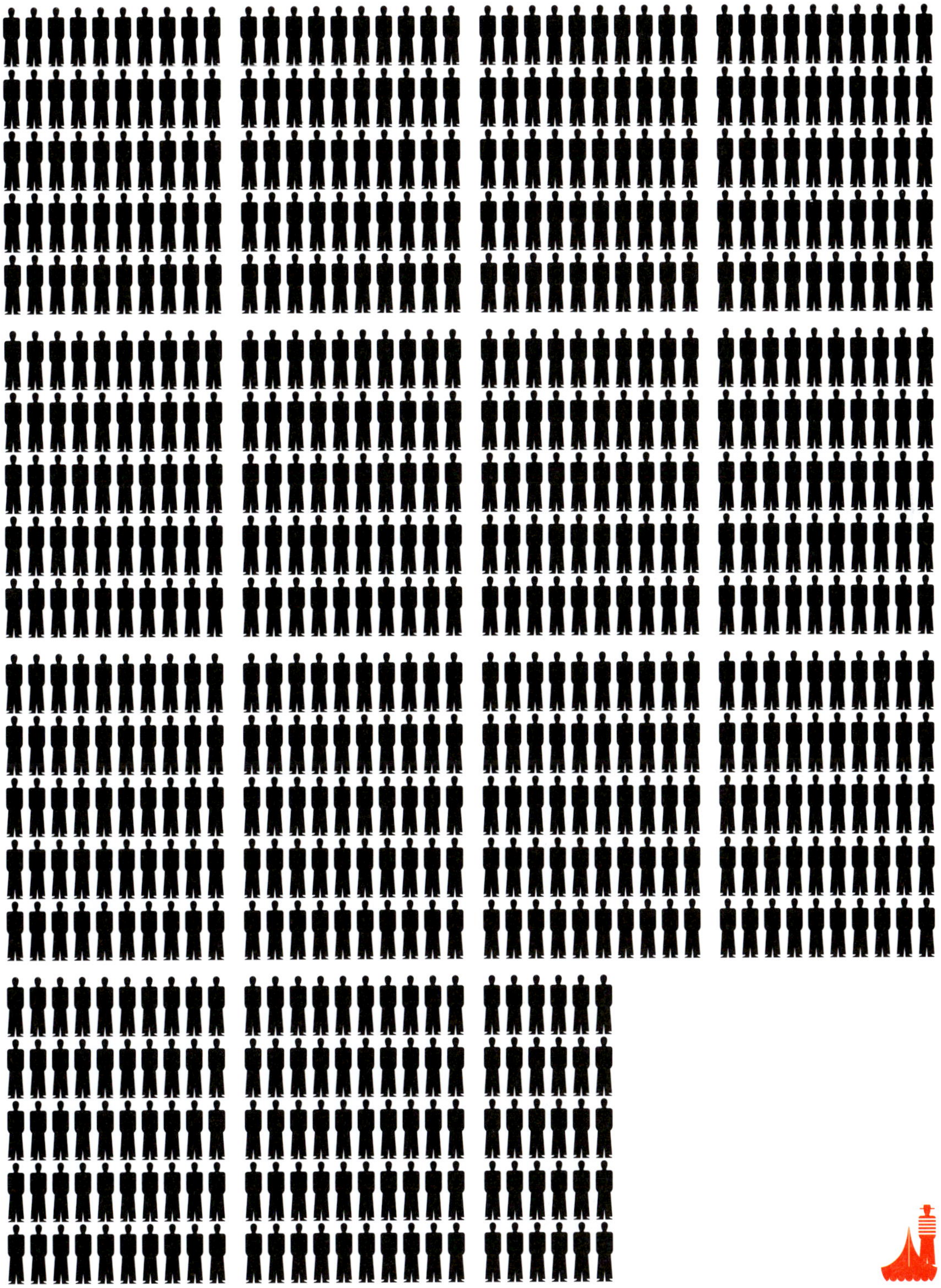

Venice, for example, has experienced a tripling of visitors in the past 25 years.[17] As rapidly as tourists arrived, the residents of the UNESCO World Heritage town moved away. Getting around in Venice becomes very difficult when each inhabitant is confronted with 730 visitors. To regulate access, the city is introducing electronic turnstiles at different entry points and charging an entrance fee of € 3 to € 10 for day-trippers. Gates are installed at the city's entry points and about 500 cameras will pick out stray, non-ticketed tourists.[18] Cruise ships have already been banned from the historic center after a cruise ship crashed into a dock in 2019.

The planet's upper and middle classes, those who have enough time and money to spend on tourism, account for about 3.0 billion people, or one-third of the human population. Every (non-pandemic) year in July and August, this group is on the move and flocks down to the world's most beloved cities and beaches.[19]

Tourism after World War II, in a time when large parts of European society were still involved in physical labor, was mainly serving recreation. This resulted in hours of

World Heritage Sites per Person

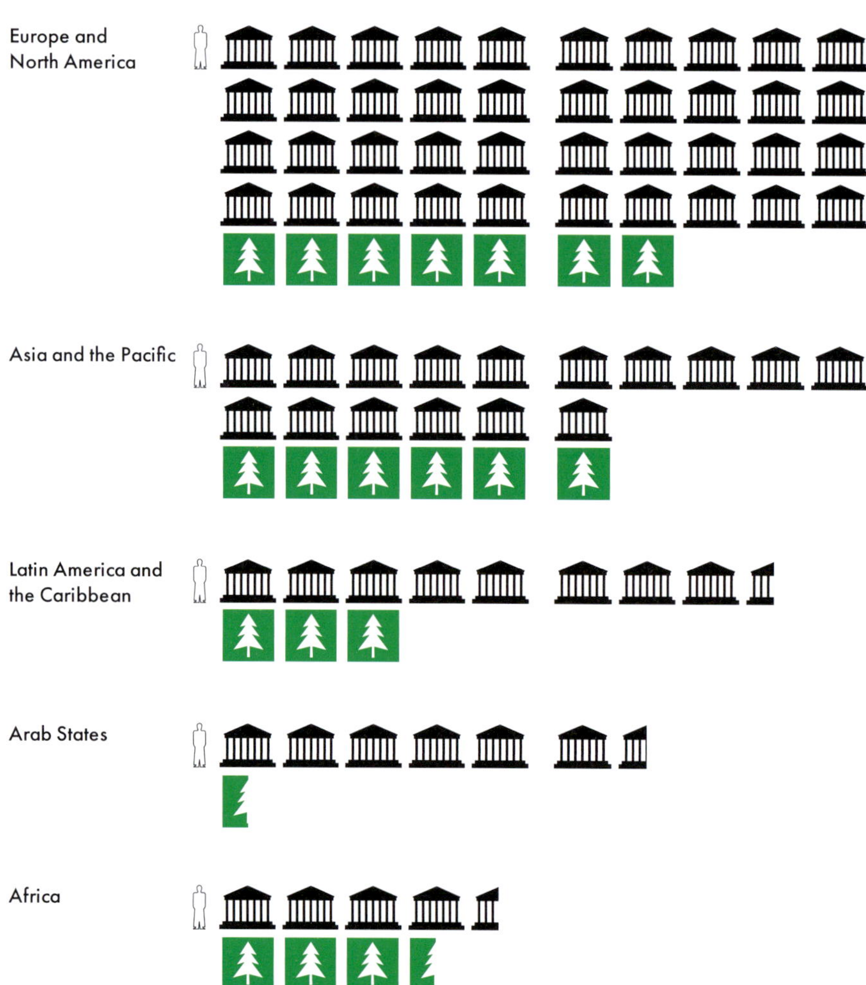

each symbol represents 1 World Heritage Site per 100,000,000 people (2022)
black: cultural World Heritage Site
green: natural World Heritage Site (mixed and shared sites are not included)

tanning on sandy beaches. Today, with most people clicking their days away at desk jobs, leisure means activity time. This trend is reinforced by social media, which has given tourism and leisure activities another boost. Instead of a week-long bore at the beach, people prefer to post pictures of themselves abseiling, rafting, water-skiing, and paddleboarding – or, of equal merit, post a selfie with the Mona Lisa or Stonehenge. Cultural tourism has offered a new way to profit from the otherwise old and forgotten stuff lying around one's country. In 1972, the same year the book *The Limits to Growth* was published, the Convention Concerning the Protection of the World Cultural and Natural Heritage was adopted by UNESCO.[20]

Today, the list of UNESCO World Heritage sites has become an index of must-sees, and is proudly brandished by each country in competition with each other for more tourists. Gaining the status of a World Heritage Site is rather competitive and costly, and has generated a lobby industry, preventing poorer countries from gaining a listing. Today there are 1,154 UNESCO World Heritage Sites, and almost half of them – 545 sites – are located in Europe.[21]

The forces of global modernization not only threaten cultural and natural sites, but also human habits and rituals. In 2008 UNESCO therefore introduced a list of "intangible cultural heritage." This raised the Viennese coffeehouse culture to the level of World Heritage when it was added to the list in 2011. Thus sipping a cup of coffee in one of the many old coffeehouses in Vienna is a contribution to an intangible world heritage. As of 2022, the list contains 584 elements, from flatbread-making in Azerbaijan to Mooba dance in Zambia.[22]

On the upside, tourism results in peaceful encounters between people from the South and people from the North. It is an economy that allows the direct flow of money from the North to the South – directly from human to human, from one hand to the other. If done with dignity and mutual respect, tourism is a brilliant way of getting to know each other with mutual benefits.

The airplane and affordable air travel have been the engine behind this social and cultural globalization. As container ships are the basis of global trade, so are airplanes the basis of global human exchange. With the rise of air travel, Earth's population increasingly grew together due to personal contacts and an exchange of knowledge. For example, the percentage of exchange students enrolled at Australian universities grew from 17% in 2005 to 28% in 2019.[23] In the case of Australia, a country with no land borders, this stark increase is solely on account of air travel. The top three countries of students' origin are China, India, and Nepal.

And again, all the speed, comfort, and freedom of traveling around the world comes at a cost to our environment. Aviation accounts for 2.5% of global CO_2 emissions.[24] To make air travel environmentally friendly or even pull it totally out of the fossil trap will be extremely difficult since kerosene, the airplanes' fuel, has a very high energy density and is thus very difficult to replace. One of many options that are being worked on now is to produce synthetic fuels based on renewable resources.

Travel Times and Distances

Traveling from New York to Singapore took about three weeks in the 1930s, approximately the same time it took from Spain to Asia Minor (today's Turkey) in the ancient Roman Empire.[25] Today the time to travel from New York to Singapore is about 19 hours by plane. The development of long-range "jumbo jets" changed air travel fundamentally (the Boeing 747, introduced in 1970, was the first of these). In the past 65 years, the scheduled flight from London to Sydney has been reduced from a 2.5-day journey with 7 stops to a 19-hour nonstop flight.[26] The same journey took almost one month in Neurath's time in the 1930s.

Using today's fastest form of transportation, the rocket, it takes about 3 days to get to the moon and about 3 months to the planet Mars.[27] But the last trips to the moon were quite a while ago. Between 1968 and 1972, seven missions took 12 US citizens to the moon.[28] For 50 years it has been quiet up there. Having people running around on the surface of the moon proved to have little scientific value. Yet the vastness of the universe is alluring. Out there is infinite space, while Earth seems to become ever more confined and boring, because every little corner has been claimed and conquered. A second space age is thriving. The steep decrease in crewed missions since the 1990s seems to have reversed itself in this decade. In the past two years, 23 crewed missions have already been sent, which is almost half as many as during the entire past decade.

London – Sydney

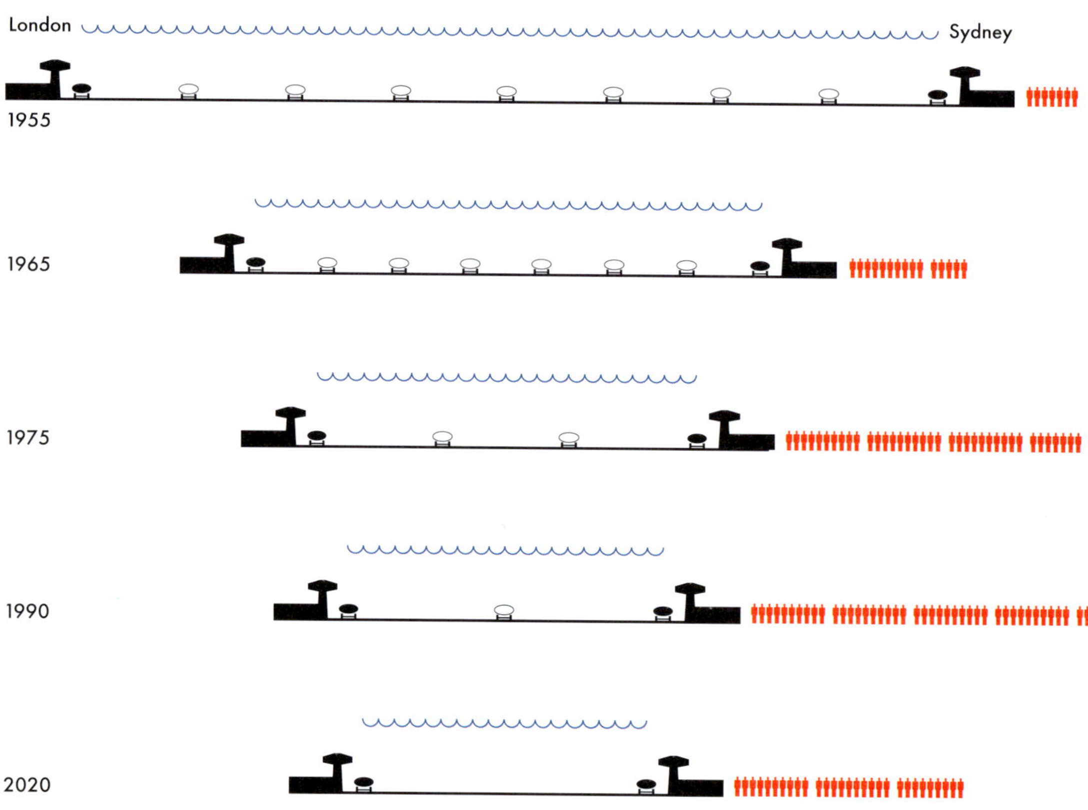

each cloud symbol represents 1 hour of travel time
each tank truck symbol represents 1 stopover
each person symbol represents 10 passengers in the fastest aircraft

14 out of these 23 have been carried out by private (American) companies which are rather new players in the field of crewed space travel and have different incentives.[29] Space mining and space tourism are high on their agenda, breathing new life into the idea of humans as an interplanetary species. The next human to set foot on the moon is planned for 2025, and the first human to set foot on Mars is scheduled for 2029.[30, 31] Going to outer space checks all the boxes of a modern project: it's high-risk, high-energy, high-tech, high-cost, high-speed, and large coverage.

Crewed Space Missions

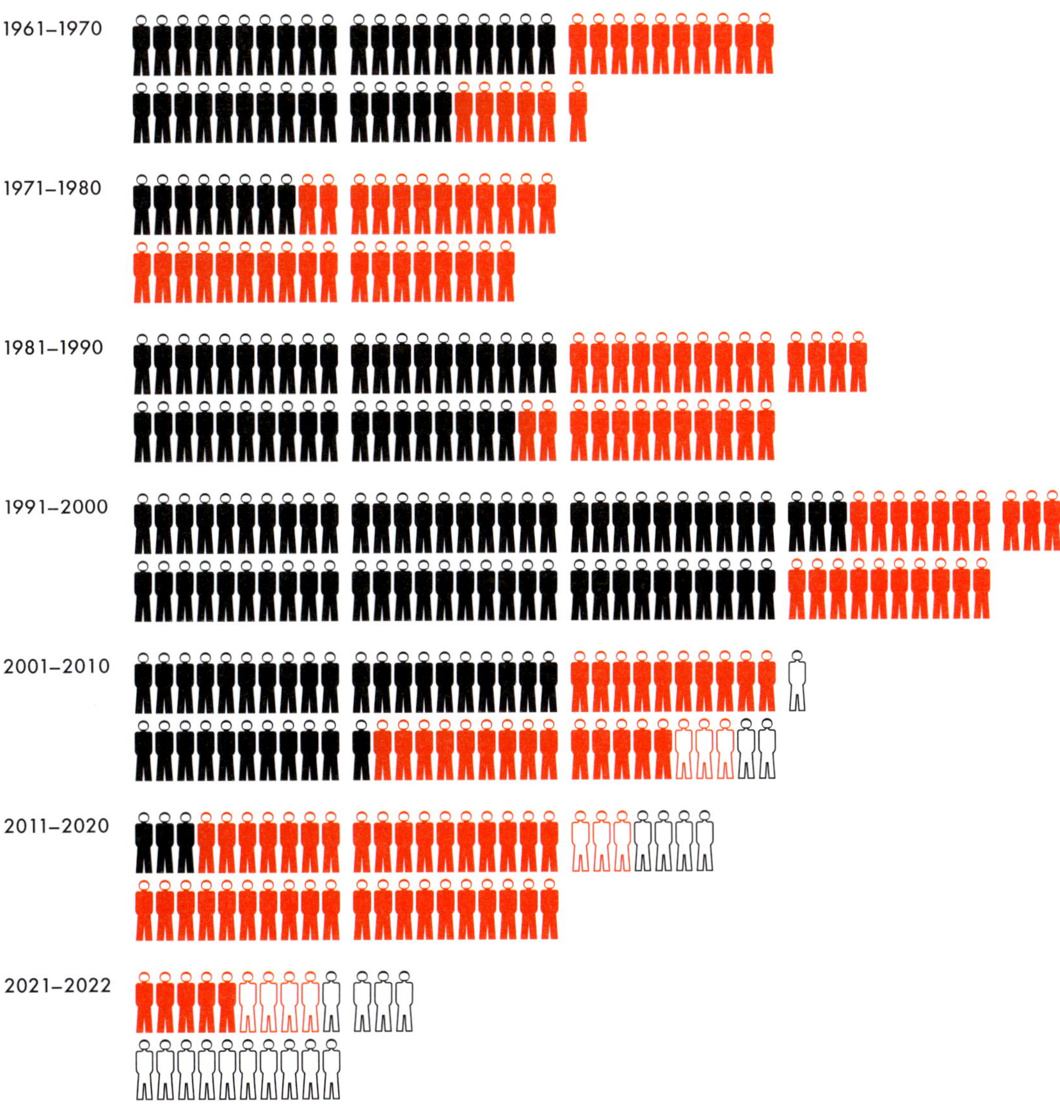

each symbol represents 1 crewed space mission

black filled: NASA / USA
red filled: Roscosmos / Soviet Union, later Russia
red outlined: CMSA / China
black outlined: private operators (Scaled Composites, Virgin Galactic, SpaceX, and Blue Origin)

Sports and Emancipation

In 1900, at the second summer Olympic Games in modern times, women were allowed to participate for the first time. 22 women (about 2% of participants) and 975 men took part in those Games in Paris.[32] At the 2020 Olympic Games in Tokyo, women accounted for 48% of the athletes. This (near) equality had taken the Olympic community 120 years of gradual improvement. Yet in terms of viewership and financial appreciation, there are still worlds between the two sexes. While the highest transfer sum for a male soccer player – Neymar – was € 222 million (2017),[33] the top transfer sum for his female colleague Keira Walsh was a meager € 0.47 million (2022).[34] More shockingly, in 2021 the total global female soccer transfer budget comprised only € 1.3 million,[35] compared to almost € 5 billion for male soccer transfers.

Hosts of the Summer Olympic Games, 1896–2021

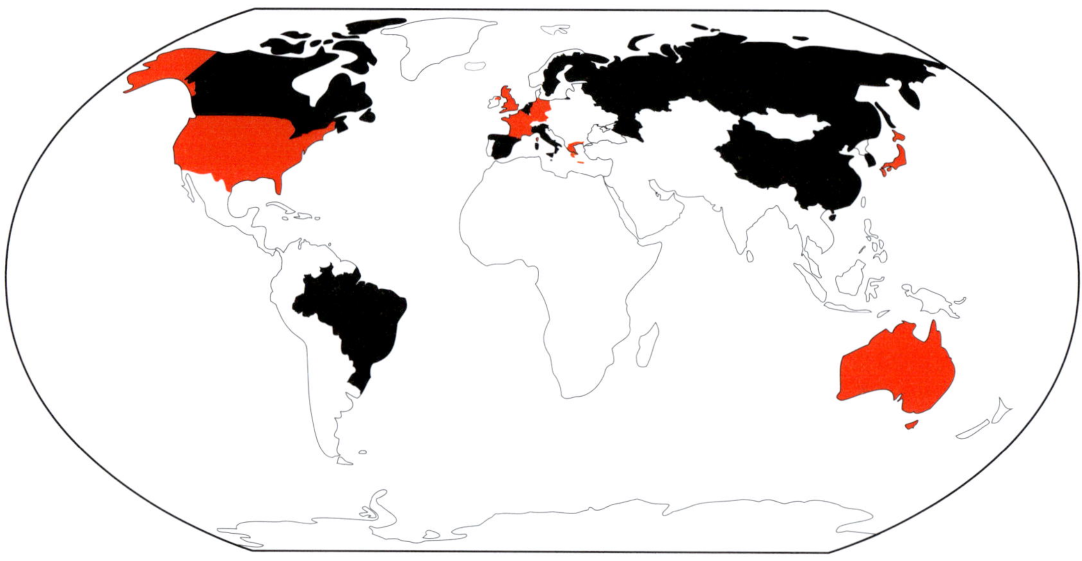

black: countries in which the Olympic Games have been held once
red: countries in which the Olympic Games have been held more than once

Sports, and especially soccer in the case of Europe, can allow a quick escape from poverty and a rise in status, as in the case of Rio Mavuba, who was born stateless in the international waters off Angola's coast during a civil war. After arriving in France as refugee, he propelled himself to soccer stardom, was transferred for millions of euros, and was granted French citizenship. Mavuba played on France's national team for 10 years. Yet for most refugees this remains a distant dream, especially if they are female.

Social progress is not always linear, as the history of women's soccer shows. Up until the outbreak of World War II, women's soccer was an accepted sport throughout the West, until things started to change after the war. A radical example is Germany. In 1955 the German Football Association (West Germany) officially banned women's soccer, since the male-dominant sport was of the opinion that soccer was "fundamentally foreign to the nature of women."[36] In 1970 the ban was lifted, with restrictions. Women were only allowed to play when it was warm outside, matches were limited to 60 minutes, and a smaller and lighter ball had to be used.[37] This resulted in severe disadvantages of the German teams at international games. Gradually the rules were

Participants at Summer Olympic Games

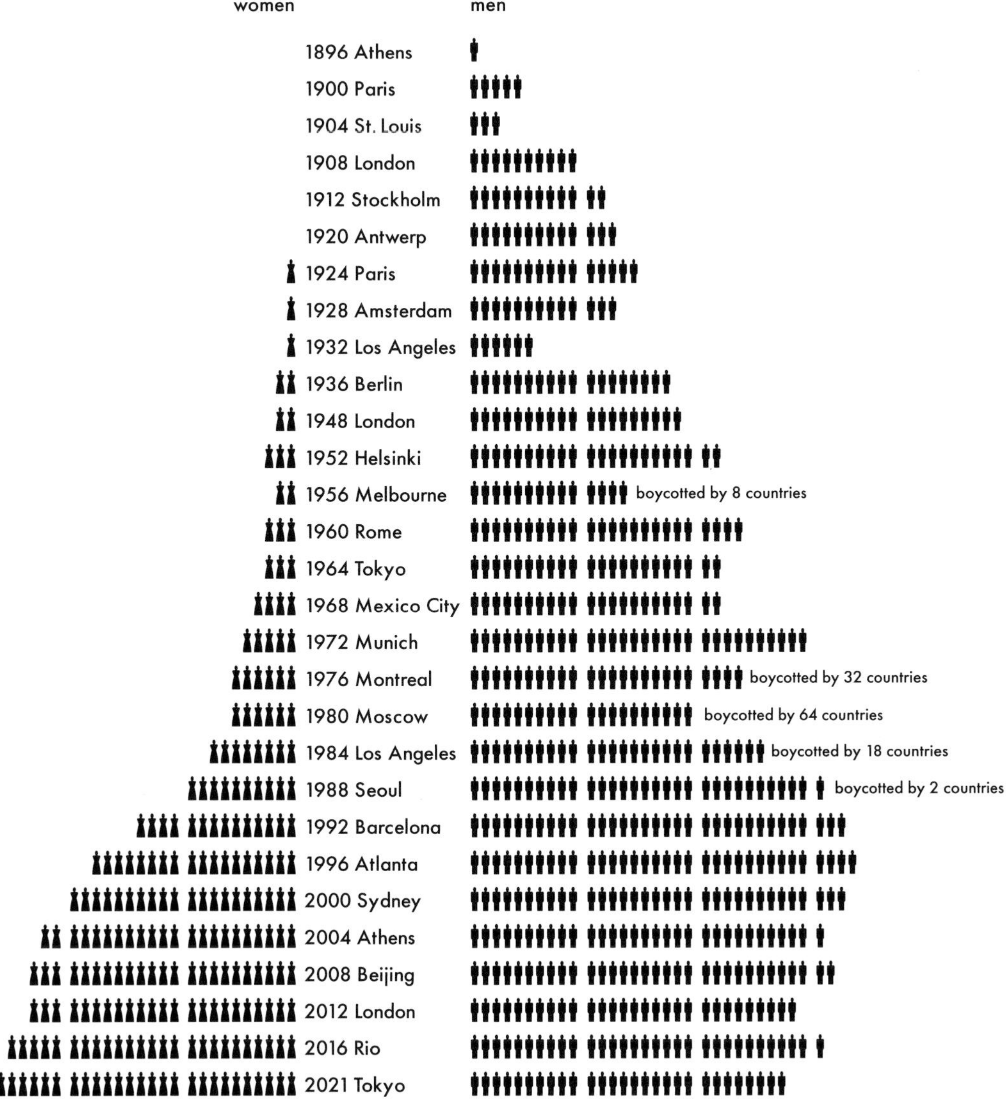

each symbol represents 200 athletes

adjusted to the same ball size and duration of play as in men's soccer. Only in 1996 did women's soccer become fully recognized again and accepted as an official Olympic discipline, 96 years after men's soccer.

Today in most countries of the world, women are allowed to practice sports. Only in Afghanistan under the rule of the radical Islamic Taliban regime have sports for women recently been banned. The challenges ahead are how to integrate transgender and intersex athletes in a fair and open way in competitions. First steps are being taken, and the International Committee announced in 2021 that it will no longer require athletes to undergo hormone level modifications to compete.[38] Even if progress is slow and sometimes halted or even reversed, there is and will be progress in the long run. The modern human seems to be stubborn, self-absorbed, and a slow learner, but can at least learn.

Sports and Health

In the West, sports have become a mass phenomenon, gaining status during the transition from a manufacturing-based economy to a service-based economy. Until the 1980s, factory work exhausted people enough that they preferred to watch sports on TV or in a stadium to practicing them. The immobile office work of today even demands a certain amount of exercise to maintain enough muscular mass to prevent back and shoulder pain. The human body, used for thousands of years to earn a living, being literally the engine that constructed Stonehenge, the pyramids of Egypt, and the Acropolis, turned into a burden that needs to be kept in good shape.

Today a healthy, muscular body is not needed for work, but as personal advertisement. All around the globe, a fit-looking body is regarded as beautiful and "sells" better on the job and marriage market. At the start of the 21 st century, a new spirit took hold of the Western middle class, the individual desire for a long and healthy life. Members of the "quantified self" movement constantly evaluate the fitness of the human body with the help of self-tracking technology.[39] Wearable sensors mine physiological information in real time to automatically generate a personal data set of blood-sugar levels, heart rate, or average speed, which can be analyzed and compared throughout time and shared with follow sportswomen and -men. These sensors can be worn in

Infant Mortality, Acute Respiratory Infections, and Accidents

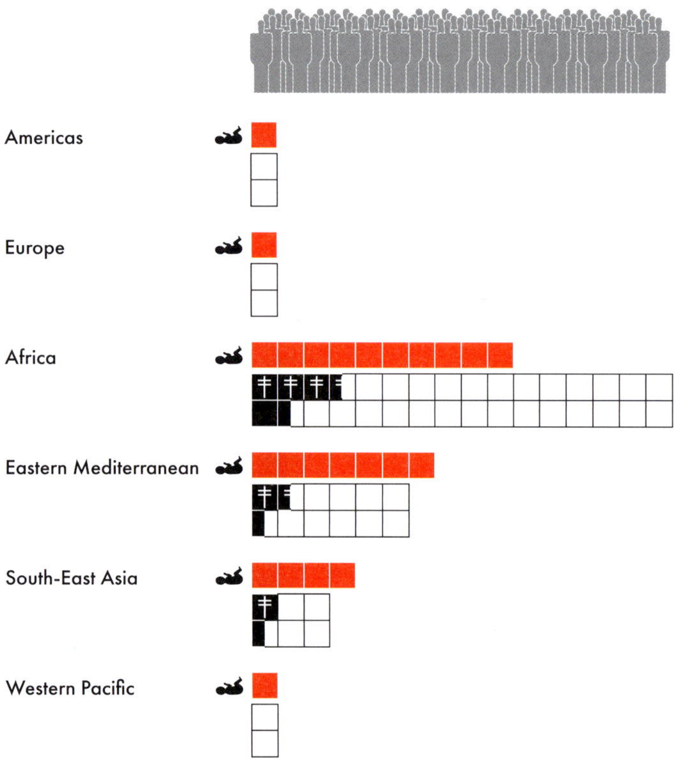

each square represents 1 death per 10,000 population annually (2019)

first row: infant death rate (0–27 days)
second and third row: death rate above the age of 1 and below the age of 4
with double cross: from acute lower respiratory infections (e.g., pneumonia)
black: from external causes (injuries)
outline: others

Smoking and Lung Cancer in the USA

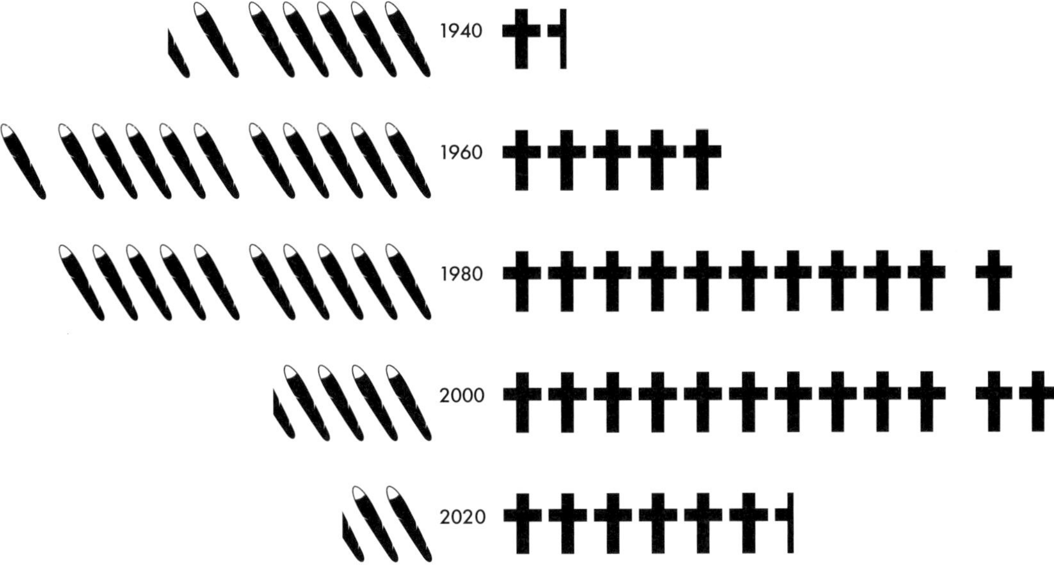

each cigar symbol represents one cigarette per day per adult
each cross symbol represents one death from lung cancer per 10,000 people

the form of glasses, jewelry, wristwatches, fitness bands, tattoo-like devices, patches, and textiles.

Recently, official health statistics have been adjusted from quantity to quality of living. In 2005 the European Union introduced the metric of "healthy life years" (HLY), which measures people's health expectancies in addition to their life expectancy – thus not how long a person will live, but how long that person will live a healthy life. Since the increase in average life expectancy has hit a ceiling of around 90 years in the West, extending the number of healthy years within those 90 is now the new (statistical) ambition.[40]

This trend was followed swiftly by the introduction of laws in Western countries. In 2004, Ireland became the first country in the world to introduce a nationwide ban on smoking in workplaces.[41] Today about 150 out of 203 countries have national smoke-free regulations.[42] Next to the social aspect of a healthier society, countries have an economic interest in having a healthy population that is less of a burden on the healthcare system. Also, health insurers have a large economic interest in keeping customers healthy, which results in fewer claims. Smokers pay up to 200% more for life insurance and 20% more for their extra health insurance in the US.[43] Obesity is surcharged by insurers, as is a risky lifestyle, which paradoxically includes almost all outdoor sports. Thus insurers definitely prefer the stationary bike in the health club to the mountain bike trail. Insurers don't believe in "more risk, more fun," but in "less risk, more money."

Moreover, a healthy body and a long life are becoming increasingly connected to a healthy planet. Personal fitness and personal health depend, especially in the urbanized regions of the world, on the fitness and health of planet Earth. Air pollution

Healthy Retirement Years of Women and Men

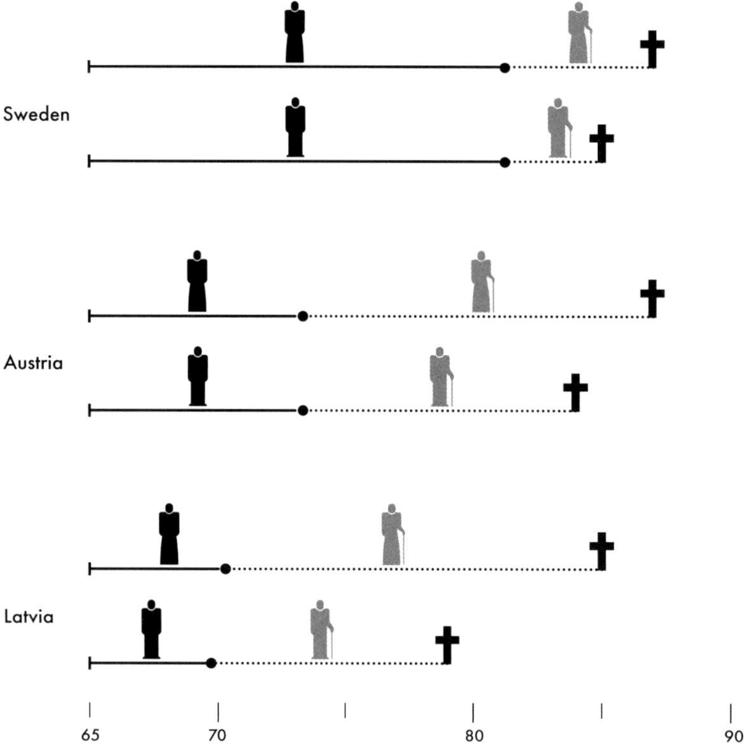

solid line: healthy retirement years
dotted line: retirement years with limitations on activity
(2019)

through smog and particulate matter caused by the use of combustion engines is a serious threat to humans. It is estimated that 8 million people died of air pollution from fossil fuels in 2018.[44] This amounts to 1 out of 7 deaths in that year, which should not come as a surprise, given that 99% of the Earth's population breathes air that exceeds the limits established by the WHO's guidelines.[45]

The atmosphere is the medium that connects and surrounds all the inhabitants of planet Earth. It is the soup in which all humans swim. The more that humans pollute this soup, the more toxic it becomes. Here, personal fitness reaches its limits and starts to become communal fitness. If not all inhabitants take care of planet Earth's fitness and the health of the atmosphere, the "quantified self" movement is rendered useless.

Sports and Warfare

Most of today's sports have their origin in military exercises. As warfare, many sports depend heavily on, and develop with, technology. Modern outdoor athletes wear clothes that resemble uniforms. Textiles are multi-layered high-tech membranes, helmets are shock-resistant, sporting goods are made from titanium or carbon fiber, and all that is championed by high-tech electronics. These electronic devices – in the form of watches, sunglasses, and helmet cameras – have sensors, cameras, and meters and connect the athlete to others who are out there or at their home base, measuring the user's vital signs. Looking at these outdoor athletes, only their extremely colorful costume differentiates them from (camouflaged) soldiers. The drill, the discipline, and the comradeship are equally inherent to sportspeople and are also an element that makes doing sports so attractive to many.

E-sports (electronic sports) depend much less on physical training and are even closer to the contemporary battlefield. The main tools of these sports are a computer mouse, joystick, or console, and the arena is a computer-generated virtual world. Contemporary soldiers use exactly the same tools, with the only difference that they pilot drones, robots, and boats to targets in the real world, killing real people. In this regard, e-sportspeople might be more fit to participate as mercenaries in a future war.

The video game also sees its inception after Neurath's time, beginning in the 1950s with simple games such as Tennis for Two, which used an oscilloscope as a screen. Due to an extra boost by the COVID-19 pandemic, the global electronic gaming industry has grown to be the largest revenue source of any media, far ahead of the music and film industry.

The earliest video game competition was between Stanford students in 1972, playing a game called Spacewar. The winners of this competition won a year's subscription to *Rolling Stone* magazine, and there was free beer.[46] In 2021, the global e-sports competition for Dota 2, a multiplayer online battle arena, had a prize pool of US$ 40,018,400 and sent the winning team of three Russians and two Ukrainians home with $ 18 million.[47]

E-sports move the battlefield entirely into the digital realm. The industry is working on an ever more immersive experience with the use of virtual and augmented reality headsets, holograms, and again sensors that measure the real player's body performance. Many games have their own economic system that is based on trading and even have their own kind of currency.

This is certainly a view into the living rooms of the Western world. Especially, and again, the societies of the world which still rely heavily on their own muscle power to work in agriculture or manufacturing do not have the time or energy to practice sports (neither indoor, nor outdoor / neither offline, nor online).

Digital Times

Digital Media

The full-scale digitalization of information is the true revolution of the 21st century. Otto Neurath reflected on the age of the gearwheel as part of a complex machinery that eventually replaced human muscular strength. This was followed by the age of the binary code that will eventually replace human brain power. Bit by bit, all information is translated into binary code. Not only are all books in all libraries being scanned; all statues, architecture, sculptures, and the Earth itself are now being scanned in 3-D.

Writing Systems

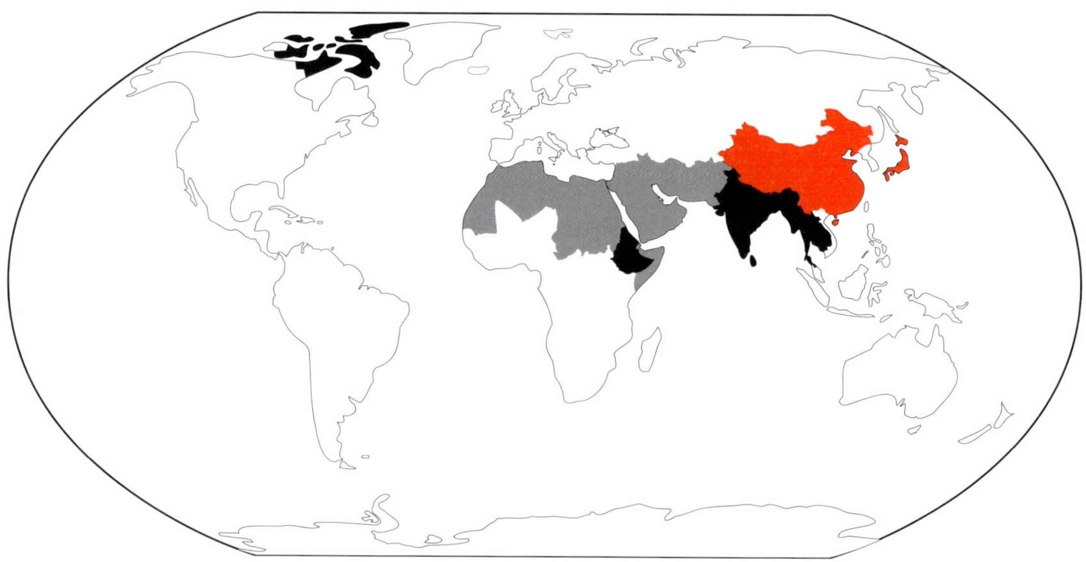

red: logographic and syllabic writing
black: abugida a.k.a. alphasyllabary (segmental writing system in which consonant-vowel sequences are written as units)
gray: abjad a.k.a. consonant (writing system in which only consonants are represented)
white: alphabetic

The transfer and storage of information has a long history. 5,200 years ago, cuneiform writing, one of the oldest scripts, was developed. It started out as a kind of set of pictograms with over 1,000 characters, and developed into an abstract script with only 41 characters. This simplification and abstraction of the writing allowed humans to process the information faster and with less storage capacity (at that time meaning fewer clay tablets).

Today about 15 to 20 major writing systems are in use, being alphabetic, logographic, alphasyllabic, and consonant writing, with characters written in all imaginable directions.[1] This book is written in the Latin alphabet, from left to right, in the English language. This is probably the most broadly understood means of information transfer via writing in the world.

The first computer in the 1940s heralded a new era and another step toward simplification: the era of the binary code. At the same time that Otto Neurath was working on his book based on the Isotype, a new pictorial language, Conrad Zuse was working on the world's first working programmable digital computer based on binary code. While

the one was trying to develop a language the illiterate could also read, the other was working on a machine with a code that not even the literate could read anymore. It seems that Zuse won the race, and today all information is digital and highly abstract – or, as the computer would translate the word "abstract": 01100001 01100010 01110011 01110100 01110010 01100001 01100011 01110100.

The fact is that Zuse and Neurath both won their race. While Zuse developed a device that could read and process the binary code, Neurath developed an International Picture Language that makes these programs instantly accessible by simultaneously shortcutting all human languages and cultures. Starting a program on any device starts with tapping on an icon. Thus, Neurath's invention enables humans to access and activate Zuse's invention.

Still, the final pictorial language is the binary code, 0 and 1. Paper in fact disappeared. You, dear reader, may be holding this book in your hands, but it is only a simulacrum of the real thing, which was written on a PC in Microsoft Word and its layout done in Adobe InDesign. Instead of using linoleum cuts, the pictograms were drawn in Adobe

Illustrator. These programs are agents that interpret the binary code into an output the author can understand, translated into lines, surfaces, colors, pictograms, and fonts. For the nostalgic reader, the work is printed and sold as a book.

But less and less printing is being done. The global production of newsprint is back to where it was in the 1960s, while since then the Earth's population has more than doubled.[2] The global production of printing and writing paper is following this trend and has declined to the level it was at when the Internet was introduced in the mid-1990s. Turning digital, media is becoming ever more fluid and faster. Printed newspapers, the 19th-century medium issued once a day, were replaced by radio newscasts broadcast every hour. Today's standard online newsfeeds are refreshed every 10 minutes, but gossip news sites like Twitter are fed constantly; they can be sent and read at any place with a connection to the World Wide Web via a smartphone.

The relatively low cost of smart mobile phones and their infrastructure made them a ubiquitous tool all around the world in record time. Between 2000 and 2020, mobile phone subscriptions in Chad increased from almost zero to 53%, while the old

Global Paper Production

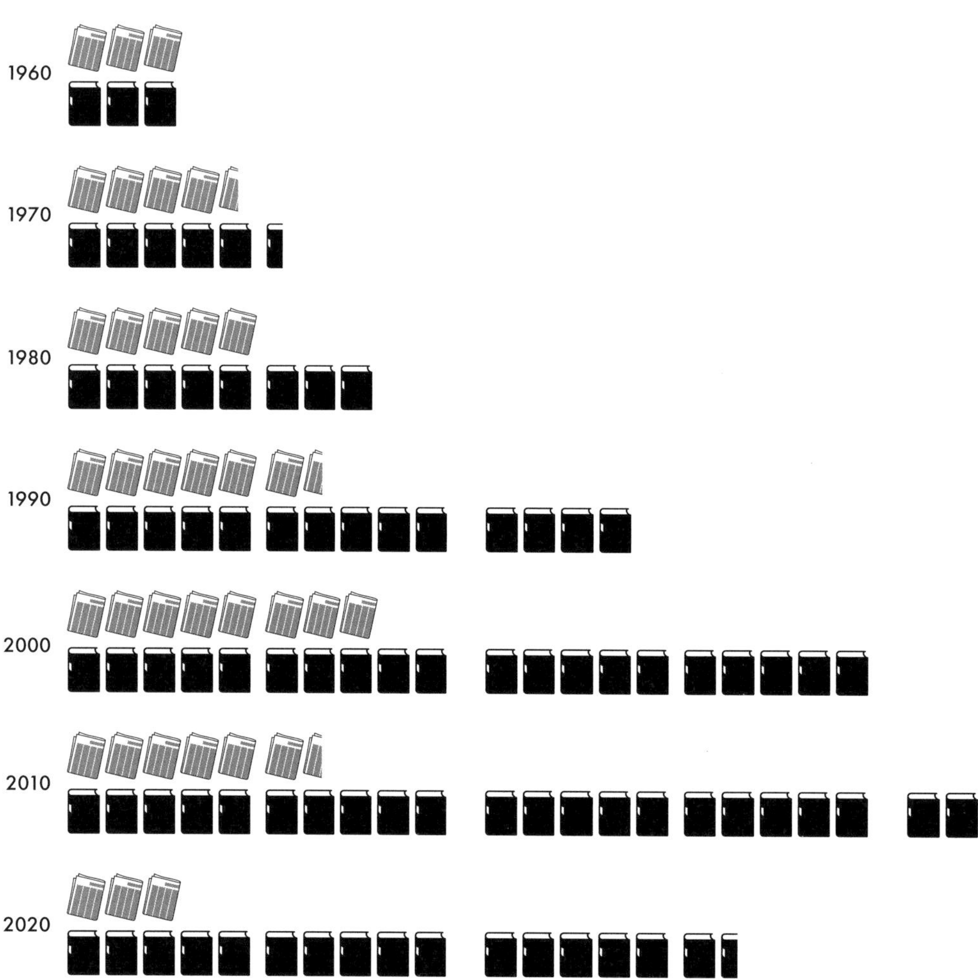

each newspaper symbol represents 5 million tonnes of newsprint paper
each book symbol represents 5 million tonnes of printing and writing paper

Modern Media in the USA

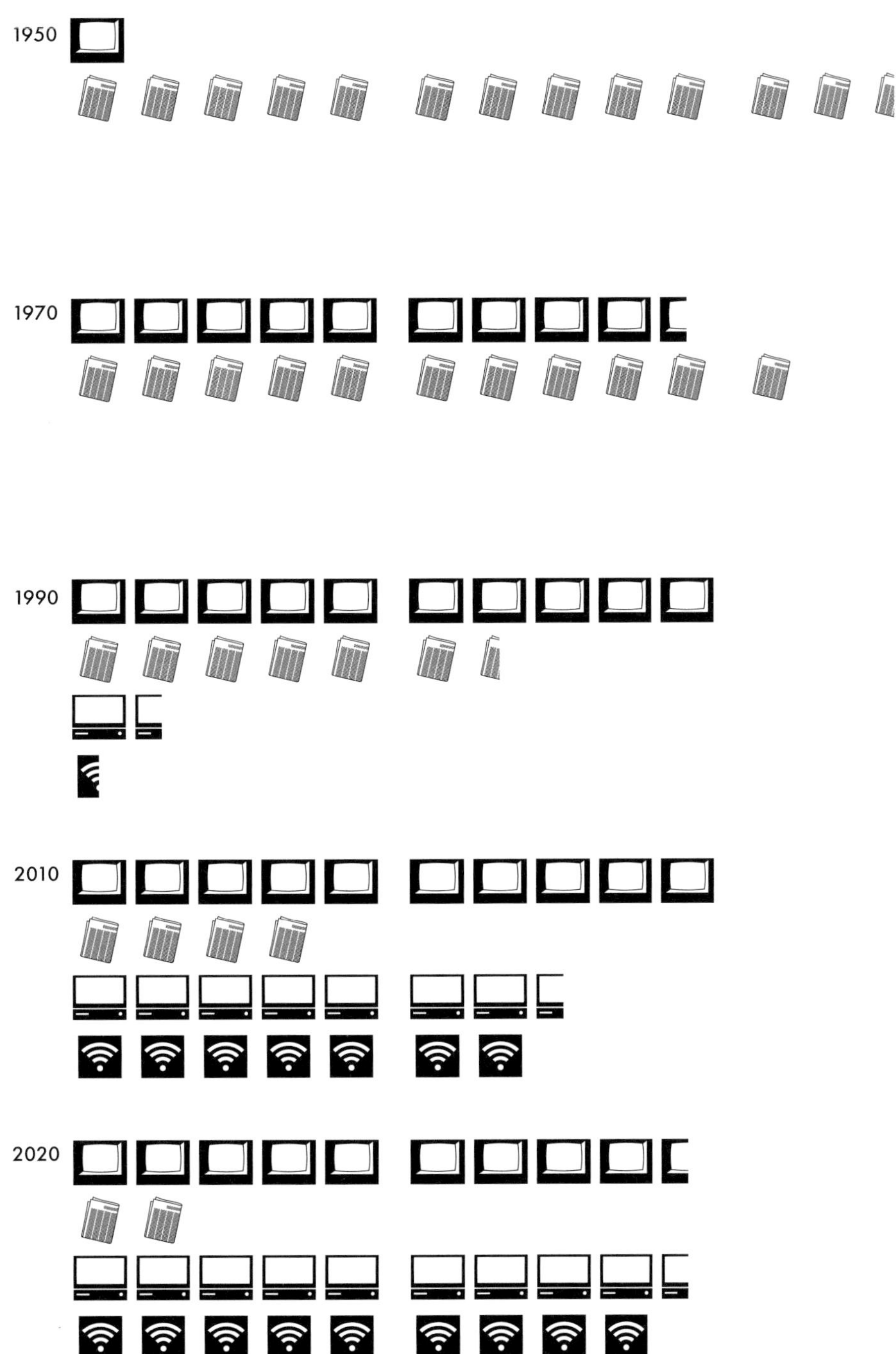

each newspaper symbol represents the number of newspapers per 10 households
each TV, computer, and Internet symbol represents 10% of US households

landline telephone never reached the 1% mark.[3] The mobile phone was right from its beginning a very personal device and is, with its number, directly connected to a person. In 2021 Germany introduced the possibility of using the smartphone as an ID card, driver's license, and social security card. Soon the phone might also replace the passport.[4]

Centuries-old media like gossip and books, but also recent media that relied on paper or specific devices, like newspaper, radio, TV, and video games, have already been absorbed by the smartphone. Likewise, interpersonal and intercultural communication is being absorbed and conducted more smoothly with the help of translation programs. Future smartphones equipped with artificial intelligence (AI) hold the promise of reversing the biblical Tower of Babel event. With the aid of simultaneous translation, anyone can talk in any desired language, thus communicating flawlessly with anyone on the planet. The smartphone as Babel fish with all its quirks and dangers.

Digital Space

Today, various encounters, from family meetings to United Nations assemblies, are held remotely. "Social media" became a term for online platforms on which the very personal events of the day are photographed and commented on by the user (= person sending). Meetings held in person are becoming rare and an ever more special occasion. In the West, where the Internet is fast and reliable, office work is more and more often being done remotely, and it seems possible that the office building, the icon of modern architecture, will become a typology of the past. Communication and infrastructure have always had an impact on the spatial arrangement of cities and the constitution of society.

Social Media Platforms with More Than 1 Billion Users

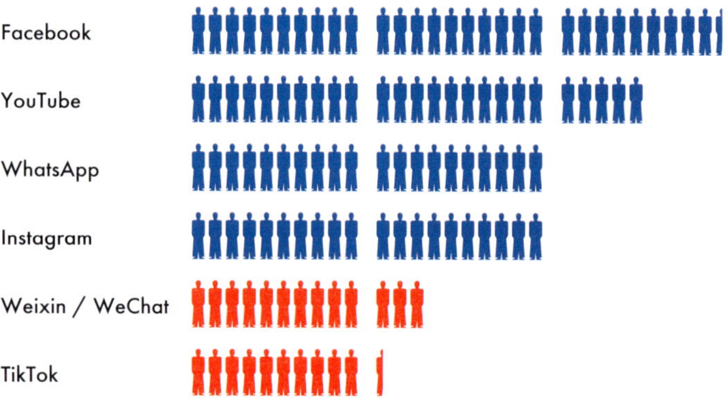

each symbol represents 100,000,000 monthly users of all social media platforms with more than 1 billion active users (2023)

blue: developed in the USA
red: developed in China

Currently, 99% of all data traffic, thus also the Internet, is carried by cables.[5] Submarine cables that span the oceans play a vital role in this infrastructure. Similarly on land, data streams are carried by cables. Wireless services rely on cellular base stations that transmit the phone signal the final 2–3 km to mobile phones and portable computers. This system relies on proximity to a cable or a transmitter, like a railway system with tracks and stations.

Satellites

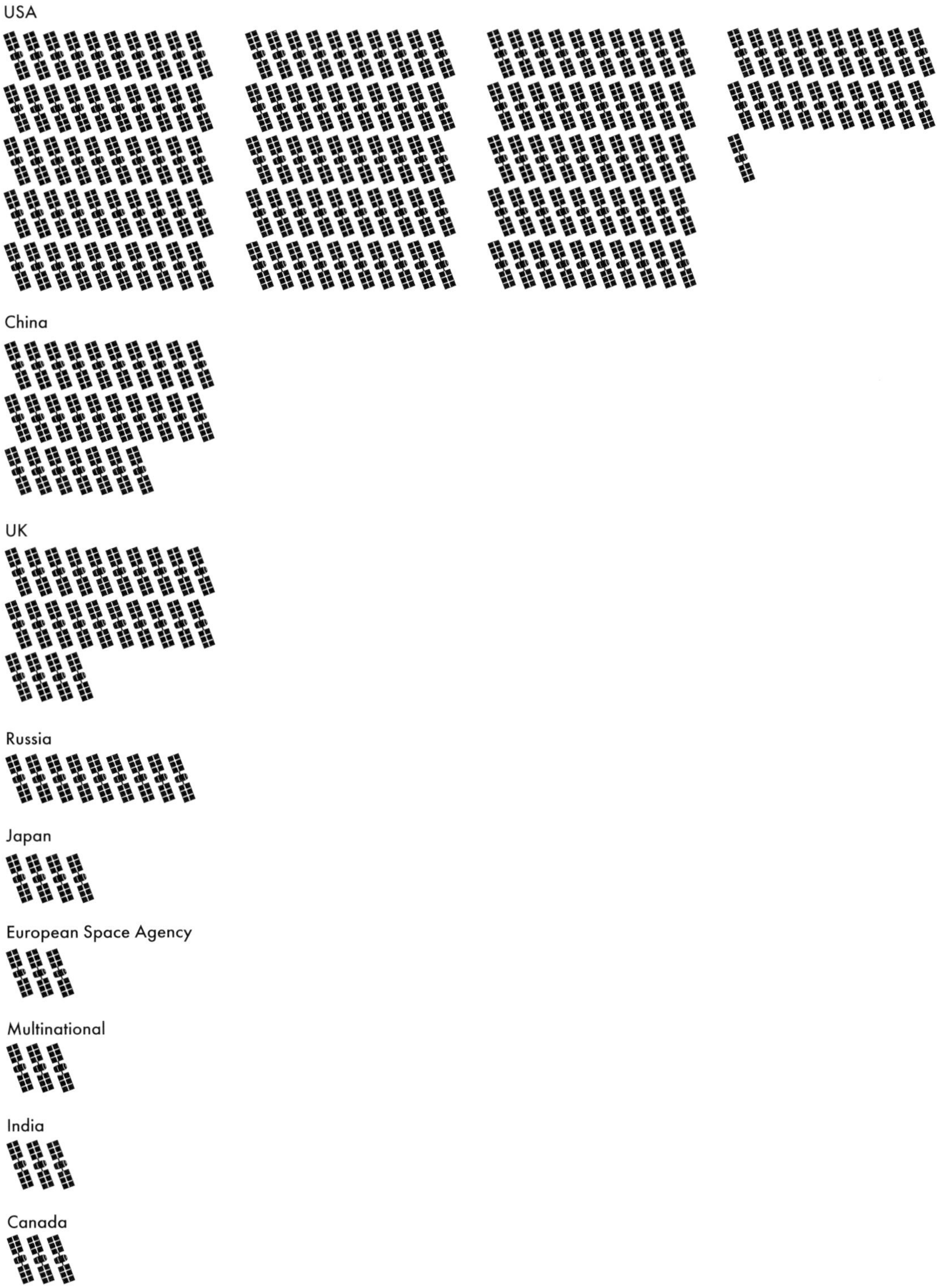

USA

China

UK

Russia

Japan

European Space Agency

Multinational

India

Canada

each symbol represents 20 satellites of all countries or institutions with more than 50 satellites (2022)

Today several private companies are trying to break with this system and launch small and micro-satellites to provide Internet access from the heavens. The most famous of these, Starlink, consisted in its first phase of 1,600 satellites and in its final stage of many thousands.[6] A satellite-based Internet service would eliminate the advantage of proximity, and all of Earth's surface would be served equally. This could have a severe impact on settlement patterns across the globe. The emergence of the metropolis was based on the accumulation and superimposition of high-quality infrastructure and communication nodes. Harbors, high-speed trains, international airports, TV and radio studios, and high-speed Internet all coincide in large cities and give them their advantage over towns and villages. Before the arrival of the satellite, no available infrastructure was as ubiquitous as air.

Satellites serve every place on Earth in the same quality. Theoretically, only three geostationary satellites are needed – these satellites orbit the Earth at the same angular speed as its own rotation, and thus are fixed above a single spot – to cover 90% of the Earth's surface. The main applications of the roughly 5,000 satellites orbiting Earth in 2022 are communications (54%), remote sensing of space and Earth (17%), research and development (11%), military (7%), navigation (4%), and science (3%).[7] The above-mentioned introduction of microsatellites led to an explosive increase in communication satellites, skewing the data toward quantity. The satellites responsible for remote sensing in particular fulfill an essential objective of modernity. These satellites are constantly scanning the Earth and trying to eliminate uncertainty, thus attempting to gain control. With the increasing help of self-learning computer programs, it becomes possible to study the planet and learn from its behavior to predict future events such as earthquakes, volcanic eruptions,[8] and flooding. Other examples for the use of sensing satellites are drought-monitoring, soy yield predicting, and forecasting of traffic congestion. This ability to gather and evaluate data to predict future events keeps the spirits high that technology could be not only the ailment but also the cure. It is as if by inventing the thermometer, we have invented the fever it measures. Humans have created a technical sky – a crystal ball – that talks to them as it observes them and their activities.

Digital Disinformation

Print media, radio, and television rely on centralized systems and large investments. For governments and non-government institutions, it is easy to verify the value of information that is broadcast. Entire jobs with their own ethical code have been developed around media.

The Internet with its various news platforms, social media platforms, and forums allows each and every one of us to be a journalist. What sounded like a beautiful promise when the Internet was still young has turned out to become part of an information war.

Autocratic states like Russia have realized that the freedom of speech, one of the human rights democratic countries are so proud of, allows them to play with the mindset of the people and turn them against each other and against democracy. Yevgeny Prigozhin, the founder of the Wagner Group, is also funding Glavset (aka Internet Research Agency), a troll factory that in 2015 allegedly employed 1,000 people in a single building in St. Petersburg, Russia.[9] The group started out by praising Russia and furthering Vladimir Putin's interests by spreading Kremlin propaganda and disinformation about opponents in the Russian-speaking community in parts of the former Soviet Union. The group's most famous and successful exploit was interfering in the 2016 US presidential election by spreading false information about Mr. Trump's opponents.[10]

Freedom of the Press

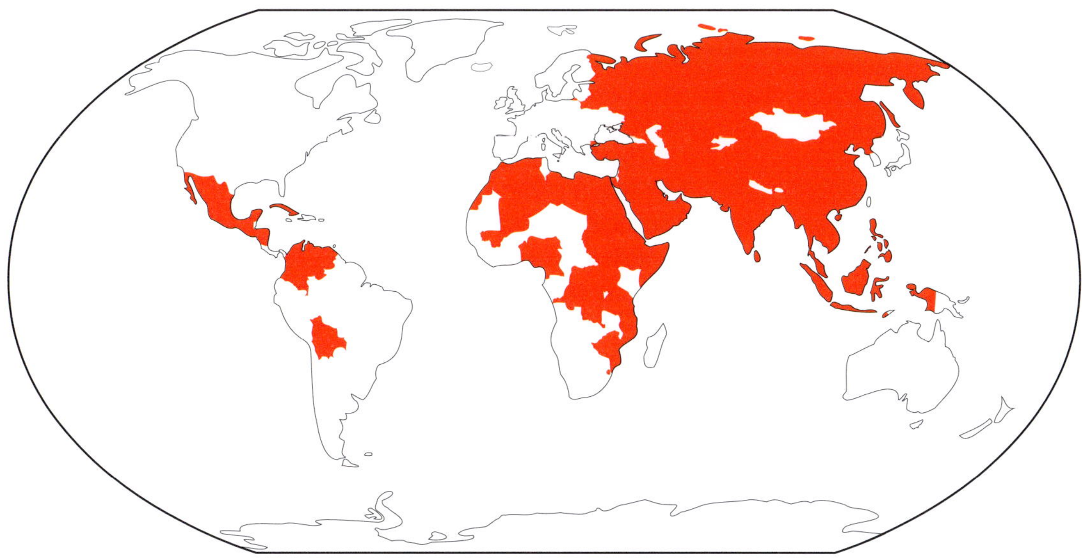

red: countries with a "difficult situation" and a "very serious situation" regarding freedom of the press (2022)

Troll factories feed thousands of fake social media accounts, blogs, and even TV channels with information daily. The fact that Glavset is funded by Wagner Group owner Yevgeny Prigozhin underscores troll factories' importance as an essential weapon in digital warfare. As on the battlefield, creating confusion is already a small victory.

China, on the other hand, is more concerned with filtering the information that it receives. The Great Firewall, a security system that filters all information entering China, was developed with the help of US companies in the early 2000s. Paradoxically, it is being used to block some of the Internet's most popular sites like Google, Facebook, and Twitter – which are owned and operated by US companies.[11]

Many other countries such as Turkey, Cuba, and Iran have all their own methods of blocking and filtering information that enters the country via the Internet. Western countries fear the destabilizing effect on democracy, but have little leverage against misinformation spreading predominantly via Western online platforms. Freedom of speech and freedom of the press need to be respected, which requires changes in laws to force companies to check the quality of their content.

Democracies have yet to learn how to deal with the freedom of the Internet. Autocracies seem to be much faster in exploiting the media to their advantage, as the rise of the Third Reich showed. Disinformation can be used to weaponize a population against perceived threats and enemies. The aim of disinformation is to drive wedges into existing cracks in liberal democracies.

Today, not only texts are altered, but images and videos as well. "Deep fake" videos are so flawlessly crafted that they are difficult to distinguish from videos of real humans. The future could bring "live fake" and "pre-live fake" posts that would cast doubt on any recorded event. War over the truth is as old as humankind, but it seems to be becoming ever more severe with all the types of media that could potentially support it. This development is deeply anti-modern. Modernity is about standards and agreements that go beyond national, economic, and cultural interests. Freedom of the press and speech are such a standard, as are the various codes of conduct agreed upon by journalists.

Superstition

No matter how modern and highly educated a society is, superstitions will never disappear. Humans love good stories, since imagination linked to emotions is the biggest asset of human intelligence. But sometimes this imagination goes wild.

The fear of the 13th floor, as described by Neurath, is still very vivid. Based on a 2002 record of buildings from Otis, a US elevator brand, about 85% of their elevators in high-rise buildings around the world don't have a 13th floor.[12] Ironically, this irrational fear and avoidance of the number 13 has already been scientifically analyzed and given a name: triskaidekaphobia. While this mainly occurs in the West, tetraphobia, the practice of avoiding the digit 4, is very much alive in Southeast Asia, since the word "four" sounds like the word for "death" in many of the languages spoken in the region.

The human brain is a wonderful but mysterious organ. As much it can be used to invent powerful machines like rockets that can fly to planet Mars, that's how much it can make thoughts drift away into strange waters. It has always been difficult for people to believe events and stories they have not witnessed with their own eyes. The biblical story of "Doubting Thomas," one of the 12 apostles, who refused to believe the resurrection of Jesus until he could see and feel Jesus' crucifixion wounds, is a reminder of this.

Science replaced religion as the gatekeeper of truth. Science does not believe in miracles, but only in evidence. With science evolving and atomizing in a multitude of fields, the population is confronted with discoveries far beyond imagination. Atoms, black holes, supernovae, viruses, and climate change are all examples of scientific findings with very concrete evidence but either too small, too large, too far away, or too intangible to be experienced by human senses.

A global society confronted with this multitude of stories is more than ever confounded by it, and doubts arise. In general, doubts are good because they sharpen the critical mind. Yet some people find through doubting rather strange and abstruse beliefs – conspiracy theories. The Internet enables these people to group together and contemplate alternatives to the common truth. Results are that the moon landing by the US was staged in a film studio, that the 9/11 attack on the World Trade Center was planned by the CIA, and that planet Earth is not a sphere but a disc, the "flat Earth theory."[13]

Living in what has been dubbed a post-truth society has made possible the creation of multiple truths concerning the same event, allowing everyone to believe in the truth which most comfortably fits with their ideals and preconceived understanding of the world.[14] Humans are often change-averse, or reluctant to adopt new paradigms. This was true for Copernicus and his heliocentric system, the roundness of the Earth, and Darwin's tree of life.

One of the common denominators of conspiracy theories is the general doubt or even fear about technology and science and its abilities and/or its misuse. The introduction of 5G broadband cellular networks happened to coincide with the outbreak of the

COVID-19 pandemic; therefore, conspiracy theorists drew a link between COVID-19 and 5G. This led to arson attacks – people setting fire to transmitter masts in various European countries to fight COVID-19. How crazy it may sound, but people really believe that radiation from 5G transmitter masts weakens the immune system, making the body more vulnerable to the virus, or even believe that 5G causes COVID-19.[15]

Even the vaccination against the COVID-19 pandemic, which probably saved millions of people's lives, is not spared from human imagination. Conspiracy theorists imagine that the jab is changing the DNA of the human body, that a microchip is implanted to remotely control the population, and/or that the pandemic does not exist at all, but is a way for big pharma to make money.

The world is, by and large, a confusing, peculiar place; and having someone to blame, knowing that things are being caused, rather than simply happening, brings a lot of comfort. Religion once offered this feeling – to a devout Catholic, it might be God's will, or a test of one's faith, as the story of Job tells. However, with no God, we are forced to embrace the whims of the universe and all its chaos. Hanging on

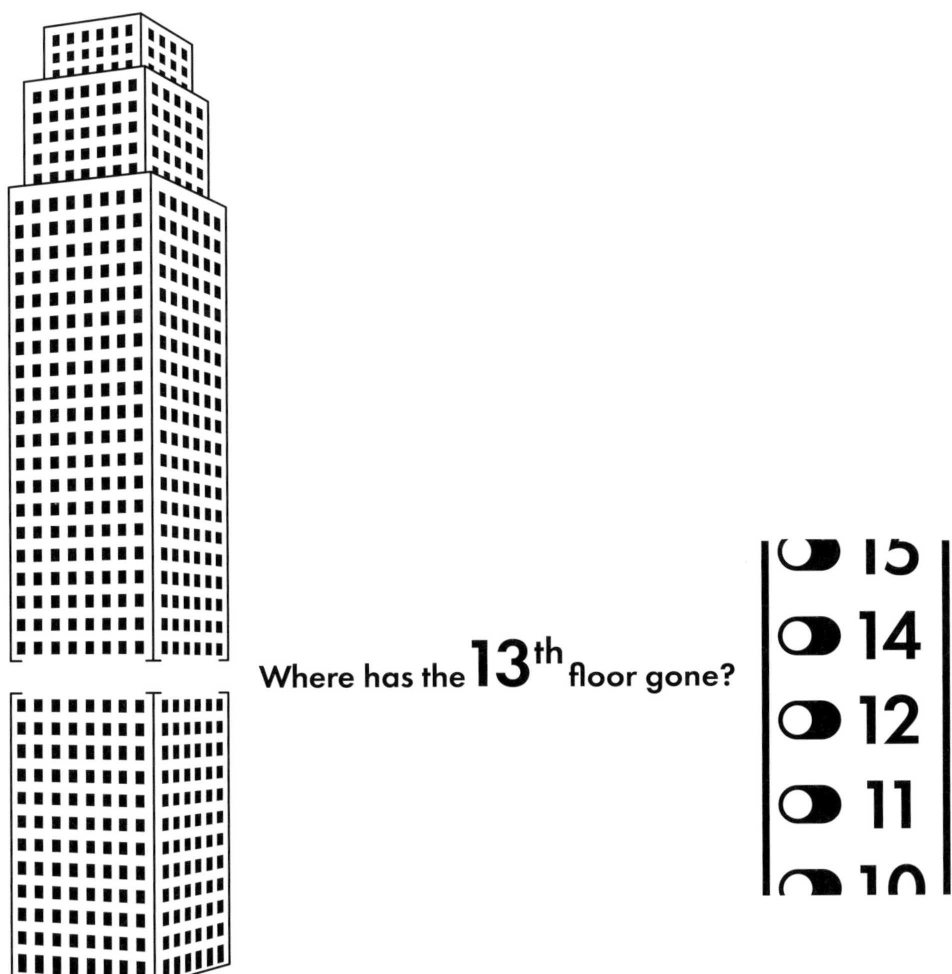

the illustration of the missing 13th floor is the last illustration Otto Neurath used in his book *Modern Man in the Making*

to conspiracy theories derives from the deeply human urge to categorize and order things to create stories that "make sense," at least for some of them.

In times like these, it is remarkable to read in Neurath's book that "during and immediately after World War I the number of books on spiritualism, astrology and such subjects increased." Especially in times of crisis, people seem to lose faith in the sciences and thus in modernity. Yet it might only be that people don't want to bet everything on one horse, and instead look for other faiths and alternatives to the raison d'être in order to keep more options on the table. Since it is often technology that causes a crisis – airplanes, tanks, and gas in the case of World War I, nuclear energy in the case of Chernobyl, and high population density in megacities in the case of COVID-19 – it seems reasonable to ask why technology would come to the rescue.

Me. We.

While working on the illustrations for *Joy and Fear,* I came to the disturbing realization that I am always an integral part of any diagram – a realization that I'm sure applies to you, the reader, as well. Each figurine is an individual, but at the same time represents all of us. In the 157 illustrations in this book, we all take part twice – once as an individual human and once as part of the global population at large. Each illustration is a flip-picture that talks to one and many at the very same moment.

The effect of these pictograms finds its verbal equivalent in a poem by Muhammad Ali. During his commencement speech at Harvard in 1975, students asked him to give them a poem. He responded, "Me. We." – one of the shortest poems ever. The "Me" with its desires, dreams, and fears is easy to grasp. It is the "We" – us as part of the 8 billion others – to which we struggle to connect.

Yes, modernity is a sneaky beast; it addresses us as individuals, but feeds on quantities, processes them, and produces ever larger numbers. To modernity, quantity is everything. Even qualities are defined by quantities. The World Happiness Index, water quality, air quality, and the quality of food are all measures along thresholds of specific quantities like minutes of laughter, pH levels, CO_2 levels, and the number of germs.

Me as an individual and We as 8 billion Me's deliver the gigantic quantities modernity is longing for. We munch away 74 billion chickens per year,[1] we own about 5 billion smartphones,[2] and we buy about 2 billion T-shirts per year.[3]

I must admit that I was shocked too many times while working on this book. Many illustrations that were continued exceeded the size of the page; instead of fitting on an A4 page (~20 × 30 cm), they barely fit A0 (~80 × 100 cm). The quantities got completely out of hand. Just look at pages 75–79, which show the iron ore production of six countries. It is incredible how steep the increase in iron production in China has been over the last 20 years; that country was not even on Neurath's chart because of its insignificant iron ore production at that time.

I doubt that Neurath could have imagined such a surge in numbers, and to be honest, in many cases I cannot and do not want to imagine that it will go on like that. I am simply worried that planet Earth is unable to deliver what we are asking of her – so much iron, so much lithium, so much wheat. On the other hand, modernity has brought a constant increase in the ease of living – ease of access, ease of washing dishes, ease of manual labor – which has contributed to many more pleasant and healthy years on Earth for millions, if not billions, of people.

Joy and Fear provides snapshots of the existing version of modernity. Its broad approach is necessary to expand our field of view and survey the current state of modernity. After climbing down from this viewing platform, we are continuing to be modern and are thus continuing to produce large quantities. Hopefully, this short break with its chilling view will stimulate us to produce different and positive quantities.

In 80 years, maybe someone else will attempt to continue this project and pick up where *Joy and Fear* left off. Whatever happens, each of us will end up in this book in one way or another as a Neurath figurine. Me will change; thus We are changing, and with us modernity as well.

Text Sources

Author's Note

1 Otto Neurath, an Austrian-born thinker, sociologist, and political economist, produced *Modern Man in the Making* in collaboration with Marie Neurath (at that time still Reidemeister) and artist Gerd Arntz. Published in 1939, *Modern Man in the Making* was intended to show the emergence of the "New Human" with the help of Neurath's International Picture Language (Isotype) often arranged in timelines that showed developments from the mid-18th century to the 1930s.
2 Heiskala, Risto; "From Modernity through Postmodernity to Reflexive Modernization: Did We Learn Anything?", *International Review of Sociology*, 2011
3 airandspace.si.edu
4 The title *Joy and Fear* derives from Otto Neurath's subtitle for the Dutch version of *Modern Man in the Making*, which was called *De Moderne Mensch Ontstaat: Een Reportage Van Vreugde en Vrees. Vreugde en Vrees* can be translated as *Joy and Fear.*
5 Neurath, Otto; *Modern Man in the Making*, A. A. Knopf, 1939

Modernity Kills

1 Neurath, Otto; *Modern Man in the Making*, A. A. Knopf, 1939
2 www.osti.gov
3 discover.lanl.gov
4 thebulletin.org
5 thebulletin.org
6 thebulletin.org
7 www.thoughtco.com
8 futureearth.org
9 Meadows, Dennis, et al.; *The Limits to Growth*, Potomac Associates – Universe Books, 1972
10 scied.ucar.edu
11 www.britannica.com
12 world-nuclear.org
13 www.reuters.com
14 www.history.com
15 large.stanford.edu
16 world-nuclear.org
17 world-nuclear.org
18 www-pub.iaea.org
19 www-pub.iaea.org/MTCD/Publications/PDF/te_1105_prn.pdf
20 www.nirs.org
21 fas.org
22 www.state.gov
23 "Although a success, Tsar Bomba was never considered for operational use. Given its size, the device could not be deployed by a ballistic missile. Instead, the bomb had to be transported by conventional aircraft, which could easily be intercepted before reaching its target. Thus, Tsar Bomba was viewed as a propaganda weapon." www.britannica.com/topic/Tsar-Bomba
24 www.chemeurope.com
25 www.ipcc.ch

Population and Urbanization

1 www.theigc.org
2 www.cato.org
3 www.vox.com
4 www.thenewatlantis.com
5 Meadows, Dennis, et al.; *The Limits to Growth*, Potomac Associates – Universe Books, 1972
6 Ehrlich, Paul R.; Howland Ehrlich, Anne; *The Population Bomb*, Sierra Club – Ballantine Books, 1968
7 openknowledge.worldbank.org
8 apnews.com
9 www.researchgate.net
10 evolution.berkeley.edu
11 en.wikipedia.org
12 www.pewresearch.org
13 data.worldbank.org
14 data.worldbank.org
www.unfpa.org/swp2022
"India is set to surpass China as the world's most populous nation, with almost 3 million more people by the middle of this year, data released by the United Nations on Wednesday showed.
Based on the projections, India's population by mid-year will reach 1.4286 billion, compared to China's 1.4257 billion – 2.9 million fewer – according to the United Nations Population Fund's (UNFPA) 'State of World Population Report' for 2023." edition.cnn.com/2023/04/19/asia/india-china-population-intl/index.html
15 population.un.org
16 data.worldbank.org
17 www.weforum.org
18 data.worldbank.org
19 population.un.org
20 worldpopulationreview.com
21 see *illustration sources*, p. 33
22 espas.secure.europarl.europa.eu
23 www.downtoearth.org.in
24 www.researchgate.net
25 data.worldbank.org
26 web.archive.org
27 www.bbc.co.uk
28 data.worldbank.org
29 www.un.org
30 www.demographic-research.org
31 www.dni.gov
32 guardian.ng
33 www.enelfoundation.org
34 www.researchgate.net
35 en.wikipedia.org
36 www.fpri.org
37 www.enelfoundation.org
38 ourworldindata.org
39 www.pnas.org
40 population.un.org
41 permaculturism.com

Agriculture

1 www.census.gov
2 data.worldbank.org
3 www.sciencedirect.com
4 www.ers.usda.gov
5 www.bls.gov
6 Spielman, D.; Pandya-Lorch, R.; Hazell, P.; in *Proven Successes in Agricultural Development*, ed. Spielman, D.; Pandya-Lorch, R.; International Food Policy Research Institute, Washington, DC, 2010, pp. 67–97
7 en.wikipedia.org
8 ourworldindata.org
9 data.worldbank.org
10 cias.wisc.edu
11 www.jstor.org
12 ourworldindata.org
13 www.dvtiernahrung.de
14 www.destatis.de
15 en.wikipedia.org
16 www.bbc.com
17 www.theguardian.com
18 www.fao.org
19 en.wikipedia.org
20 www.cdc.gov
21 historyofyesterday.com
22 see *illustration sources*, p. 53 bottom
23 www.fleischwirtschaft.de
24 ourworldindata.org
25 www.fao.org
26 www.cifor.org
27 www.farmlandgrab.org
28 landmatrix.org
29 *The Economist*, October 2, 2021
30 www.theguardian.com

Manufacturing

1 www.imf.org
2 data.worldbank.org
3 econofact.org
4 www.mckinsey.com
5 www.pewresearch.org
6 Neurath, Otto; *Modern Man in the Making*, A. A. Knopf, 1939 – page 50
7 www.safeguardglobal.com
8 www.statista.com
9 en.wikipedia.org
10 see *illustration sources*, p. 63 top
11 data.worldbank.org
12 www.iisd.org
13 www.thehindu.com
14 apps.who.int
15 core.ac.uk
16 www.ukft.org
17 www.davidpublisher.com
18 www.npr.org
19 www.tbsnews.net
20 www.minimum-wage.org
21 commonslibrary.parliament.uk
22 data.worldbank.org
23 see *illustration sources*, p. 66
24 sewport.com

Raw Materials

1 www.vorwaerts.de
2 www.rsc.org
3 www.usgs.gov
4 www.handelsblatt.com
5 www.wiwo.de
6 www.reuters.com
7 data.worldbank.org
8 www.kitco.com
9 Neurath, Otto; *Modern Man in the Making*, A. A. Knopf, 1939 – page 67
10 www.theguardian.com
11 mneguidelines.oecd.org
12 pubs.usgs.gov (2023)
13 seekingalpha.com
14 pubs.usgs.gov (2023)
15 pubs.usgs.gov (2023)
16 www.worldbank.org
17 about.bnef.com

Fossil Fuels

1 Tolkien, J. R. R.; letter to his son Christopher, 1945; available at: www.tolkienestate.com
2 eu.theadvertiser.com
3 www.britannica.com
4 www.opec.org
5 history.state.gov
6 www.woodgas.com
7 www.researchgate.net
8 unearthed.greenpeace.org
9 see *illustration sources*, p. 92
10 see *illustration sources*, p. 92
11 www.nationmaster.com
12 web.archive.org
13 www.oica.net
14 www.fuelfreedom.org
15 www.unep.org
16 www.unep.org
17 en.wikipedia.org
18 apps.who.int

Global Trade

1 www.ncbi.nlm.nih.gov
2 www.oecd.org
3 www.ft.com
4 Broeze, Frank; *The Globalisation of the Oceans*, Liverpool University Press, 2002
5 Witthöft, Hans Jürgen; *Container. Transportrevolution unseres Jahrhunderts*, Herford Verlag, 1978
6 www.iso.org
7 www.iso.org
8 www.cargo-partner.com
9 www.icontainers.com
10 www.economist.com
11 www.cornwalllive.com
12 www.reuters.com
13 web.archive.org
14 www.wired.co.uk
15 www.livemint.com
16 www.bbc.com
17 www.bbc.com
18 www.deccanherald.com
19 www.maritime-executive.com
20 dataports-project.eu
21 www.economist.com
22 bilgeclean.ca
23 www.dw.com
24 www.itf-oecd.org
25 Neurath, Otto; *Modern Man in the Making*, A. A. Knopf, 1939 – page 81
26 asia.nikkei.com
27 asia.nikkei.com
28 www.ers.usda.gov
29 www.ers.usda.gov
30 www.fas.usda.gov
31 www.fao.org
32 www.fao.org
33 www.theglobaleconomy.com

War

1 www.china.org.cn
2 www.sipri.org – excluding China (no data available)
3 www.sipri.org
4 www.aerotime.aero
5 www.theguardian.com
6 Neurath, Otto; *Modern Man in the Making*, A. A. Knopf, 1939 – page 89
7 www.thenews.com.pk
8 www.files.ethz.ch
9 www.militarytimes.com
10 guide-humanitarian-law.org
11 edition.cnn.com
12 www.typeinvestigations.org
13 www.politifact.com
14 www.typeinvestigations.org
15 guide-humanitarian-law.org
16 www.rferl.org
17 www.thetimes.co.uk
18 www.economist.com
19 www.theguardian.com
20 www.eda.admin.ch

Politics

1 see *illustration sources*, p. 126
2 www.cfr.org
3 antilogicalism.files.wordpress.com
4 www.forbes.com
5 www.v-dem.net
6 commons.ungeneva.org
7 www.unhcr.org
8 www.unhcr.org
9 www.unhcr.org
10 www.refworld.org
11 data.worldbank.org
12 latinamericanpost.com
13 pulitzercenter.org
14 web.archive.org
15 en.wikipedia.org
16 www.unhcr.org
17 Deutinger, Theo; *Handbook of Tyranny*, Lars Müller Publishers, 2023
18 www.thenationalnews.com
19 www.hurriyetdailynews.com
20 www.unhcr.org
21 www.brookings.edu
22 en.wikipedia.org
23 ec.europa.eu/eurostat/databrowser/view/NAMA_10_FTE__custom_4232263/bookmark/table?lang=en&bookmarkId=fafb4e3b-f3aa-4907-9102-16be8df6f775
24 cadmus.eui.eu
25 www.tandfonline.com
26 gulfnews.com
27 carnegieendowment.org
28 www.aljazeera.com
29 Neurath, Otto; *Modern Man in the Making*, A. A. Knopf, 1939 – page 72
30 www.nytimes.com
31 www.dw.com
32 www.hrw.org
33 Neurath, Otto; *Modern Man in the Making*, A. A. Knopf, 1939 – page 70
34 piketty.pse.ens.fr
35 www.reuters.com
36 books.google.at
37 www.economist.com
38 www.vice.com
39 piketty.pse.ens.fr
40 Piketty, Thomas; *Das Kapital des 21. Jahrhunderts*, C. H. Beck, 2014 – page 566
41 see *illustration sources*, p. 140
42 https://ec.europa.eu/eurostat/databrowser/view/NAMA_10_FTE__custom_4232263/bookmark/table?lang=en&bookmarkId=fafb4e3b-f3aa-4907-9102-16be8df6f775
43 wid.world
44 www.ncbi.nlm.nih.gov

Consumerism

1 For example, the Austrian Civil War in 1934 (lasting 4 days).
2 www.britannica.com
3 www.britannica.com
4 Cohen, Lizabeth; *A Consumers' Republic: The Politics of Mass Consumption in Postwar America*, Vintage Books, 2003
5 Quote by Charles Kettering, general director of General Motors Research Laboratories, 1929; available at: www.bbc.com
6 rarehistoricalphotos.com
7 www.youtube.com
8 see *illustration sources*, p. 148
9 see *illustration sources*, p. 148
10 see *illustration sources*, p. 149
11 www.theguardian.com
12 planetcare.org
13 pubs.acs.org

14 www.theguardian.com
15 en.wikipedia.org
16 www.science.org
17 wrap.org.uk
18 www.plateconference.org
19 www.commonobjective.co
20 see *illustration sources*, p. 150
21 see *illustration sources*, p. 150

Convenience and Lifestyle
1 globaldatalab.org
2 archive.nytimes.com
3 Neurath, Otto; *Modern Man in the Making*, A. A. Knopf, 1939 – page 51
4 wagecentre.com
5 Neurath, Otto; *Modern Man in the Making*, A. A. Knopf, 1939 – page 120
6 www.oica.net
7 www.theglobaleconomy.com
8 www.weforum.org
9 www.worldbank.org
10 see *illustration sources*, p. 158

Family
1 Neurath, Otto; *Modern Man in the Making*, A. A. Knopf, 1939 – page 113
2 ec.europa.eu
3 en.wikipedia.org
4 ec.europa.eu
5 Neurath, Otto; *Modern Man in the Making*, A. A. Knopf, 1939 – page 115
6 see *illustration sources*, p. 165
7 medium.com
8 www.guttmacher.org
9 www.latimes.com
10 www.independent.co.uk
11 www.gapminder.org
12 data.worldbank.org
13 www.unfpa.org
14 Today there are only five countries without compulsory education: Bhutan, Oman, Papua New Guinea, Solomon Islands, and Vatican City. And primary education is officially with tuition only in Papua New Guinea, South Africa, Somalia, Guinea, Zimbabwe, and Zambia.
15 www.unicef.org
16 www.coparents.com
17 borgenproject.org
18 Neurath, Otto; *Modern Man in the Making*, A. A. Knopf, 1939 – page 58
19 see *illustration sources*, p. 171
20 www.whitehouse.gov
21 data.worldbank.org
22 data.worldbank.org
23 www.ssa.gov
24 www.numbeo.com
25 www.ilo.org
26 data.worldbank.org

Leisure
1 historyofinformation.com
2 en.wikipedia.org
3 books.google.cz
4 www.weforum.org (2021)
5 www.sciencedirect.com
6 www.rug.nl
7 wiserobotics.com
8 reparti.free.fr
9 countryeconomy.com
10 www.sciencedirect.com
11 wttc.org
12 www.passportindex.org
13 see *illustration sources*, p. 180
14 wttc.org
15 While square and beehive typologies are typical for some regions, the round prevailed. repository.up.ac.za
16 www.europarl.europa.eu
17 see *illustration sources*, p. 182
18 www.lonelyplanet.com
19 www.pewresearch.org
20 whc.unesco.org
21 whc.unesco.org
22 ich.unesco.org
23 data.oecd.org
24 ourworldindata.org
25 Neurath, Otto; *Modern Man in the Making*, A. A. Knopf, 1939 – page 124
26 see *illustration sources*, p. 186
27 mars.nasa.gov
28 see *illustration sources*, p. 187
29 see *illustration sources*, p. 187
30 www.space.com
31 www.marca.com
32 olympics.com
33 en.wikipedia.org
34 www.footballtransfers.com
35 digitalhub.fifa.com
36 worldsoccertalk.com
37 www.reuters.com
38 www.nbcnews.com
39 rize.io
40 ec.europa.eu
41 www.ncbi.nlm.nih.gov
42 commons.wikimedia.org
43 www.bestow.com
44 www.seas.harvard.edu; ourworldindata.org
45 www.who.int
46 kotaku.com
47 www.esportsearnings.com

Digital Times
1 commons.wikimedia.org
2 see *illustration sources*, p. 198
3 www.worlddata.info
4 www.personalausweisportal.de
5 dgtlinfra.com
6 www.starlink.com
7 maxpolyakov.com
8 Neurath, Otto; *Modern Man in the Making*, A. A. Knopf, 1939 – page 110
9 www.rferl.org
10 edition.cnn.com
11 www.politico.com
12 web.archive.org
13 physicsworld.com
14 journals.sagepub.com
15 www.ncbi.nlm.nih.gov

Me. We.
1 www.fao.org/faostat/en/#data/QCL (2021)
2 www.statista.com/statistics/203734/global-smartphone-penetration-per-capita-since-2005/
3 www.bluecotton.com/blog/articles/55-things-you-probably-didnt-know-about-t-shirts/

Illustration Sources

Modernity Kills
12
www.atomicarchive.com

13
www.atomicarchive.com

14
thebulletin.org

15
en.wikipedia.org

17
radio.nilu.no

18
www.iaea.org

19
www.bund.net

20
en.wikipedia.org

21
ahf.nuclearmuseum.org

22
www.bund.net

Population and Urbanization
26
population.un.org

28
fred.stlouisfed.org
www.ons.gov.uk
www.statista.com
Denman, James; McDonald, Paul; *Unemployment Statistics from 1881 to the Present Day*, Central Statistical Office, 1996; available at: escoe-website.s3.amazonaws.com

29
population.un.org
data.footprintnetwork.org

30, 31
data.worldbank.org

32
population.un.org

33
www.un.org

34
unstats.un.org
ourworldindata.org
population.un.org
data.worldbank.org
www.citypopulation.de
worldpopulationreview.com
de.wikipedia.org
en.wikipedia.org
www.ide.go.jp
ocw.mit.edu
www.unicef.org
www.milbank.org
www.cdc.gov
web.iima.ac.in
www.statista.com
www.infoplease.com
web.archive.org

35
www.un.org

36 top
data.worldbank.org
en.wikipedia.org

36 bottom
www.leekuanyewworldcityprize.gov.sg
en.wikipedia.org
unhabitat.org
www.un.org

37
population.un.org

39
www.bp.com
data.worldbank.org

Agriculture
42
ourworldindata.org
www.bls.gov

44
ourworldindata.org
www2.census.gov
www.fao.org
www.nass.usda.gov
agcensus.mannlib.cornell.edu

45
data.worldbank.org

46
Neurath, Otto; *Modern Man in the Making*, A. A. Knopf, 1939

47
www.fao.org
foodensity.com
appsso.eurostat.ec.europa.eu
www.kakaoverein.de
unctad.org
www.kakaoforum.de
www.icco.org/wp-content
www.voicenetwork.eu
www.indexmundi.com
ricestat.irri.org:8080
apps.fas.usda.gov
global.chinadaily.com.cn
trendeconomy.com
resourcetrade.earth
www.ico.org
www.agrifutures.com.au

48
data.worldbank.org

49
data.worldbank.org
www.fao.org

50
www.fao.org

51
www.fao.org

53 top
www.cjd.ed.ac.uk

53 bottom
cdn.who.int

54
landmatrix.org

55
www.worldbank.org

56
www.pbl.nl

Manufacturing
58
Neurath, Otto; *Modern Man in the Making*, A. A. Knopf, 1939

59
ec.europa.eu
skillspanorama.cedefop.europa.eu

60
statisticsanddata.org
apps.who.int

61
stats.oecd.org
www.in2013dollars.com

62
data.worldbank.org

63 top
data.worldbank.org
www.globalpetrolprices.com
data.un.org

63 bottom
apps.who.int

64
www.davidpublisher.org
bb.org.bd
www.bgmea.com.bd

65 top
www.jstor.org

65 bottom
www.wto.org
shenglufashion.com

66
documents1.worldbank.org
cottonanalytics.com
www.fao.org
www.oerlikon.com
www.oecd-ilibrary.org
www.expertmarketresearch.com
textileexchange.org
documents1.worldbank.org
www.cottonguide.org
staging.icac.org

68
www2.census.gov
books.google.at
apps.fas.usda.gov
stats.oecd.org
www.fao.org

Raw Materials
72
Neurath, Otto; *Modern Man in the Making*, A. A. Knopf, 1939

73
www.worldsteel.org
www.fao.org
stats.oecd.org

75
www.usgs.gov

80, 81
pubs.usgs.gov

82
www.worldsteel.org
www.bp.com

83
www.amec.org.au

Fossil Fuel
86
www.britannica.com

87
www.bp.com

88
www.bp.com
vaclavsmil.com

89
hypertextbook.com
www.natural-gas.com.au
pubs.rsc.org
www.woodgas.com
www.ior.com.au

90
www.bp.com

91
globalenergymonitor.org

92
maecourses.ucsd.edu
www.iea.org

93
www.ceer.eu
www.statista.com

94
wedocs.unep.org

95
wedocs.unep.org

Global Trade
98
www.vsm.de
digital-commons.usnwc.edu
www.perseus-web.fr
danskemaritime.dk
shipbuildinghistory.com

101
www.mckinsey.com
www.scf.com.au

102
agtransport.usda.gov
www.crsl.com
unctadstat.unctad.org
ex.hhs.se

103
www.worldshipping.org

104
papers.ssrn.com

105
www.marineinsight.com

106
maritimecyprus.com

107
transportgeography.org

108
Neurath, Otto; *Modern Man in the Making*, A. A. Knopf, 1939
www.fao.org

110
Neurath, Otto; *Modern Man in the Making*, A. A. Knopf, 1939

111
stats.oecd.org
apps.fas.usda.gov
publications.industry.gov.au
publications.industry.gov.au

112
Neurath, Otto; *Modern Man in the Making*, A. A. Knopf, 1939
www.fas.usda.gov

War
116
commons.wikimedia.org

117
armstrade.sipri.org
www.prio.org

118–122
www.iiss.org
www.fao.org
www.bp.com
www.world-mining-data.info
www.prio.org
ucdp.uu.se
csis-website-prod.s3.amazonaws.com

Politics
126
commons.wikimedia.org
www.eiu.com

127
Neurath, Otto; *Modern Man in the Making*, A. A. Knopf, 1939
commons.wikimedia.org

128
commons.wikimedia.org

129
www.refworld.org

130
fragilestatesindex.org

131
www.polgeonow.com

132
www.unhcr.org
Deutinger, Theo; *Handbook of Tyranny*, Lars Mueller Publishers, 2017

133
www.unhcr.org

134
data.worldbank.org
datacatalog.worldbank.org

136
piketty.pse.ens.fr

138 top
www.heritage.org
www.imf.org

138 bottom
www.credit-suisse.com

139
gsociology.icaap.org
www.statista.com
data.worldbank.org

140
Piketty, Thomas; *Das Kapital im 21. Jahrhundert*; C. H. Beck, 2014

141
piketty.pse.ens.fr

Consumerism
144
www.commonobjective.co
publications.parliament.uk
www.epa.gov
www.un.org

145
www.bbvaresearch.com
data.worldbank.org
books.google.at
www.eea.europa.eu
www.kba.de
jean.godi.free.fr
data.worldbank.org
en.wikipedia.org

147
datatopics.worldbank.org
en.wikipedia.org
www.bir.org
data.worldbank.org

148, 149
Geyer, R., Jambeck, J. R., & Law, K. L.; "Production, Use, and Fate of All Plastics Ever Made," *Science Advances*, 2017; available at: advances.sciencemag.org

150
www.epa.gov
www.census.gov
www.commonobjective.co

Convenience and Lifestyle
154
www.cisco.com

155
globaldatalab.org
tcdata360.worldbank.org
www.farsnews.ir
data.worldbank.org
washmatters.wateraid.org
money.cnn.com
www.theguardian.com
de.statista.com
tradingeconomics.com
www.nationmaster.com
worldpopulationreview.com
expandedramblings.com

156
www.census.gov

157
www.itu.int
appsso.eurostat.ec.europa.eu
www.oica.net
en.wikipedia.org
www.acea.be

158
www.sowi.uni-stuttgart.de
www.basicthinking.de
www.ard-zdf-massenkommunikation.de
www.agkino.de

160
www.geschichtewiki.wien.gv.at
de.statista.com
Wolfschluckner, Sabrina; "Das Kaffeehaus als Seismograph gesellschaftlicher Veränderungen. Wien ab 1950," diploma thesis for teaching certification in History, Social Studies, Political Education, and Spanish, University of Vienna, 2014

161 top
www.fao.org

151 bottom
www.wikiwand.com
de.wikinew.wiki
en.wikipedia.org

Family
164
ec.europa.eu

165
commons.wikimedia.org

166
commons.wikimedia.org

167
commons.wikimedia.org

168
data.unicef.org
169
data.worldbank.org

170
www.ons.gov.uk
statswales.gov.wales

171
en.wikipedia.org
tradingeconomics.com

172
en.wikipedia.org
www.nationmaster.com
data.worldbank.org

Leisure
176
ifr.org

177
stats.oecd.org

178
www.sciencedirect.com
www.rug.nl

179
reparti.free.fr
ifr.org

180
mkt.unwto.org

181
www.researchgate.net

182
wanderwisdom.com
allaboutvenice.com
www.scribd.com

183
wanderwisdom.com
allaboutvenice.com
www.scribd.com

184
www.fao.org
data.worldbank.org

186
transportgeography.org

187
en.wikipedia.org

188
en.wikipedia.org

189
www.whereig.com
www.statista.com

190
www.who.int
www.who.int
childmortality.org
www.un.org
www.healthdata.org

191
www.iarc.who.int
cancerstatisticscenter.cancer.org
ghdx.healthdata.org

192
www.oecd.org

Digital Times
196
commons.wikimedia.org

197
Own research

198
www.fao.org

199
www.pewresearch.org
variety.com
www.statista.com
books.google.at
www.statista.com
www.ibisworld.com
www.statista.com
data.worldbank.org
datacatalog.worldbank.org
www.statista.com
thenextweb.com
news.usc.edu
www.zippia.com
www.theatlantic.com
americancentury.omeka.wlu.edu
stratechery.com

200
www.statista.com
thenextweb.com

201
www.ucsusa.org

203
rsf.org

205
Neurath, Otto; *Modern Man in the Making*, A. A. Knopf, 1939

The author has made every effort to reflect all sources correctly. If, however, despite careful checking, errors have occurred, please contact the publisher.

Theo Deutinger (b. 1971)
is an architect, writer, curator, and designer of sociocultural studies. He is the founder and head of *The Department* (TD), a practice that combines architecture with research, visualization, and artistic thinking. With *The Department* he works on all scales from global planning, spatial master plans, and architecture to graphic and curatorial work. Deutinger is known for his theoretical writings on the transformation of European urban culture and his publications such as *Handbook of Tyranny*. His work has been shown at the Design Biennale Kwangju (Korea, 2011), the 14th Venice Architecture Biennale (Italy, 2014), and the Storefront for Architecture in New York (USA, 2019), among others. Theo Deutinger lives and works in Austria.

Special thanks to Christopher Clarkson for his great contribution to this work.

Thanks to Max Bruinsma, Christopher Burke, Roger Fouquet, Günther Sandner, and Michael van Schaik for their input.

Thanks to Monique Leenders for her support.

Joy and Fear
An Illustrated Report on Modernity

Author: Theo Deutinger
Research: Christopher Clarkson, Luca Deutinger, Theo Deutinger, Shelia Jap, Pia Prantl, Kerstin Reyer
Fact-checking: Charlotte Kaulen
Copyediting: Michael Pilewski
Proofreading: Michael Pilewski
Project coordination: Kristina Lemke, Fanny Rakeseder
Design: Theo Deutinger in collaboration with Integral Lars Müller / Lars Müller and Esther Butterworth
Production: Esther Butterworth
Printing and binding: Printer Trento, Italy
Paper: Arctic Volume White 1.12, 130 g/m^2

Lars Müller Publishers is supported by the Swiss Federal Office of Culture with a structural contribution for the years 2021–2024.

Lars Müller Publishers
Zurich, Switzerland
www.lars-mueller-publishers.com

ISBN 978-3-03778-743-4

Distributed in North America by ARTBOOK | D.A.P.
www.artbook.com

Printed in Italy

For their support we thank:

Federal Ministry
Republic of Austria
Arts, Culture,
Civil Service and Sport

creative industries fund NL